A2-Level
Psychology

A2 Psychology is seriously tricky — no question about that.
To do well, you're going to need to revise properly and practise hard.

This book has thorough notes on everything you need to know for the
AQA A specification, plus plenty of detailed psychological studies.

There are also warm-up and exam-style practice questions for every topic,
with a separate section of advice on how to do well in the exams.

And of course, we've done our best to make the whole thing vaguely entertaining for you.

Complete Revision and Practice
Exam Board: AQA A

Published by CGP

Editors:
Katie Braid, Polly Cotterill, Katherine Craig, Rob MacDonald, Kate Redmond, Jane Sawers

Contributors:
Radha Bellur, Lauren Burns, Richard Carciofo, Elisa M Gray, Nigel Holt,
Christine Johnson, Kate Robson, Denise Say, Stuart Wilson

ISBN 978 1 84762 276 1

With thanks to Charley Darbishire and Glenn Rogers for the proofreading.

With thanks to Laura Jakubowski for copyright research.

Groovy website: www.cgpbooks.co.uk

Jolly bits of clipart from CorelDRAW®
Printed by Elanders, Newcastle upon Tyne.

Based on the classic CGP style created by Richard Parsons.

Contents

*We deliberately haven't put any answers in this book,
because they'd just be saying what's already in the book.
So instead, here's how to write answers and do well.*

Introduction to A2 Psychology

These pages are here to give you a quick intro to A2 Psychology — recapping some stuff that you did at AS and giving you a brief overview of what exciting topics A2 has got in store for you. Are you sitting comfortably? Then let's begin...

A2 Psychology is Made Up of Two Units

A2 Psychology is made up of two units — imaginatively named **Unit 3** and **Unit 4**.

Unit 3

Unit 3 contains eight topics — **Biological Rhythms and Sleep**, **Perception**, **Gender**, **Relationships**, **Aggression**, **Eating Behaviour**, **Intelligence and Learning**, and **Cognition and Development**. The good news is you only have to answer questions on **three** of these topics and you get to choose which ones you do.

Unit 4

Unit 4 covers **Psychopathology** (where you'll have to choose **one** disorder to study out of **three**) and **Psychology in Action** (where you'll study one application of psychology from a choice of three). There's also a visit to the old favourite, **Research Methods**.

You learnt about the different **approaches** that are used to study psychology during AS level. You'll need these again for A2, so here's a quick recap:

The Cognitive Approach Focuses on Internal Processes

1) Cognitive psychologists focus on **internal processes** to understand behaviour — for example, how we perceive or remember things.

2) They compare the human mind to an advanced **computer** system, so they use **computer models** to try to understand human cognition (thinking).

3) Using concepts from information processing, cognitive psychologists describe the brain as a **processor** — it receives **input**, **processes** it, and produces an **output**. Obviously it's a bit more complicated than that, but the general idea is the same.

4) Cognitive psychology studies are often laboratory-based and **artificial**, so they can lack **validity** in the **real world** (**ecological validity**).

If brains are like computers, Sarah's crashed the day she packed for her holiday.

Developmental Psychology is About How Humans Develop... Obviously...

You covered **developmental psychology** at AS level and it's back again for A2. Bet you're pleased about that.

Developmental psychology is a bit of a jumble of ideas from different approaches. It deals with how people **develop** and **change** over their lifetime. It also involves looking at how children are **qualitatively different** to adults in their understanding, abilities and feelings.

Chloe had just seen that solid food was next on her timetable and she couldn't wait.

Researchers like **Piaget** and **Samuel and Bryant** looked at children's **cognitive** development. They studied the way children approach problems depending on their age and the stage of development they've reached.

They found that the brain appears to have a **timetable** of **what** we can do and **when** we can do it — e.g. children don't start speaking or progress with potty training until they reach a certain stage of development.

Introduction to A2 Psychology

The **Biological Approach** Explains Behaviour as a Product of **Nature**

The biological approach involves three **key assumptions**:

⭐1 **Human behaviour** can be explained by looking at internal, biological stuff, like hormones and the nervous system.

⭐2 Experimental research that uses **animals** can be generalised to **human behaviour**.

⭐3 **Abnormal behaviour** can be removed using **biological treatments** — e.g. medication for mental illnesses such as schizophrenia.

So, as far as this approach is concerned, it's what's inside that counts...

1) Researchers look at **genetics**, **hormones**, the **brain**, and the **nervous system** to explain behaviour.

2) It's very scientific — research is mostly carried out in **laboratory experiments**.

3) Common research techniques include **animal studies**, **brain scans** and **correlational studies**.

Individual Differences is About **Differences** Between... erm... **Individuals**

You've met **individual differences** before as well. It's another one that's made up of bits from loads of approaches. The main thing that researchers want to find out is **how** and **why** we're all **different** from each other. You might think it's pretty obvious that we're all different, but psychologists have got to find something to fill the day.

1) Other areas of psychology tend to assume that people are broadly the **same** — e.g. developmental psychologists assume that we all go through the same basic stages of development.

2) However, this usually isn't the case. Not everyone hits the stages of development at the same **age**, and we all differ to some extent in our **psychological characteristics** — for example, our levels of motivation, aggression and intelligence, etc.

3) So, the individual differences approach looks at what **causes** these differences.

For example, Brian and his friend Flippy differ from each other in a few ways.

Social Psychologists Look at How We **Interact** with Each Other

Last one, hurrah. Social psychology isn't new to you either — you covered it for AS.

1) This approach is all about how we **influence** each other's thoughts, feelings and behaviour — either as **individuals** or as **groups**.

2) Major areas of research include **conformity** and **obedience**.

> Probably the most famous experiment in social psychology is **Milgram's Behavioural Study of Obedience** (1963). In the experiment he tested people's obedience by asking participants to give someone electric shocks if they made mistakes in a learning task. Most of his participants carried on giving the shocks, even when they thought they were causing harm. He concluded that most people will follow orders even if it means doing something they don't think is right. Pretty scary stuff.

3) Other areas of research include **persuasion**, **attitudes** and **relationships**.

4) Common research methods include **correlational studies**, **observational studies** and **experimental methods**. If you don't remember what these are don't stress — there's a whole section on research methods starting on page 110.

And that's all there is to A2 Psychology...

OK, that's a lie. Clearly there's a lot more to A2 psychology than just these two pages. There's the whole rest of this book. And there's nothing for it than to make your way through it one page at a time. But don't fret — if you look after the pages then the sections will look after themselves (as the saying almost never goes) and very soon you'll be ready for the exam.

The Scientific Process

You've already met the stuff on this page at AS. It's the nuts and bolts of science though — and that's pretty important stuff. So, if you're not sure how we develop and test scientific theories then read on...

Science Answers Real-life Questions

Science tries to explain **how** and **why** things happen — it **answers questions**. It's all about seeking and gaining **knowledge** about the world around us. Scientists do this by **asking** questions and **suggesting** answers and then **testing** them, to see if they're correct — this is the **scientific process**.

What happens if you spend too long on your own? Send your hypotheses on a postcard please.

1) **Ask** a question — make an **observation** and ask **why or how** it happens.

2) **Suggest** an answer, or part of an answer, by forming a **theory** (a possible explanation of the observations).

3) Make a **prediction** or **hypothesis** — a **specific testable statement**, based on the theory, about what will happen in a test situation.

4) Carry out a **test** — to provide **evidence** that will support the prediction (or help to disprove it).

Suggesting explanations is all very well and good, but if there's **no way to test** them then it just ain't science. A theory is **only scientific** if it can be tested.

Science is All About Testing Theories

It starts off with one experiment backing up a prediction and theory. It ends up with all the scientists in the world **agreeing** with it and you **learning** it. Stirring stuff. This is how the magical process takes place:

1) The results are **published** — scientists need to let others know about their work, so they try to get their results published in **scientific journals**. These are just like normal magazines, only they contain **scientific reports** (called papers) instead of celebrity gossip. All work must undergo **peer review** before it's published.

- **Peer review** is a process used to **ensure the integrity** of published scientific work. Before publication, scientific work is sent to **experts** in that field (**peers**) so they can assess the **quality** of the work.

- This process helps to keep scientists **honest** — e.g. you can't '**sex-up**' your conclusions if the data doesn't support it, because it **won't pass** peer review.

- Peer review helps to **validate conclusions** — it means published theories, data and conclusions are more trustworthy. But it **can't guarantee** that the conclusions are 100% right. More **rounds** of predicting and testing are needed before they can be taken as '**fact**'.

- Sometimes **mistakes** are made and bad science is published. Peer review **isn't perfect** but it's probably the best way for scientists to **self-regulate** their work and to ensure **reliable** scientific work is **published**.

2) Other scientists read the published theories and results, and try to **repeat them** — this involves repeating the **exact experiments**, and using the theory to make **new predictions** that are tested by **new experiments**.

3) If all the experiments in all the world provide evidence to back it up, the theory is thought of as scientific 'fact' (**for now**).

4) If **new evidence** comes to light that **conflicts** with the current evidence the theory is questioned all over again. More rounds of **testing** will be carried out to see which evidence, and so which theory, **prevails**.

If the Evidence Supports a Theory, It's Accepted — For Now

Our currently accepted theories have survived this '**trial by evidence**'. They've been tested **over and over and over** and each time the results have backed them up. **BUT**, and this is a big but (teehee), they never become totally undisputable fact. Scientific **breakthroughs or advances** could provide new ways to question and test a theory, which could lead to **changes and challenges** to it. Then the testing starts all over again...

And this, my friend, is the **tentative nature of scientific knowledge** — it's always **changing** and **evolving**.

The Role of Science

So what's it all about then — why do scientists get to flounce around in long white swishy lab coats, with their goggles pushing back their flamboyant hairstyles and the smell of ammonia wafting after them?

Science Helps Us Make **Better Decisions**

Lots of scientific work eventually leads to **important discoveries** that could **benefit humankind**. Oh yes.
These results are **used by society** (that's you, me and everyone else) to **make decisions** about the way we live.
All sections of society use scientific evidence to make decisions:

1) **Politicians** use science to devise policy. E.g. **cognitive behavioural therapy** is available on the NHS because there's evidence to show it can help people with **depression**.

2) **Private organisations** use science to determine what to make or develop — e.g. evidence has shown that the number of people being diagnosed with **depression** is increasing, so drugs companies might put **more money** into this area of research.

3) **Individuals** also use science to make decisions about their **own lives** — e.g. evidence suggests that we should exercise and eat healthily, but it's up to individuals to **decide** whether they take that advice or not.

Other **Factors** Can **Influence** Decision Making

Other factors can influence decisions about science or the way science is used:

Economic factors

- Society has to consider the **cost** of implementing changes based on scientific conclusions — e.g. the **NHS** can't afford the most expensive drugs without **sacrificing** something else.
- Scientific research is **expensive** so companies won't always develop new ideas — e.g. developing new drugs is costly, so pharmaceutical companies often only invest in drugs that are likely to make **money**.

Social factors

- **Decisions** affect **people's lives**. How psychologists decide what's **normal** and what's **abnormal** affects how people are treated — e.g. homosexuality was defined as an **abnormal behaviour** until 1987.

Environmental factors

- Scientists believe **unexplored regions**, like parts of rainforests, might contain **untapped drug** resources. But some people think we shouldn't **exploit** these regions because any interesting finds might lead to **deforestation, reduced biodiversity** and **more CO$_2$** in the atmosphere.

Science Has **Responsibilities**

Yes, you've guessed it — **ethics**. Science has to be **responsible** in many ways. Scientists aren't allowed to test something just because they can. They have to think about the **ethical considerations** surrounding the experiment design and how the results could affect society.

1) **Design** — e.g. experiments involving **animals** are tightly controlled and monitored. **Studies** are checked to ensure they aren't placing individuals in **unnecessary danger**. If a study shows a drug has a highly **beneficial effect**, it's stopped and those in the **placebo** (negative) group are given the drug too.

2) **Results** — e.g. scientists' understanding of some **genetic disorders** could lead to tests to detect members of the population that carry the genes for them. But would people want to know?

Society does have a say in what experiments take place. **Controversial experiments** involving ethical issues have to be approved by scientific and **ethics councils** before they are allowed to be carried out.

So there you have it — how science works...

Hopefully these pages have given you a nice intro to how science works — what scientists do to provide you with 'facts'. You need to understand this, as you're expected to use it to evaluate evidence for yourselves — in the exam and in life.

Biological Rhythms

George Gershwin. Gloria Estefan. 90s dance maestros Snap. They all had rhythm, and so do you. You don't have to write a song on it (unless you really want to) but you do need to know about it. And these lovely pages are here to help.

Biological Rhythm Cycles **Vary** in **Length**

Biological rhythms can be classified according to how long their cycle lasts.

1) **Circadian rhythms** — have cycles that generally occur **once every 24 hours**. For example, we will usually go through the **sleep-waking cycle** once every day.

2) **Infradian rhythms** — have cycles that occur **less than once every day**. For example, the menstrual cycle. **Sabbagh and Barnard (1984)** found that when women live together their menstrual cycles may **synchronise**. It isn't clear why, but it may be linked to **pheromones** (chemicals that can affect the behaviour or physiology of others).

3) **Ultradian rhythms** — have cycles that occur **more than once every 24 hours**. For example, the sleep cycle has several repeating stages of light and deep sleep (see p.8). Research using **EEGs** (electroencephalograms) to monitor brain activity during sleep has shown that a **regular** sleep pattern is really important. Disrupting these cycles can have very **serious consequences** — see the next page.

Stan and Paul had more than enough rhythm for everyone.

Biological Rhythms are **Regulated** by **Internal and External Influences**

The timing of biological rhythms is determined by factors both **inside** and **outside** our bodies.

Endogenous pacemakers

1) Some aspects of our biological rhythms are set by **genetically determined** biological structures and mechanisms **within the body**.

2) The **suprachiasmatic nucleus** (SCN), part of the **hypothalamus**, seems to act as an **internal clock** to keep the body on an approximate 24-hour sleep-waking cycle.

3) It is sensitive to light and regulates the **pineal gland**, which secretes **melatonin** — a hormone which seems to induce sleep. When there is **less** light, more melatonin is produced. When there is **more** light, secretion is reduced and waking occurs.

4) **Menaker et al (1978)** lesioned this structure in hamsters — their sleep-waking cycle was **disrupted**.

Exogenous zeitgebers

1) These are influences outside of the body that act like a **prompt**, which may trigger a **biological rhythm**.

2) **Light** is the most important zeitgeber. **Siffre (1975)** spent six months in a cave. He had **no clocks** and **no natural light** as zeitgebers. His sleep-waking cycle **extended** from a 24-hour to a 25-30 hour cycle. It therefore seems that natural light is needed to fine-tune our normal 24-hour cycle.

Endogenous and Exogenous Factors **Interact**

Endogenous and exogenous factors **interact** to regulate the timing of our biological rhythms.

1) In some cases, endogenous factors may **completely determine** a cycle. **Pengelly and Fisher (1957)** found that squirrels will hibernate even when kept in laboratory conditions very different from their natural environment.

2) However, many animals can **react more flexibly**, especially humans who are able to adapt to their surroundings. We can make ourselves stay awake and **change the environment** to suit our needs, e.g. by using artificial light.

3) **Cultural factors** are also important. For example, Eskimos often live in permanent daylight or permanent night-time but can maintain **regular daily sleep cycles** — so the cycle can't just be determined by levels of light acting on the pineal gland.

4) **Individual differences** can also affect the rhythms. **Aschoff and Wever (1976)** found that in a group of people isolated from daylight, some maintained their **regular** sleep-waking cycles. Other members of the group displayed their own very **extreme** idiosyncrasies, e.g. 29 hours awake followed by 21 hours asleep. This also shows that factors must interact to control or influence biological rhythms.

Biological Rhythms

Disrupting Biological Rhythms can have Negative Consequences

1) In the natural environment, zeitgebers normally **change slowly**, e.g. light levels during the year change gradually.
2) However, in modern society, zeitgebers can change quickly. This can have **negative effects** on our ability to function — slowing **reaction times**, impairing **problem-solving skills**, and limiting our **ability to concentrate**.

Jet lag

1) Jet planes allow fast travel to **different time zones**. Leaving the UK at 9am means that you'd get to New York at about 4pm UK time. New York is 5 hours behind the UK, so the local time would be about 11am.
2) Consequently you'll feel sleepy at an **earlier (local) time**. If you then went to sleep you would wake-up earlier and be **out of sync** with local timing. It appears easiest to **adapt** by forcing yourself to stay awake.
3) It can take **about a week** to fully synchronise to a new time zone. **Wegman et al (1986)** found that travelling east to west (**phase delay**) seems easier to adapt to than travelling west to east (**phase advance**).
4) **Schwartz et al (1995)** found that baseball teams from the east coast of the USA got **better results** travelling to play in the west than teams based in the west did when travelling to play in the east.

Shift work

Modern work patterns mean some people work shifts throughout the 24-hour period, disrupting their sleep cycle.

Czeisler et al (1982) studied workers at a factory whose shift patterns appeared to cause sleep and health problems. The researchers recommended **21-day shifts** (allowing more time for workers to adapt), and changing shifts **forward in time** (phase delay). After implementing the changes **productivity** and **job satisfaction** increased.

Research on Biological Rhythms has Limitations

1) Findings from animal studies can't accurately be **generalised** to humans — humans have greater **adaptability**.
2) Studies that have deprived humans of natural light have still allowed **artificial light**, which may give many of the **benefits** of natural light — this reduces the **validity** of these studies.
3) Things like **individual differences** need further study. Some people are more alert early in the day, and others later on, and the speed with which we **adapt to disruptions** can vary. It's difficult to determine whether a person's lifestyle is a **cause or effect** of their biological rhythms.
4) If we fully understand what causes the problems linked to jet lag and shift work, we can **minimise** or **avoid them**, reducing accidents in work environments. However, there are different ways to deal with these problems, e.g. taking time to **naturally adjust**, or using **drugs** to reduce the effects of sleep deprivation.

Practice Questions

Q1 What is the difference between circadian, infradian and ultradian rhythms?
Q2 Explain what is meant by 'endogenous pacemakers' and 'exogenous zeitgebers'.
Q3 Why does jet lag occur?
Q4 Why is shift work disruptive to biological rhythms?
Q5 Give two criticisms of research on biological rhythms.

Exam Question

Q1 a) Outline the roles of endogenous pacemakers and exogenous zeitgebers in biological rhythms. [8 marks]

b) Discuss research studies that have examined the role of endogenous and exogenous factors in human biological cycles. [16 marks]

"I didn't mean to fall asleep Miss — the melatonin made me do it..."

It's scientific fact that if you're a rock star, your biological rhythm immediately changes to 'Here I Go Again' by Whitesnake. Actually, that's not scientific at all. Nor is it fact. When you can answer the practice questions, and you've had a crack at the essays, think about what your rock rhythm would be... Are you ready? It's 'Here I Go Again', by Whitesnake. Fact.

Sleep States

Sleep — a topic that's surely close to all our hearts. We spend about a third of our lives asleep, so it must be pretty important. Amazingly, no one's quite sure why. I reckon I know though — it's because staying in bed all day is brilliant.

Sleep Can Be Split into Stages of Different **Brain Activity**

Electroencephalograms (EEGs) measure electrical activity in the brain, and are used to record the stages of sleep.

1) Adults pass through the stages about **five times a night**, with each cycle lasting about **90 minutes**. Who'd have thought we were so busy...

2) As you fall into deeper sleep, brain activity becomes **higher voltage** and **lower frequency**. These are the stages of slow wave sleep (SWS):

   Stage 1 is a bit like deep relaxation, with lowered heart rate, muscle tension and temperature. It's quite easy to wake people up.

   Stage 2 has slower and larger EEG waves, with some quick bursts of high frequency waves called **sleep spindles**.

   Stage 3 has even larger, slower waves.

   Stage 4 has the largest, slowest waves of all, because it's the deepest stage of sleep. Metabolic activity is pretty low in general, and the sleeper is very hard to wake.

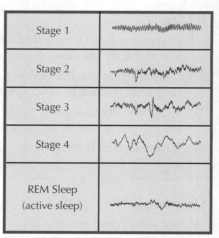

3) After stage 4 the cycle reverses back through stages 3 and 2. A period of **active sleep** occurs instead of stage 1.

4) During the active stage, metabolic activity increases, and the body appears almost paralysed except for **rapid eye movement (REM)**. The EEG pattern is almost like when you're awake. The cycle is repeated about five times during the night, but we only enter stages 3 and 4 in the first two. Periods of REM increase with each cycle.

There are Lots of **Different Theories** of Sleep

Evolutionary approaches relate to the **environment, evolution** and **survival of the fittest**.
1) **Webb (1968)** suggested that everyday sleep is similar to **hibernation** — sleep conserves energy at times when it's harder to get resources (i.e. at night time). Using energy would be **inefficient**.
2) **Meddis (1977)** suggested that sleep helps keep animals **safe**. By being quiet and still, they are less likely to attract predators (especially at night). However, sleep also makes animals **vulnerable** to predators if discovered.
3) Not sleeping at all would be very advantageous, but as it seems to occur in all animals, it must have an **important function** — although how much sleep animals have **varies**. Animals that **graze** often and must avoid predators **sleep less**, while **predators**, that don't eat as frequently and aren't hunted, **sleep more**.

- The evolutionary approach, focusing on survival and environmental adaptation, is useful for understanding **how and why** behaviours occur. Behaviours have evolved to help survival and adapt us to our environment.
- Evolution occurs over **long periods** so it's hard to test theories about why some behaviours have been **naturally selected**. So, it's difficult to **prove them wrong**, making them **less useful** from a scientific perspective.

Restoration approaches suggest that sleep restores the body's ability to **function**, after being busy during the day.
1) **Oswald (1980)** suggested that SWS/non-REM sleep is for restoring bodily functions linked to **physical activity**, and REM sleep is for restoring **brain functions**.
2) **Horne (1988)** distinguished between two types of sleep: **core sleep**, which is made up of stage 4 SWS (for body restoration) and REM sleep (for brain restoration), and **optional sleep**, which is made up of the other sleep stages. Although optional sleep is not necessary, having it can help to conserve energy.

- It seems that important **brain and body restoration** occurs during sleep. Babies, whose brains are developing, spend more time in REM sleep and release more **growth hormone** during SWS.
- **Shapiro et al (1981)** found that long-distance runners had more SWS after a race, implying that the exercise **increased** the need for bodily restoration.
- However, **Horne and Minard's (1985)** study found that when participants did physical and cognitive activity they fell asleep **more quickly**, but did not sleep for longer. It may be that there was a **reduction** in the amount of **optional sleep** that they had.

Sleep States

Several Techniques are Used in Sleep Research

The following equipment and techniques are often used in **sleep laboratories**:

1) Equipment such as **EEGs** measure electrical activity in the brain and provide **quantitative reports** which can easily be compared to others. They have high **reliability** and changes in sleep stages can be easily identified.

2) Other equipment used includes **EOGs** (electrooculograms) which measure the electrical activity of the **eyes**, and **EMGs** (electromyograms) which measure the electrical activity in **muscles**.

3) **Self reports** involve participants keeping a record of their dreams or estimating their length. They're useful for gaining information which couldn't be collected in any other way, but they're limited by the **accuracy of recall**.

4) **Observations** of patterns and directions of **eye movements** can be recorded and related to sleep stages.

5) Variables, such as noise and distraction, are **controlled** to increase the **reliability** of the research. However, research in sleep laboratories creates an **artificial environment**, which may affect the participants' sleep patterns and so reduce **validity**.

Our Sleeping Patterns Change During Our Lifespan

The **amount** we sleep and our **patterns** of sleep **change** as we get older.

1) The **older** we get the **less** we tend to sleep — babies sleep up to 20 hours a day, whilst most adults average 7-8 hours and people over 50 average only 6 hours.

2) Also, as we get older we tend to have **less REM sleep** — Kleitman (1963) found that newborn babies may spend 8-9 hours every day in REM sleep. Children have less REM sleep than infants, and adults have less than children.

3) Kales and Kales (1974) found that elderly people are more likely to **wake up** several times during their night's sleep than younger people.

Comments

1) Most evidence for changes in sleep patterns comes from laboratory research using **EEG recordings**. These recordings are obtained by attaching **electrodes** to participants. This creates an **unfamiliar sleeping environment** for the participants, which may **disrupt** their usual **sleep patterns**.

2) However, Empson (1989) suggests that after the first night participants **adjust** to the conditions and their sleep is representative of their usual patterns.

3) More research is needed to find out the **reasons** for lifespan changes in sleep. For example, REM sleep in childhood may be linked to brain development.

Practice Questions

Q1 Summarise the four stages of slow wave sleep.

Q2 What is active sleep?

Q3 How does the average amount of sleep that we have every day change over our lifespan?

Q4 Give a limitation of sleep research using EEG recordings.

Exam Question

Q1 a)	Outline the stages of human sleep.	[4 marks]
b)	Outline the lifespan changes in human sleep.	[4 marks]
c)	Evaluate research on the functions of sleep.	[16 marks]

REM sleep — not the same as dozing off with your headphones on...

Don't know about you but I'm not looking forward to getting down to six hours sleep a night — talk about falling standards. Bring back the good old days of 20 hours snoozing out of 24. Anyway, seeing as you've got so much more time awake than ever before, I suggest that you put it to good use and learn about the nature, functions and lifespan changes of sleep. Enjoy.

SECTION ONE — BIOLOGICAL RHYTHMS AND SLEEP

Disorders of Sleep

There are lots of different sleep disorders — some are common, like insomnia, others are more unusual, like narcolepsy. And then there's sleepwalking — which can lead to some very bizarre situations. You need to know about all three.

Insomnia *is a* Sleep Disorder

1) People with **insomnia** have **difficulty falling asleep**, **difficulty staying asleep**, or **both**.

2) They may feel **sleepy** and **irritable** during the day, with **impaired concentration** — this can affect their daily life and their relationships.

3) Insomnia may be **acute**, lasting a few nights, or **chronic**, lasting for weeks, months or years.

4) Research has suggested that about **10%** of adults may suffer from **chronic** insomnia.

5) There are different types of insomnia:

Primary Insomnia

Primary insomnia is insomnia that **isn't linked** to any existing **physical** or **psychological** conditions. Instead, it may be caused by:

1) **Stimulants.** Stimulants such as caffeine or nicotine increase arousal and can lead to insomnia. This can also lead to a vicious circle of frustration and anxiety.

2) **Disruptions to circadian rhythm.** Jet-lag, shift work and sleeping at irregular times (e.g. staying-up late at weekends) may all disrupt sleep patterns and lead to insomnia.

Secondary Insomnia

Secondary insomnia is the result of existing **physical** or **psychological** conditions. For example:

1) **Physical complaints.** A number of physical complaints such as arthritis, diabetes and asthma can cause insomnia.

2) **Psychological conditions.** A number of psychological conditions, e.g. depression, can cause insomnia.

3) **Stress or anxiety.** Worrying about something causes anxiety (higher bodily arousal), which may in turn cause insomnia. Failure to get to sleep can cause frustration, which creates more anxiety, making it even harder to get to sleep and producing a vicious circle.

4) **Medication.** Some medications may have side effects which disrupt sleep. Also, medications taken to improve sleep may cause problems if their effects are too long-lasting (leaving the person sleepy the next day), or if their effects wear off too early. Some people may become dependent on sleeping pills and suffer even worse insomnia if they stop taking them.

Insomnia *is* Influenced *by* Many Factors

An episode of insomnia can be influenced by many factors. For example:

1) **Sleep apnoea.** This is a condition where a person's airways become temporarily **blocked** whilst they are sleeping, causing their **breathing** to be **interrupted**. This **disrupts** their **sleep pattern** — either causing a person to wake up or to move into a lighter stage of sleep. Sleep apnoea is linked to snoring and may be caused by various abnormalities in brain or respiratory functioning. It's also linked to obesity — especially in males.

2) **Personality traits.** Characteristics like being **overly sensitive**, **worrying**, having a very **serious attitude** to life issues and being **overly dependent** on other people can lead to insomnia.

3) **Depression and anxiety.** These increase **emotional arousal** — which may then increase **physiological arousal**, causing insomnia.

Claire broke the news gently — Jake's nap time snoring was the cause of the insomnia epidemic in Class 1.

Research into insomnia is **difficult** as there are **many variables** that can cause or influence the condition. This problem is compounded by the fact that some of the variables are **hard to control**. Much of the research that's been done has produced **correlational evidence** rather than showing cause and effect.

Disorders of Sleep

Sleepwalking *is a Sleep Disorder...*

Sleepwalking is a disorder associated with **stage 3** and **stage 4** sleep. It affects approximately **15% of children** and **2% of adults**. The causes of sleepwalking are not fully known but it's thought it can be triggered by...

- **Sleep deprivation**, especially in people with a history of sleepwalking
- An **irregular sleep schedule**
- **Stress** or anxiety
- Some **drugs**, e.g. anti-psychotics or stimulants

Dauvilliers et al's (2005) study suggests there may be a **genetic component** to sleepwalking as well — they found higher concordance rates for the disorder in identical twins than in non-identical twins.

...and so is Narcolepsy

Narcolepsy is a disorder causing sudden episodes of **day-time sleepiness**, leading to a person falling asleep for a short period of time (seconds or minutes). They may also experience **features** of sleep such as **weak muscles** (**cataplexy**) and **dream-like imagery**. Narcolepsy affects **0.02-0.06%** of the population, most of whom develop the condition in early adulthood. The causes of narcolepsy may include:

- **Reduced levels of hypocretin**. Hypocretin is a chemical that's involved in regulating arousal levels. It's thought narcolepsy may be caused by the body's immune system attacking the cells that produce hypocretin, reducing the body's ability to regulate sleep.

Alfie might claim it was narcolepsy but he was fooling no-one. They knew a lazy seal when they saw one.

- **Genetics**. Studies have shown a 25-31% concordance rate for the condition between identical twins — this suggests a genetic link. This concordance rate is fairly low, so environmental influences must also be important. It could be that a virus, e.g. that causes measles, may trigger a genetic predisposition to narcolepsy. So a person would need the genetic predisposition for narcolepsy as well as contact with the virus before developing the condition — meaning the cause would be both genetic and environmental.

Practice Questions

Q1 What is insomnia?
Q2 What is the difference between primary insomnia and secondary insomnia?
Q3 How can depression influence insomnia?
Q4 List three possible causes of sleepwalking.
Q5 List some possible causes of narcolepsy.

Exam Question

Q1 a) Outline explanations for insomnia. [6 marks]

b) Describe and explain how sleep apnoea and personality traits can influence insomnia. [12 marks]

c) Evaluate the evidence for one explanation for narcolepsy. [6 marks]

Revision — *it cures insomnia and induces narcolepsy in one go...*

Now stay with it — you need to remember this stuff. It's not too bad really, three sleeping disorders — insomnia, narcolepsy and sleepwalking, with explanations for all of them. Once you've learnt that, you can give yourself a pat on the back, make yourself some cocoa and have a little nap if you like — because you've reached the end of this very short section. Huzzah.

Theories of Perception

*Perception is how we make sense of things around us. Without it the world would be a mish mash of meaninglessness —
so it's pretty important. With that in mind, you'd better have a look at some theories of perception. Here they come...*

Perception *is the Process of* Giving Meaning to Stimuli

1) Our senses are constantly detecting **stimuli** in the environment around us.

2) The information the stimuli provide has to be **processed** in order to **make sense of it**.

3) This processing is known as **perception**.

4) Theories of how the information is understood are known as **theories of perception**.
You need to know about two of them — Gibson's **direct theory** and Gregory's **indirect theory**.

*'Bottom up' means
information is pieced
together to make
sense of it.*

Gibson's Direct Theory *of Perception is a* Bottom Up *Theory*

1) **Gibson's** (1979) **direct theory** of perception suggests that stimuli provide **visual information**
which the cognitive system then **processes**, allowing the person to make sense of the stimuli.

2) Previously stored knowledge **isn't needed** — the information provided by the stimuli is enough.

3) Gibson argues that this is possible because of the large amount of information provided by the **optic array**:

The Optic Array

The optic array is the **pattern of light** that enters the eye, allowing things to be seen. It's a really **complicated**
pattern — it's made up of all the light rays reflecting off all the objects and surfaces in view, so it holds
lots of information. To make things even more complex, it **changes** each time you **move**. The optic array
gives rise to **texture gradients**, **horizon ratios** and **optic flow patterns**. These are all involved in perception.

Texture gradients

Objects that are **far away** take up less of
the optic array and are **closer together** than
objects that are near. This is known as the
texture gradient. It provides information
on the **depth** and **distance** of objects.

Horizon ratios

Objects that are the **same height** are cut in
the **same place** by the horizon, regardless of
how far away they are. This is known as a
horizon ratio and provides us with information
on the **size** and **distance** of objects.

Optic flow patterns

As we move, the place we're moving towards appears to be stationary whilst other objects appear to
move past us. Objects that are **close** to us seem to be moving **quickly**, whilst those **far away** seem to
move much more **slowly**. For example, when you travel in a car, signposts and nearby buildings zoom by
in comparison to mountain ranges in the distance. This is due to **changes in the optic array** as we move.
These are known as **optic flow patterns**. They give us information on the **position** and **depth** of objects.

Although the optic array **changes** when a person **moves**, the information provided by texture gradients,
horizon ratios and optic flow remains **constant**. This enables us to perceive the world around us.

4) The optic array explains our perception of the **position** of objects relative to each other. However,
it doesn't address how we're able to perceive what objects **are** or how they should be **used**.

5) Gibson proposed that we perceive how an object should be used from the object itself.
An object **affords** (offers) **itself** to certain **behaviours**, e.g. a bed affords itself to lying down.

6) The **affordances** of objects can **change** depending on the **circumstances**, e.g. a box might
afford itself to storing something or afford itself to being stood on to reach a high object.

Comments on Gibson's Theory

1) Gibson studied perception in real-world situations, so his theory has **ecological validity**. His theory
also has **practical applications** — the concept of optic flow has been used to help train pilots.

2) However, the idea of **affordances** has been **criticised**. Many psychologists believe that the uses
of some objects can't be perceived without drawing on **stored knowledge** or **experience**.

Theories of Perception

Gregory's Indirect Theory of Perception is a Top Down Theory

'Top down' means perception is steered by context and prior knowledge.

1) **Gregory's (1966) indirect theory** of perception suggests that stimuli often **don't** provide the cognitive system with **enough information** for it to make sense of a situation.

2) This could be because the stimuli are **ambiguous** or because the information they provide is **limited**.

3) Instead, stimuli are treated as **hypotheses** which are tested within different **contexts** using **stored knowledge**.

4) **Visual illusions** provide support for Gregory's theory:

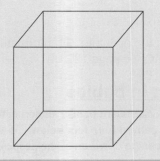

The diagram on the left shows a **Necker cube**. As you look at it your perception of which face is the **front face** changes. Gregory suggests that this is your brain **testing different hypotheses**. As there's **no context** to help you decide which the front face is, your brain continues to switch between them. This **supports** Gregory's theory that stimuli alone don't always provide enough information for the cognitive system to work out what's going on.

Comments on Gregory's Theory

1) There's plenty of evidence to support Gregory's theory — however, it's based on **laboratory experiments** so **lacks ecological validity**.

2) The theory can explain **errors** in perception — for example, those caused by **optical illusions**.

3) However, many psychologists reckon that if perception is based entirely on hypothesis testing we would make **more errors** in perception than we do.

Perception is Probably a Combination of Top Down and Bottom Up Processes

1) Many psychologists believe that perception stems from a **combination** of **top down** and **bottom up** processes.

2) **Bottom up** processes are most likely when the information provided by stimuli is **unambiguous** and **plentiful**.

3) **Top down** processes become more dominant when the amount or the quality of information provided by stimuli is **reduced**. We become more dependent on **stored knowledge** and **past experiences**.

4) When this happens, unconscious 'educated guesses' play a greater part in perception.

Practice Questions

Q1 What is perception?
Q2 Give an example of a bottom up theory of perception.
Q3 What is the optic array?
Q4 What do texture gradients provide information on?
Q5 Which features of the optic array provide information on the size of objects?
Q6 Why does Gregory's (1966) theory lack ecological validity?

Exam Question

Q1 Outline and evaluate Gregory's indirect theory of perception.   [24 marks]

Bottom up theory — not the same as bottoms up. That's for after the exam.

Before you get to the celebratory times after finishing exams you need to get through the not-so-great times of learning for the exam. And as part of that, you definitely need to take the time to learn about Gibson's and Gregory's perception theories. So stuff your brain with info on affordances, visual illusions, hypotheses and the like — not forgetting that mysterious optic array.

Development of Perception

The odd visual illusion aside, we're pretty good at perception and can make sense of most things most of the time. Hmmm, I wonder if we're born with this skill or if we learn it. Oh yes — it's nature vs nurture time again.

There Have Been Lots of **Studies** on The **Development of Perception**

There's been much debate over whether our perceptual abilities are **innate** (inbuilt) or are **learned** through experience. In other words, whether they're down to **nature** or **nurture**. Studies have been carried out to investigate the development of perceptual abilities such as **depth perception** and **visual constancies**.

Some Studies Suggest **Depth Perception** is **Innate**

Depth perception allows us to change a 2D image on the retina (the inner lining of the eye) into 3D information. We do this using cues such as relative size, texture gradients and optic flow patterns (see page 12).

Gibson and Walk (1960) — depth perception in babies

Method:	A '**visual cliff**' was created using a layer of glass with **two levels** of a checkerboard pattern underneath. The shallow level had the pattern just below the glass, the deep level had the pattern **four feet below**. 36 six-month old babies were placed on the shallow side and encouraged by their mothers to crawl on to the deep side.
Results:	Most babies **wouldn't** crawl on to the **deep side** of the visual cliff.
Conclusion:	Babies can perceive depth so **depth perception** is the result of **nature**, not nurture.
Evaluation:	The **validity** of this study is questionable as the babies were six months old and could have **learnt** depth perception by this age. **Campos (1970)** tested **babies** by measuring their heart rate when they were on different sides of the cliff. He found that the heart rate of two-month old babies (who **couldn't crawl**) was the **same** on both sides, suggesting they didn't perceive any change in depth. Nine-month old babies (who **could crawl**) had a **increased** heart rate on the deep side, suggesting they had learned depth perception, i.e. through **nurture**.

Studies Have Suggested That **Visual Constancies** are **Innate**

1) As you look at an object, an image of it forms on the **retina**, allowing it to be seen.

2) The **closer** an object is, the **larger** the image it creates on the retina. However, when the brain interprets the image it's able to identify the object as being closer rather than larger. This is known as **size constancy**.

3) Similarly, when an object is rotated, e.g. a door opening, the **shape** of the image on the retina **changes** but the brain doesn't interpret this as the object changing shape. This is known as **shape constancy**.

4) Size and shape constancy are both **visual constancies** and important perceptual abilities.

5) Several studies have been carried out to determine whether visual constancy is a result of **nature** or **nurture**:

Slater and Morrison (1985) — shape constancy in babies

Method:	**Newborn** babies were shown a square held at **different angles**. At some angles the image on the retina would be a **trapezium**. Once the baby was familiar with the square they were shown a trapezium **alongside it**.
Results:	The babies were more likely to look at the new **trapezium** than the square.
Conclusion:	Babies can distinguish between the trapezium and the square held at an orientation where it looks like a trapezium. So, babies have an **innate** ability to apply **shape constancy** to objects.

Bower (1964, 1966) — size constancy in babies

Method:	**Two-month-old** babies were conditioned to look at a **30 cm cube** held **1 m away** from them, by being given a reward each time they looked at it. Once they could do this they were presented with new stimuli. Firstly they were shown a **90 cm cube** held **1 m away**. This would create a **larger** retinal image than the original cube. Then they were shown a **90 cm cube** held **3 m** away, producing the **same size** retinal image as the original. Lastly, the **original 30 cm cube** was held at a distance of **3 m**, producing a **smaller** retinal image than before.
Results:	The babies preferred to look at the **original 30 cm cube** held at a distance of **3 m** than the 90 cm cubes.
Conclusion:	Babies can distinguish between objects of different sizes regardless of the size of the image they create on the retina. So, babies have an **innate** ability to apply **size constancy** to objects.

Development of Perception

Cross Cultural Studies Have Been Carried Out On Perceptual Abilities

1) If perceptual abilities are the result of **nature** they're likely to be present in **everyone** regardless of culture.

2) However, if they're the result of **nurture** they're likely to **vary** between people of different cultures.

3) So, **cross-cultural studies** can help to determine whether perceptual abilities are the result of **nature** or **nurture**:

1) The **Müller-Lyer illusion** shows two lines of the **same length** that can appear to be different lengths due to inward or outward facing arrow heads (see diagram on right).

2) **Segall et al (1966)** showed the illusion to a sample of **urban** South Africans and a sample of **rural** Zulus.

3) Most of the urban South Africans identified the line with the **inwardly pointing arrows** (**a**) as being **longer** than the line with the **outwardly pointing arrows** (**b**). The Zulus were **less susceptible** to the illusion, with a high proportion identifying the lines as being the same length.

4) Segall suggested that the urban South Africans, who were used to an environment dominated by **straight lines** (e.g. in buildings, furniture, roads, etc.), interpreted the diagram in **3D**.

5) In 3D, **line a** resembles an object receding **away** from the observer (e.g. the inner corner of a room). **Line b** resembles an object projecting **towards** the observer (e.g. the outer corner of a building).

6) As **line a** appears to recede away from the observer the brain interprets it as being **further away** than **line b**.

7) So, the brain interprets **line a** as being **larger** than the image it forms on the retina (**size constancy**) and **perceives** it to be **longer** than **line b**.

8) The **Zulu** people were **less familiar** with buildings made from **straight lines** — their huts were circular. Segall suggested that they saw the lines in **2D**, so didn't apply size constancy and didn't perceive any difference in the length of the lines.

9) He saw this difference in perception across cultures as evidence that perceptual abilities are **developed** in response to the **environment**, i.e. perception is the result of **nurture**.

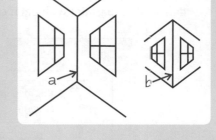

Practice Questions

Q1 What did Gibson and Walk's (1960) 'visual cliff' study test?
Q2 What is size constancy?
Q3 What is shape constancy?

Exam Question

Q1 a) Outline one cross-cultural study into the development of perceptual abilities. [8 marks]

b) Discuss the nature-nurture debate in relation to explanations of perceptual development. [16 marks]

I perceive you might not care whether it's down to nature or nurture...

...however, I also perceive that the examiners don't care that you don't care. I'm perceptive like that. And I perceive that, regardless of your cultural background, your perceptual abilities will lead you to concur. So, in short, learn these pages.

Face Recognition and Visual Agnosia

Of all the very clever things we can do, being able to recognise thousands of different faces is surely one of the most useful. So you'd think someone would have come up with a theory of how we do it. And you'd be right. Read on...

Bruce *and* Young's *(1986) Theory Suggests How We* Recognise Faces

1) **Face recognition** is an important perceptual ability — allowing us to **form relationships** and **function socially**.

2) It lets us tell the **difference** between thousands of faces, even though they have the **same basic features**, e.g. eyes.

3) We're also able to **identify familiar faces** — those of friends, family or famous people.

4) **Bruce and Young** (**1986**) suggest that the process of face recognition is **different** from recognition of other objects. Their model outlines a number of different **components** involved in face recognition:

  - **Structural encoding** — physical features are interpreted to determine **basic information** (e.g. age, gender). This allows a **structural model** of the face to be built up.
  - **Expression analysis** — facial features are analysed to work out the person's **emotional state**.
  - **Facial speech analysis** — facial movements (e.g. lip movements) are used to help **interpret speech**.
  - **Directed visual processing** — processing of **specific features** (e.g. whether the person has a beard).
  - **Face recognition units** — these contain information about the structure of **familiar faces**.
  - **Person identity nodes** — these contain information known about the **person** (e.g. their job, interests).
  - **Name generation** — this helps us to retrieve the **name** of a familiar person and relate it to their face.
  - **Cognitive system** — this contains **extra information** (e.g. the context in which a face is likely to be seen). It also helps determine which of the **other components** involved in face recognition are activated.

5) Bruce and Young suggested that some of these components are activated in a **specific sequence**, whilst others can work in **parallel** with each other. The diagram below shows how they suggest the components are linked.

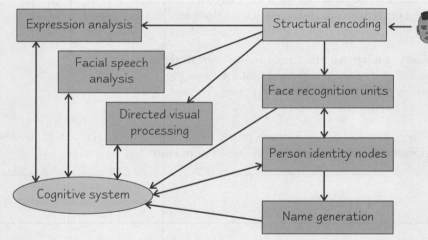

It might well be familiar, but no-one ever seemed to look at Troy's face.

  - For example, **structural encoding** is always the **first** component to be activated. After this either **face recognition units**, **facial speech analysis**, **expression analysis** or **direct visual processing** may be activated. These components work in **parallel**.

  - However, **person identity nodes** can only be activated **after** the **face recognition units**, and only **after this** can **name generation** be activated. These components work in **sequence**. Makes sense — you can't come up with information about someone until you've realised they're familiar.

The Components Used *Depend on Whether the Face is* Familiar *or* Not

Bruce and Young's model proposes that we use **different components** to process **new** and **familiar** faces.

1) They suggest that processing of a **new face** involves **structural encoding**, **expression analysis**, **facial speech analysis** and **directed visual processing**.

2) Recognition of **familiar faces** uses **structural encoding**, **face recognition units**, **person identity nodes** and **name generation**.

Face Recognition and Visual Agnosia

People with **Prosopagnosia** Have Trouble **Recognising Faces**

1) **Prosopagnosia** is a condition where people have difficulty **recognising familiar faces**.

2) It's usually caused by **brain damage**, but some evidence suggests that it could also be **congenital** (present at birth).

3) There are **different types** of prosopagnosia, with the most serious forms leaving people unable to recognise their spouse, close family and friends. Some patients can't even recognise their own face.

4) Some studies of prosopagnosia have provided support for Bruce and Young's model of face recognition:

- **Farah (1994)** studied a patient (LH) who developed prosopagnosia as a result of **brain damage** caused by a **car crash**.
- Along with a control group of participants who didn't have prosopagnosia, he was shown pictures of **faces** and pairs of **spectacles** and then given a **recognition memory test**.
- LH performed **as well** as the control group in recognising **spectacles** but much **worse** than the control group in recognising the **faces**.
- This suggests that prosopagnosia is caused by damage to the area of the brain involved in **face recognition** but not **object recognition**.
- This supports Bruce and Young's proposal that face recognition and object recognition are **separate processes**.

- **Kurucz and Feldmar (1979)** saw a patient with prosopagnosia who was **unable** to identify **familiar faces** but could interpret the **emotional state** of the person.
- This suggests that recognition of familiar faces and interpretation of emotional states are processes that work **independently** of each other.
- This supports Bruce and Young's concept of expression analysis and face recognition units as **separate components** that work in **parallel** with each other — one can be functional even if the other isn't.

5) These case studies suggest that the various types of prosopagnosia are caused by problems with one or more of the components of Bruce and Young's model. For example, the patient in Kurucz and Feldmar's study would have suffered damage to **face recognition units** or **person identity nodes** but **not** to the **expression analysis component**.

There's Some **Evidence** That Bruce and Young's Model **Isn't Correct**

Some studies suggest that Bruce and Young's model **isn't accurate**. For example:

1) **de Haan et al (1991)** found that when given the names and faces of famous people, a patient with amnesia was able to correctly match **88%** of the **faces** to the **names** even though they couldn't give any other information about the person.

2) This doesn't support Bruce and Young's model — the study suggests that activation of **face recognition units** was followed by **name generation**, bypassing **person identity nodes** entirely.

Practice Questions

Q1 What is the role of expression analysis in Bruce and Young's (1986) theory of face recognition?
Q2 Which components of Bruce and Young's (1986) model contain information about familiar faces?
Q3 What is prosopagnosia?

Exam Question

Q1 a) Outline Bruce and Young's (1986) theory of face recognition. [8 marks]

b) Using case studies, discuss the evidence for and against Bruce and Young's theory. [16 marks]

Prosopagnosia's not so bad — there are some faces you want to forget...

So, final two pages for this section. Best to go out with a flourish and learn them really well I think. Especially as there's only ONE theory here. I'm unbelievably kind to you when you think about it. Anyway, enough about me. You need to learn Bruce and Young's theory and the info on prosopagnosia, including the case studies. And then you're done with perception.

Formation, Maintenance and Breakdown

Relationships are a bit of a song and dance at the best of times. But learn these lovely pages and you'll be able to explain — WITH evidence — why you went off on one when Kevin nicked one of your chips without asking.

We Might Form Relationships for **Selfish Reasons**

1) **Reward/need satisfaction theory** states that we form friendships and relationships to receive **rewards** or **reinforcement** from others.

2) Relationships provide **rewards** (approval, sex, status, love, money, respect, agreement with our opinions, smiling, information, etc.) that satisfy our **social needs** (for self-esteem, affiliation, dependency, influence, etc.)

3) So, in terms of operant conditioning, being in a relationship is **positively reinforced** because it is rewarding.

4) **Byrne and Clore's (1970)** Reinforcement-Affect theory suggests that both **operant** and **classical conditioning** play a part in relationships. The theory states that we **learn** to associate people with **positive or enjoyable situations**, even if they are not **directly rewarding** us in these instances.

Economic Theories Consider Relationships to be a **Trading Process**

1) **Social Exchange Theory** (Thibaut & Kelley, 1959) suggests that people try to **maximise rewards** (e.g. attention, self-esteem, happiness) from a relationship and **minimise costs** (e.g. time, effort, emotional support).

2) If the relationship is to continue, then the rewards must not be **outweighed** by the costs — we should end up in **profit**. So, relationships are formed using a sort of 'cost-benefit' analysis.

3) But if we are striving to **get more** and **give less**, this may result in an **unequal relationship**.

1) **Equity theory** suggests that people expect relationships to be **fair and equal**.

2) They want to receive rewards from relationships that are **in balance** with the rewards they provide for the other person.

3) If a relationship is unequal or unfair then it produces **discomfort and distress** in both partners, even if you are the one getting more and giving less.

4) The disadvantaged person may try to **make things fairer** if it seems possible.

"This doesn't seem very fair."
"Well... it is, so keep pushing."

Relationships can be **Perceived Very Differently**

People within a relationship may have different feelings about the relationship and have different levels of satisfaction.

Hatfield et al (1979) asked newlyweds to assess what they and their partner **contributed** to the relationship and their level of **contentment** with the marriage:

• The least satisfied were those who were **under-benefited** (unhappy about giving the most).

• The next least satisfied were those who were **over-benefited** (perhaps they felt a bit guilty about giving the least). Equal relationships were the **most satisfactory**.

But there may be sex differences in how we feel about unequal relationships. **Argyle (1988)** found that:

• Over-benefited **men** were almost as satisfied as those in equitable marriages.

• Over-benefited **women**, however, were much **less satisfied** than women in equal relationships.

Theories of relationship formation can also give an insight into **relationship maintenance**.

• A relationship in which your needs are satisfied would be important for you to **protect and maintain**.

• In the same sense, equity theory says that people in an unbalanced, unfair relationship may **attempt to change things** in order for the balance to be restored.

Formation, Maintenance and Breakdown

A Range of Factors can Influence the **Breakdown of a Relationship**

These are some common reasons for the breakdown of a relationship:

- **dissatisfaction** or **boredom** with the relationship
- **breaking agreed rules** (e.g. being faithful, confidentiality)
- **interference** from other relationships (e.g. family or friends)
- **abuse** (e.g. violence, drugs, alcohol)

- an attractive **alternative relationship** exists
- costs **outweigh** benefits
- **conflict** or **dispute** (e.g. over finances)
- **jealousy** over a real or imagined rival

Theories Suggest Relationships **End in Stages**

Lee (1984) conducted interviews with over 100 couples who had broken up.
He identified **five stages** in the process of the breakdown of a relationship:

1) **Dissatisfaction** in one or both partners
2) **Exposing** the dissatisfaction and identifying problems
3) **Negotiating** the exposed problems

4) **Resolution** — attempting to solve problems
5) **Termination** of the relationship if no resolution

Not all couples went through **all the stages**. It seems that less intimate relationships may progress to the termination stage **more quickly**. Stronger relationships took **longer** to go through the stages and took longer to get over.

Duck (1988) developed a **four-phase model** of the ending of an intimate relationship.

1) **Intra-psychic** phase — inside the head of **one person**. One partner becomes **dissatisfied** with the relationship.
2) **Dyadic** phase — between **two people**. The other partner is told about the dissatisfaction.
3) **Social** phase — beyond the couple. The break-up is **made public** to friends and family. **Implications** are discussed (e.g. care of children). The relationship **can still be saved** here (e.g. intervention of family, external marital support).
4) **Grave-dressing** phase — finishing the relationship completely. The ex-partners organise their lives post-relationship. They tell their own version of the break-up and of their current relationship with their ex.

However, the theories don't take **individual differences** into account and **research evidence** suggests these models don't show how **complex** relationship dissolution can be.

- **Rusbult and Zembrodt (1983)** said some people in relationship breakdowns **actively lead** the process (to resolve the problems or speed up the ending). Others are **passive** (believing things will resolve themselves).
- **Akert (1992)** said people who do the breaking up are **less likely** to be upset and show physical symptoms (e.g. loss of appetite and sleep) — not surprising really.
- Finally, these theories don't take **cultural differences** in relationships into account (see page 23).

Practice Questions

Q1 List some needs and rewards provided by relationships.
Q2 Give three examples of reasons for the breakdown of a relationship.
Q3 What are Lee's five stages of relationship breakdown?
Q4 Describe the dyadic phase of Duck's model.

Exam Questions

Q1 Outline and evaluate two or more theories of relationship formation. [24 marks]

Q2 Discuss research (theories and/or studies) relating to the dissolution of relationships. [24 marks]

People might try and tell you that a relationship is the best kind of ship...

... but that's clearly a lie. The best kind of ship is probably like that one out of Pirates of the Caribbean. It had cannons. And pirates. But I doubt psychologists are cut out for the high seas. Duck might cope, I suppose. Now, make sure you can describe the main theories concerning the formation and dissolution of relationships, and then we can quack on...

Reproductive Behaviour

If you've ever wondered why we find certain characteristics attractive in people, or why parents put so much time and effort into bringing kids up, you've come to the right pages. If you've never wondered this, these are still the right pages.

Sexual Selection Explains Certain Reproductive Behaviours

1) Within a species there are certain **characteristics** that make individuals **attractive** to potential mates.

2) For example, female peacocks find the **long**, **brightly coloured tails** of male peacocks attractive.

3) Males with very brightly coloured tails are more noticeable to **predators**. Those with very long tails find it **difficult to escape** from predators. So, long, brightly coloured tails **reduce** male peacocks' **chances of surviving**.

4) However, as female peacocks are **attracted** to this feature, males with long, brightly coloured tails have a **higher chance of reproducing** and passing their genes on to the next generation than other males.

5) This means that the characteristic **evolves** in the species even though it reduces the survival chances.

6) This evolution of characteristics which are attractive to potential mates is known as **sexual selection**.

7) In **humans**, characteristics affecting attractiveness include **physical** and **mental health** and some **physical features**.

8) These influence potential mates as they indicate ability to **reproduce** and **provide for offspring**.

There Are Different Types of Sexual Selection

Intrasexual selection

Intrasexual selection takes place when males compete (often aggressively) and the winner is rewarded with the female. The female is **passive** in this process — she doesn't choose her own mate.

Intersexual selection

Intersexual selection takes place when males compete for the **attention** of a female. The female plays an **active role**, choosing her mate.

Sperm Competition is a Form of Intrasexual Selection

1) Short's (1979) **Sperm Competition Theory** suggests that males are motivated to ensure that their sperm is **successful in fertilisation** and compete against other males to make this happen.

2) In **humans** this has resulted in men evolving to release **large amounts** of sperm during ejaculation.

3) This is a form of **intrasexual selection** and increases the likelihood of **successful fertilisation**.

Buss (1989) Carried Out Cross Cultural Research Into Intersexual Selection

Buss (1989) — gender differences in mate selection

Method:	**Questionnaires** were used to collect data from over 10 000 men and women from 37 different cultural groups. The questionnaires covered **demographic information** such as age, gender and marital status. They also asked about preferences for variables such as marriage, age differences and characteristics in a mate (e.g. intelligence, sociability and financial prospects).
Results:	**Women** valued variables associated with **gaining resources** (e.g. money, safe environment) more highly than men. **Men** valued variables associated with **reproductive capacity** (e.g. youth) more highly than women.
Conclusion:	Historically, women have had limited access to the **resources** needed to provide for themselves and their offspring. So, they've evolved to select mates who can **provide** these resources. Men have been limited by access to **fertile women**, and so have evolved to be attracted to women with a high likelihood of **reproducing**.
Evaluation:	The study supports an **evolutionary explanation** of gender differences in sexual selection. **Similar findings** were found across a range of **different cultures**. However, it **wasn't** a truly **representative** study as it was hard to include rural and less educated populations. The study also didn't take **social influences** on mate selection into account. For example, changes in society mean that women in many cultures are now able to provide for themselves and their offspring, and aren't as dependent on men for resources. Also, **homosexual relationships** aren't explained, as reproduction isn't a goal in same-sex relationships.

Reproductive Behaviour

Parental Investment Can be Explained in Terms of Evolution

1) **Parental investment** refers to any **time**, **effort** and **energy** that a parent puts towards the **conception**, **gestation** and **rearing** of a child that **reduces** their ability to invest in **other offspring**.

2) In species where gestation is **short** and offspring become independent **quickly**, **less** parental investment is needed.

3) However, in **humans**, parental investment is **more demanding** — gestation takes nine months and children don't become independent for many years.

4) **Sex differences** are an **evolutionary factor** that affects parental investment. For example:

Sex differences

1) Parental investment in humans shows **sex differences**.

2) Men only need to be involved at **conception** whilst women also have to invest during **pregnancy**.

3) There are differences when the offspring is born too, e.g. women have to invest in **breast-feeding**. Historically, men provided **protection**, **shelter** and other **resources** (e.g. food) whilst women invested more time and energy in the **day-to-day care** of children.

4) The **number of children** women can have is **limited** so they're likely to invest **heavily** in the survival of each one. Men can have many more children so investment in each individual is **less important**.

5) **Trivers (1972)** suggests the sex that invests **most** in the offspring (usually females) will **discriminate** when choosing a mate. The sex that invests **least** (usually males) will **compete** more for the higher investing mates.

6) Trivers' parental investment theory explains why men are usually **bigger** than women. Men who were **strong** and **aggressive** were more likely to win the **competition** for a higher investing female. This meant that their **genes** were more likely to stay in the gene pool.

7) Trivers' theory also offers an explanation for differences in **sexual promiscuity** between men and women. Men are more willing to engage in **one-night stands** and to have sex with lots of **different partners**, whereas women are more **choosy**. Trivers argued that this was because the parental investment per child is usually much **lower for men** than for women. Men need to make as many offspring as possible whereas women need to find a mate who will **protect** their offspring.

- Not all psychologists agree that parental investment theories explain the differences in reproductive behaviour between men and women. Some women are willing to have one-night stands, and get involved with short-term relationships. Also, **Sternglanz and Nash (1988)** argued that one-night stands aren't likely to result in pregnancy.
- It's possible that **culture** has also played a big role in shaping human reproductive behaviour. For example, it's often seen as **socially acceptable** for men to be promiscuous, but promiscuous women are **shunned**.
- **Buss (2000)** accepts **evolutionary explanations** for reproductive behaviour, but points out that sexual discrimination in women and sexual competition in men could be **problematic** for modern relationships.

Practice Questions

Q1 List some characteristics that influence attractiveness in humans.
Q2 What is meant by parental investment?
Q3 Male chimpanzees can be around 1.3 times bigger than female chimpanzees. Suggest why this might be.

Exam Question

Q1 a) Outline the relationship between sexual selection and human reproductive behaviours. [8 marks]

b) Discuss and evaluate the influence of sex differences on parental investment. [16 marks]

Research into sexual selection — sounds like a very dodgy excuse to me...

Sexual selection may sound made up, but it's actually a proper psychological term — along with sex differences and parental investment. Once you've got those straight you'll be able to wow those examiners with your reproductive knowledge.

Adult Relationships

We form relationships with lots of people throughout our lives. The relationships we form when we're young and the ones we see around us can affect our own ability to form successful adult relationships. A scary thought indeed...

Hazen and Shaver (1987) Linked **Attachment Theory** to **Adult Relationships**

1) **Childhood** experiences can influence **adult relationships** as they provide **examples** of how to behave.

2) **Hazen and Shaver** (**1987**) noticed similarities between the attachments infants form with their caregivers and the behaviour shown by adults in romantic relationships.

3) They investigated the link between the **attachment type** individuals showed as children and the way they felt about **adult relationships**:

	Hazen and Shaver (1987) — attachment and adult relationships
Method:	Descriptions of three attitudes towards adult relationships were published in a newspaper. These attitudes were based on **Ainsworth et al's attachment types**. Readers were asked to choose the attitude that best suited them. They were also asked to describe their relationships with their own caregivers.
Results:	The **attachment type** that an individual had shown as a child was **significantly related** to how they felt about **adult relationships**. Those who showed a **secure** attachment type in childhood were more likely to enjoy **secure** relationships as an adult. Those with an **anxious-avoidant** attachment type in childhood were more likely to find it **difficult to trust people** in adult relationships. Those with an **anxious-resistant** attachment type in childhood were more likely to feel **anxious** in adult relationships and find it hard to get others as close to them as they wanted.
Conclusion:	Relationships formed with parents during childhood affect relationships in adulthood.
Evaluation:	The study was based on **self-report data** which is **subjective** and therefore may be **unreliable**. The data was also **retrospective**, further reducing the reliability of the study. Also, because the study relied on people replying to a newspaper article, the sample might not be **representative** of the whole population.

Look back to AS if you can't remember about Ainsworth.

Parental Divorce Can Also Affect **Adult Relationships**

1) Many studies show that people who experienced **parental divorce** during childhood have **more negative attitudes** towards relationships than those who didn't experience parental divorce.

2) These negative attitudes include being **less optimistic** about having a successful relationship, feeling **less trustful** of partners, having a **more favourable attitude** towards **divorce** and a **more negative attitude** towards **marriage**.

3) Silvestri (1991) found that having **divorced parents** significantly increased an individual's **own chances** of getting divorced. Johnston and Thomas (1996) suggest that this could be because individuals model their adult behaviour on their parents' behaviour.

4) Alternatively, it could be a result of **learnt negative behaviour**, **disruption** caused by family tension, or **separation** from a parent or siblings during normal child developmental stages.

5) If one parent is absent the child doesn't have a **template** on which to model their own adult relationships. Franklin et al (1990) found that this can create problems with children's future adult relationships.

6) Not all children of divorced parents go on to have unsuccessful adult relationships. There are many factors which can influence the long-term effects, e.g. **quality of relationship** with parents and **support after divorce**.

7) This research can be used to **minimise** the **effect of divorce** on children.

Peer Interaction in **Adolescence** Develops **Skills** For **Adult Relationships**

1) Arnett (2007) suggests that friendships with **peers** during childhood and adolescence give opportunities to develop the **skills** needed to form **successful adult relationships**. These include how to **resolve conflict** and how to take on different **roles** needed in relationships.

2) Collins and van Dulmen (2006) support this theory and also suggest that relationships with peers give individuals the opportunity to learn **behaviours** and **expectations** involved in relationships.

3) So, experiences during childhood and adolescence influence the **quality** of adult relationships.

Adult Relationships

Different Cultures have Different Attitudes to Relationships

Western societies tend to be **individualist** and **Eastern** societies tend to be **collectivist**.

1) A **collectivist** society sees the individual as part of an **interdependent social group**. Obligations to others and the good of the group are very important.
2) Relationships are more likely to be **non-voluntary** (e.g. arranged marriages), where marriage joins **families** as well as individuals. Extended families are more likely to **live together**, providing support for each other.
3) In Western societies, the emphasis is on the **individual's** freedom, achievements and rights. So relationships are formed for individual happiness and are mostly **voluntary**, where a person chooses their partner for themselves.

The Attitudes and Values of Cultures Affect Relationships

Hsu (1981) stated that Western cultures value **change** and **new things**, but that Eastern cultures value **ancestry**, **history** and **continuity**. **Values** affect relationships in different parts of the world.

Duration
- Relationships are more likely to be **permanent** in non-Western cultures.
- In Western societies, we are more likely to split up and have **new relationships**.

Marriage
- Arranged marriages are often associated with collectivist cultures, and involve **whole families**. Arranged marriages also seem to have more **stability** than those based on 'romantic love'.
- However, **De Munck (1996)** found that in a Sri Lankan community with an emphasis on arranged marriages, **romantic love** was still considered when choosing a partner.
- **Ghuman (1994)** stated that arranged marriages were **common** among Hindus, Muslims and Sikhs in Britain, but **Goodwin (1997)** found that only **9%** of Hindu marriages he studied were arranged.
- **Levine et al (1995)** found a higher percentage of people from **collectivist** societies would marry a person with the **right qualities** whom they didn't love, compared to members of **individualistic** societies.

Divorce
- **Goodwin (1999)** calculated the US divorce rate to be **40-50%**.
- However, the Chinese regard divorce as shameful to the **families involved** as much as the divorcing couple — **fewer** marriages end in divorce. This is beginning to change though, as a result of **westernisation**.

Barry got his family's seal of approval before agreeing to anything.

Practice Questions

Q1 Describe the effect of parental divorce on a person's attitude towards adult relationships.

Q2 Give an example of a skill used in peer relationships that can also be used in adult relationships.

Q3 List some differences between trends in relationships in individualistic and collectivist cultures.

Exam Question

Q1 a) Discuss the influence that childhood experiences may have on adult relationships. [8 marks]

b) Discuss research relating to cultural differences in relationships. [16 marks]

I'm the anxious-resistant-avoidant type when it comes to exams...

Just like 40-50% of US marriages, you've reached the end of the road — or at least the end of the section. The key things to learn here are how childhood experiences affect adult relationships, and how relationships vary between cultures. Which is basically everything on these pages. Apart from Barry and the seals — you don't have to learn about him. He's very strange.

Social Theories of Aggression

This section is about aggression — GRRRR! Eeek, I scared myself a bit there. Maybe some theories will calm me down...

Deindividuation *Theory Says Being* Anonymous *Encourages Aggression*

One **social psychological** theory of aggression suggests we're **disinhibited** when we're an **anonymous** part of a **crowd**. People may feel less **personal responsibility** and less fear of **public disapproval** when they're part of the group. **Festinger et al (1952)** coined the term **deindividuation** to describe this state.

Aggression is behaviour intended to harm — including physical and psychological harm.

There's some **real-world evidence** for this effect:

1) **Mullen (1986)** analysed newspaper reports of **lynch mob violence** in the US. The **more people** there were in the mob, the **greater** the level of violence.

2) **Mann (1981)** analysed 21 reports of **suicides** and identified ten cases where a crowd had **baited** the person threatening suicide (e.g. shouting 'jump'). Baiting was more likely to happen **at night**, when the crowd was **at a distance** and when the crowd was **large** (more than 300 people).

Research studies have also supported deindividuation:

1) **Zimbardo (1969)** showed that **anonymity** affects behaviour. Participants in his study believed they were administering **shocks** to another participant in a learning experiment. **Individuated** participants wore normal clothes, large name badges and were introduced to each other. **Deindividuated** participants wore coats with hoods, were instructed in groups and weren't referred to by name. The **more anonymous** participants administered more and longer shocks.

2) **Diener et al (1976)** observed 1300 trick-or-treating children in the US. If they were **anonymous** (in costumes, masks or large groups) they were **more likely** to steal money and sweets.

This evidence supports the idea that deindividuation **increases** aggression. But there are also examples of it having **no effect** or even **reducing** aggression. For example, individuals in crowds at religious festivals often express goodwill to others. It could be that being in a group means that you **conform to group norms**. If group norms are **prosocial**, the individual may behave that way too.

Social Learning Theory *Says* Experience *Explains Aggressive Behaviour*

Social learning theory says behaviours are learnt in two ways:

1) **directly** through **reinforcement** (i.e. reward and punishment).

2) **indirectly** by seeing others being rewarded or punished for behaviours (**vicarious learning**).

Bandura (1965) conducted the **Bobo Doll Experiment** to investigate whether **aggressive behaviour** can be learnt through reinforcement and punishment.

A Bobo doll is an inflatable figure with a weight in the bottom.

Bandura (1965) — Bobo Doll Experiment

Method:	In a **controlled observation** with an **independent measures** design, children watched a video of a male or female model behaving aggressively towards a Bobo doll. Their behaviour was distinctive — e.g. they used a hammer or shouted certain things. The children either saw the model being told off (**punished**) or being rewarded with sweets (**reinforced**). In a **control condition**, the model was neither rewarded nor punished. The children were then allowed to play in a room of toys, including the Bobo doll.
Results:	Children who'd seen the model being rewarded and those in the control condition imitated **more** aggressive behaviours than those who saw the model being punished.
Conclusion:	Children learn aggressive behaviour through **observation** and **imitation**, particularly if it's rewarded.
Evaluation:	The models used distinctive actions that the children were unlikely to produce spontaneously, meaning that Bandura could be sure that **imitation** was taking place. However, the conditions were pretty **artificial** — it's unlikely that children would see adults behaving aggressively towards toys in real life, so the study lacks **ecological validity**. The study also didn't consider the differences between **playfighting** and aggression towards other people. The **previous** behaviour of the children wasn't considered, and no **follow-up** was done to see if the aggressive behaviour was long-term.

Institutional Aggression

Institutional Aggression is Often Seen as Acceptable

Aggression doesn't always involve red faces, bulging eyes and throbbing veins. It can be calm, organised, and even respectable. Certain groups in society are actually relied on to show aggression, so the rest of us don't have to...

Aggression in the police force

To uphold the **rules** and **norms** of society the police are allowed to use aggression against people breaking the law. In this situation, aggression can be seen as a **prosocial behaviour** and many people think the threat of police aggression is critical in maintaining order in society. To make sure their aggressive behaviours are **controlled** and **appropriate** to the situation police officers have to go through training — uncontrolled police aggression or abuse of police power isn't tolerated by society. The **Independent Police Complaints Commission** helps make sure that police aggression is controlled and appropriate by holding police officers accountable for their actions.

Aggression in the military

Wars are usually started and coordinated by **politicians**. Their motivations may be very different to those of the soldiers who join up to fight. For example, a soldier may join the military in order to become part of **a group** and feel a sense of **belonging**, leading to increased **self-esteem**.

Aggression, or the threat of aggression, is an important feature of a soldier's job. However, like in the police force, the aggression needs to be **controlled** and used for **specific purposes** only. For this reason soldiers receive training on **when** to behave aggressively and what **types** of aggression are appropriate. For example, the use of guns to return enemy fire is deemed acceptable, but violence towards prisoners and innocent civilians is not.

However, organised aggression isn't always respectable or accepted by society.
Terrorist groups are an example of aggressive organisations that **aren't** tolerated by society.

Aggression in terrorist groups

People who join **terrorist organisations** may be motivated by a wide range of reasons, including the sense of belonging that comes with joining a group. Many join believing it will bring them certain **benefits**, e.g. young Palestinians living in poverty are often recruited as suicide bombers with the promise of glory in the afterlife. The difference between military organisations and terrorist groups is **relative**, depending on who the target of aggression is — enemy soldiers or civilians.

Practice Questions

Q1 What does deindividuation mean?

Q2 Outline a laboratory experiment that linked deindividuation and aggression.

Q3 Give two criticisms of Bandura's (1965) Bobo Doll experiment.

Q4 Give two examples of institutional aggression.

Q5 Give three reasons why an individual might decide to join the army and fight for their country.

Exam Question

Q1 a) Outline two social psychological theories of aggression. [3 marks]

   b) Evaluate the theories of aggression outlined in part (a). [16 marks]

That wasn't aggression — my fist slipped... And then so did my foot...

It doesn't seem at all surprising that a small child will mimic behaviour that they've recently seen, especially if there's been no harmful outcome of the behaviour they witnessed. But is hitting a doll the same as hitting another child because you've seen someone on TV doing it... Hmm, not too sure about that one — it's a really big jump, and not something you can easily test.

Biological Explanations of Aggression

Aggression is a tendency that humans share with almost all species of animal, as anyone who's tried to give a cat a bath will know. It's a response that can be partially explained by biology. Not sure that'd go down well as an excuse though...

There Are **Genetic Influences** Underlying Aggression

1) Species of various animals have been **selectively bred** to produce highly **aggressive** individuals — e.g. Doberman dogs were originally bred by humans to behave aggressively towards intruders so they can be used as guard dogs.

2) This ability to select the most aggressive dogs and breed them together to give **new generations** with the **same** aggressive tendencies suggests that there are specific **genes** that determine levels of aggression.

3) In humans, evidence for a genetic component to aggression comes from **twin studies** and **adoption studies**, where **criminality** is used as a measure of aggression.

Christiansen (1977) — Twin study into aggression

Method:	A **concordance analysis** of all 3586 pairs of **twins** born between 1881 and 1910 in a region of Denmark was conducted. From this sample, **926** individuals were registered by the police for **criminal activity**. **Identical (MZ)** and **non-identical (DZ)** twins were compared for the rate at which **both** twins of the pair were registered.
Results:	**Male MZ twins** showed **35% concordance** for criminality, compared to the **12% concordance** shown between **DZ twins**. **Female MZ** twins showed **21% concordance** compared to **8%** for **DZ** twins.
Conclusion:	There's a **genetic component** to aggressive behaviour.
Evaluation:	Genetics can't be the only factor, as the concordance rate for MZ twins (who share all of their genetic material) wasn't 100%. In previous twin studies, **samples** have been used where at least one twin had committed a crime. This gave **inflated** concordance rates. However, by studying **all** the twins born in a specified time frame, this study gives a more **representative** rate of concordance. As with all twin studies, **shared environment** for MZ twins is a **confounding variable**.

Mednick et al (1984) — Adoption study into aggression

Method:	A **concordance analysis** of 14 427 Danish **adoptees** was conducted. Rates of concordance for **criminality** between the adoptees and their **adopted** and **biological parents** were compared.
Results:	**13.5%** of adoptees with parents (adoptive or biological) **without** a criminal conviction had a criminal conviction themselves, compared to **14.7%** of adoptees with at least one criminally convicted **adoptive** parent, **20%** of adoptees with at least one criminally convicted **biological** parent, and **24.5%** of adoptees with at least one convicted adoptive **and** one convicted biological parent.
Conclusion:	A **genetic link** is supported. However, the **concordance rates** are quite **low**, suggesting that there are **other** factors that lead to criminality.
Evaluation:	Adoption studies allow **separation** of the genetic and environmental influences. However, criminal convictions may not be a **valid indicator** of aggression — the convictions could have been for non-violent crimes. Also, just because a person has not been **convicted** of a crime does not necessarily mean that they have never committed one.

Areas of the **Brain** Have Been Linked to Aggression

Different areas of the **brain**, including the **temporal lobe** and the **limbic system**, have been linked to different forms of aggressive behaviour. One part of the limbic system, the **amygdala**, has been found to have a particularly strong connection to aggression. Animal studies have shown that **electrical stimulation** of different parts of the amygdala can either **cause** or **reduce** aggression. **Lesions** to the amygdala have been found to cause cats to **attack**, but caused dogs to become **more submissive** and **less aggressive** — they needed **more stimulation** to provoke a response.

There is some evidence for the role of the amygdala in **human** aggression too. **Charles Whitman**, a sniper who killed 14 innocent people and wounded 31 others, left a note that pleaded for his brain to be examined after death for possible dysfunction. An autopsy showed that he had a **temporal lobe tumour**, pressing on his amygdala.

Biological Explanations of Aggression

Hormones May Also Be Involved in Aggression

High levels of **testosterone** (an androgen) are linked to aggression.

1) Levels of testosterone have been **compared** in **males** and **females**, and in **violent** and **non-violent** criminals.

2) **Males** in general, and **violent criminals** in particular, have **higher** levels of testosterone. This may explain their higher levels of **aggression**.

3) However, there's a problem with establishing **cause and effect** — this data is only **correlational**. Another factor could be causing aggressive behaviour, or it could be that being aggressive raises levels of testosterone.

Cindy wasn't the aggressive type, but if she ever saw that hairdresser again...

Van Goozen et al (1994) studied the effects of testosterone **directly**. This avoided having to depend on correlational data, which made it easier to establish cause and effect.

	Van Goozen et al (1994) — Aggression in sex-change participants
Method:	In a **repeated measures** design, 35 female-to-male and 15 male-to-female transsexuals completed **questionnaires** to assess **proneness to aggression**. They completed the questionnaires before and after receiving hormone treatment to 'change' their sex. Female-to-male transsexuals were given testosterone (an androgen) and male-to-female transsexuals were given anti-androgens. Treatment lasted 3 months.
Results:	**Female-to-male** transsexuals reported an **increase** in aggression proneness, whereas **male-to-female** transsexuals reported a **decrease**.
Conclusion:	Levels of **testosterone** determine the likelihood of displaying **aggressive behaviours**.
Evaluation:	By controlling levels of testosterone **experimentally**, the **direction** of cause and effect between testosterone and aggression can be established. However, **self-report** measures of aggression were used, which are subjective and so may not be valid. The participants may have been conforming to **stereotypes** of their new gender roles by expressing an increase or decrease in aggression.

Practice Questions

Q1 Give two possible biological causes of aggression.

Q2 Outline the conclusion of the study by Christiansen (1977).

Q3 Describe the method used in the study by Mednick et al (1984).

Q4 Which parts of the brain have been linked to aggression?

Q5 Which hormone has been linked to aggression?

Q6 Give one advantage and one disadvantage of the method used in the study by Van Goozen et al (1994).

Exam Question

Q1 a) Outline the role of hormones in aggression. [8 marks]

b) Discuss the genetic explanation for aggression. [16 marks]

Pardon me for being aggressive — it was not me, it was my amygdala...

Not quite as snappy as the original, but I still have high hopes that it'll catch on. It's quite surprising that biological parents have more influence on criminal behaviour than the adoptive parents you've grown up with. But, as the study pointed out, the concordance rates are still quite low, so there must be other factors involved — e.g. your friends and where you live.

Evolutionary Explanations of Aggression

Aggression often (though not always) serves a purpose. That doesn't give you licence to go stomping around throwing things about though — it's not big and it's not clever. Speaking of clever, you'd best get on and learn this stuff...

There's an *Evolutionary Explanation* For Aggression

Lorenz proposed a theory of aggression based on **animal behaviour**. He used the idea of **natural selection** (that only the best adapted will survive and pass on their genes) to explain how the behaviour of animals is shaped. Lorenz suggested his theory could also be applied to **humans**.

1) Aggression is an **innate tendency** that's triggered by **environmental stimuli**.

2) Aggression is an **adaptive response**. An individual will be more likely to pass on their **genes** if they're able to gain the **upper hand** in competition for food, mates or territory.

3) Aggression is **ritualised**. A behaviour won't be passed on in the genes if it gets an animal **killed** before it produces offspring. So, there are ritual behaviours in place to stop confrontations being fatal, e.g. wolves end a fight by the loser exposing his jugular vein as a sign of **submission**. This puts the winner in prime position to kill their rival, but in fact the winner takes no further action. If animals were **routinely killed** during everyday power struggles or mating contests, it's likely the species would become **extinct**.

Lorenz's theory has been **criticised** on the fact that aggression **isn't always** adaptive and ritualised — there are many species that **do** fight to the death. Also, the relevance of the theory to **humans** is limited, as **cultural** influences are highly influential in the expression of aggression, e.g. a person's religious beliefs may shape their actions, as may the availability of weapons or the occurrence of war. However, an **evolutionary** approach may be relevant in explaining **some** aggressive human responses.

Jealousy is Aggression to *Deter a Partner's Infidelity*

1) In a survey by **Kinsey (1948)**, **50%** of married **men** and **26%** of married **women** reported having had sex with somebody else while married.

2) Infidelity can be seen as an **evolutionary adaptive strategy** for a man to increase the **quantity** of offspring carrying his genes, and for a woman to improve the **quality** of her offspring.

3) However, it's obviously **not** in the **genetic interests** of their **partners** to be cheated on — it won't be their genes being passed on to the next generation.

4) Indicators that a partner is being unfaithful often lead to **jealous rage**. Jealousy has been explained as a product of **evolution**, although this response is triggered **differently** in each sex.

Tony didn't see it as infidelity, more a service to mankind — genes as good as his should be passed on.

	Buss et al (1992) — Sex differences in jealousy
Method:	This was a **cross-cultural questionnaire study**. Participants were presented with the **hypothetical scenario** that someone they were in a serious, committed romantic relationship with had become interested in someone else. They were asked what would distress them more — imagining their partner forming a deep **emotional attachment** to that other person, or enjoying passionate **sexual intercourse** with the person.
Results:	Across all studies, **more men** than women reported **sexual infidelity** to be most upsetting. On average, **51%** of the men versus **22%** of the women chose this to be more distressing than **emotional infidelity**.
Conclusion:	Men's jealousy is innately triggered by the threat of uncertainty over the **paternity** of children produced within the relationship. However, women are more threatened by **emotional involvement** as it could mean being left for another woman, and so reducing the resources available to her children.
Evaluation:	The fact that the evidence was **consistent** across **different cultures** suggests that these different responses are **innate** rather than learned. However, the fact that the questionnaires were based around a **hypothetical** situation, and the responses available to the participants were **multiple choice**, means that the **validity** of the results is questionable — they may not accurately reflect what participants would actually do if they found themselves in that situation.

Evolutionary Explanations of Aggression

Group Aggression Also Has an Evolutionary Explanation

Aggression can be used by groups to establish dominance in **status** or to gain better **resources**. Warfare and sport are two examples of **group displays** of aggression in humans. There's an **evolutionary explanation** for them both:

Warfare

1) **Buss and Shackelford (1997)** suggest that aggression is an **adaptive response** as it encourages the **reproductive success** of the species. **Sexual selection** means that we choose between prospective mates who we will breed with. Aggression through warfare is one way to **eliminate rivals** and increase the likelihood of our genes being passed on.

2) According to **Waller (2002)**, **terrorist attacks** and **genocides** can be explained by evolutionary theory. Because humans have evolved living in **groups**, a sense of 'them' and 'us' has become important to us. Warfare and other violence against 'outsiders' are ways of defining the **boundaries** of our groups.

- **Tinbergen (1968)** pointed out that aggression in humans **doesn't always** have an **adaptive survival function**. Humans are **one of the few species** that use aggression purely to cause harm.
- Tinbergen said that advances in **technology** mean we're now able to fight each other from **long distances**. In face-to-face aggression we use **signals of appeasement** and **submission** (e.g. emotional tears blur vision and so reduce the efficiency of attack and defence — this acts as a signal of submission to the opponent). In **modern warfare**, these signals no longer apply as we can't clearly see our opponent. In other words, changes in technology have **outstripped** the evolution of adaptive behaviour.

Sport

1) **Podaliri and Balestri (1998)** studied Italian **football supporters**. They found that **aggressive chants** and **aggressive behaviour** strengthened the **cultural identity** of the different supporters, so that the differences between the groups were emphasised.

2) They argued that being **associated** with the **winning team** at a football match gives us **increased status** and makes us more **attractive** to potential partners. This has **adaptive value** because we increase the likelihood of genes from our group being passed on — aggressive behaviour has **survival value**.

3) A weakness of this approach is that similar levels of aggression are **rare** in supporters of **other types of sports**. Also the role of **testosterone** (see page 27) and **social learning theory** (see page 24) aren't considered.

Anthony had listened carefully in psychology class — drowning the opposition at the water polo game had worked very nicely indeed.

Practice Questions

Q1 Describe the findings of the study by Buss et al (1992).

Q2 Why have we evolved the adaptive response of aggression?

Q3 What were the findings of the Podaliri and Balestri (1998) study?

Exam Questions

Q1 "Aggression is an adaptive response." Discuss this statement. [20 marks]

Q2 Rob is at a football match where the crowd becomes aggressive.
How could an evolutionary approach to aggression explain this behaviour? [4 marks]

Forget infidelity — it's people with no exams that make me jealous...

The point to remember about evolutionary arguments is that a modern man or woman probably wouldn't have an affair in order to spread their genes about or improve the quality of any offspring. But these may be deeply buried motives that have been passed down from their early ancestors and still affect their behaviour today, even if they're not aware of it. Spooky.

Factors Influencing Eating Behaviour

This section is all about food and eating, so if you're feeling peckish I suggest you go and grab some biscuits before you start reading. Or a nice bar of chocolate. Maybe even some toast. Actually, forget that, where's the takeaway menu...

Cultural Influence Affects Attitudes Towards Food and Size

In the UK today we tend to assume that you have to be **skinny** to be **beautiful**. But that's actually quite a **recent** idea.

1) Throughout human history, being **voluptuous** (curvy) was considered an attractive trait in a potential partner — it signalled **health** and access to **plentiful resources** in times of scarcity. People were proud to gorge themselves on food and drink because it signalled their **wealth** and **status**.

2) However, in the last 40 years the 'supermodel' and 'size zero' figure has become popular in Western culture. Highly profitable diet, exercise and surgery industries have sprung up as a result of this popularity.

3) In many other places big is **still** seen as best though — for example, in many **African** cultures plump females are regarded as wiser and more fertile, in **Asian** cultures weight is often still linked to affluence and success, and **Pacific Islanders** (Hawaiians/Samoans) equate large physical size in both genders with beauty and status.

Food is also an important part of many **religions**:

> 1) Some **fast** to show devotion (e.g. **Muslim** Ramadan).
> 2) Some **feast** to celebrate important events (e.g. **Christian** Christmas).
> 3) Some **forbid** certain foods (e.g. **Judaism** — pork isn't eaten).
> 4) Some incorporate food in **rituals** (e.g. **Catholicism** — communion wafers).

Different cultures attach different **meanings** to foods and eating forms a major part of many **celebrations** and **ceremonies** worldwide. Imagine birthdays without cake, or Christmas without sprouts...

Attitudes to Food Can Be Affected By Mood

Anyone who has been unable to eat when **stressed** or who has 'pigged out' on junk food when they're feeling **down** will know that mood and food are **linked**.

> 1) A reduced appetite or bad diet, caused by a lack of motivation, is a common symptom of **depression**.
> 2) If you don't have the **energy** to prepare healthy meals you might be more likely to resort to unhealthy pre-packaged ready meals and quick snacks.
> 3) Some people may impulsively '**comfort eat**' or **binge eat** in the hope that a quick indulgence will make them feel better — usually choosing foods high in carbohydrates, fat, sugar and salt to provide that quick 'hit'.
> 4) This can lead to a **vicious cycle** of mood swings caused by unnatural highs and lows in blood sugar levels, which trigger further cravings.

Psychologists are currently investigating the role **emotional intelligence (EI)** plays in the relationship between mood and eating behaviour. They believe that people with a **high level** of personal EI make better food choices and are less likely to use food to regulate their mood. These people are also less likely to find that their appetite is affected (reduced or increased) by **stress**.

Emotional intelligence is the ability to recognise and manage your own emotions and those of other people.

Health Concerns Can Affect Eating Behaviour

Health concerns (e.g. high blood pressure) can affect what and how much we eat. However, eating healthily can become an **obsession** for some people:

> **Orthorexia** is an **eating disorder** where people survive on a **highly restricted diet** to try and avoid anything they think might be 'unhealthy'. This can range from pesticides, herbicides, artificial additives or genetically modified ingredients to fats, animal products, or anything except raw fruit and vegetables. In extreme cases this can lead to **malnutrition** or even **death**.

More familiar examples of eating disorders include **anorexia** and **bulimia** (see p.34–37). Sometimes these can begin with a desire to lose weight and be more **healthy**, which then gets out of hand and becomes a dangerous **obsession**.

Factors Influencing Eating Behaviour

Dieting Doesn't Always Lead to Weight Loss

It's not as easy as just going on a diet and watching the weight drop off. Whether a person **succeeds** in losing weight depends on things like motivation, willpower, genetics, lifestyle and medical conditions (e.g. diabetes or thyroid problems). Other factors include:

Support and Encouragement

1) Eating is often a part of **social interaction**, so many experts think dieting should be too.
2) Informing friends and family of weight loss goals should help reduce the **temptations** of food and encourage **positive reinforcement** (and punishment) from others. Lots of dieters also join a weight loss group or diet with a friend or partner to maintain **motivation**.
3) But this approach doesn't work for everyone — some people find constant monitoring by others stressful and use **secretive binge eating** as a defence mechanism.

They were meant to be on a diet, but Mike sensed that his wife's resolve had slipped.

Physiological Changes Due to Dieting

1) Your body has evolved to cope with **chronic food shortages** by lowering your metabolic rate and protecting fat stores in times of **starvation**. Extreme dieting triggers this response.
2) If you then return to normal eating you end up with **more excess calories** than before which are then converted to fat. To overcome the feeling of deprivation during the diet people often also **overeat** afterwards, which gives an even bigger weight gain.
3) You may then start **another.** even more restrictive diet to undo the weight gain. But this will just reduce the metabolic rate **further** and so the pattern of **'yo-yo'** dieting continues.

Polivy and Herman (1975) — Psychological effects of dieting

Method:	In a study with an independent measures design, samples of **dieting** and **non-dieting** students were placed in three '**pre-load**' conditions — drinking either one or two glasses of milkshake or nothing at all. They were then given unlimited supplies of ice cream.
Results:	The non-dieters ate **less** ice cream the more milkshakes they had drunk. The dieters ate **more** ice cream the more milkshakes they had drunk.
Conclusion:	Drinking the milkshake had damaged the dieters' determination — they gave in to total indulgence after failure. This is known as '**the counter-regulation effect**'.
Evaluation:	These findings **support** what we already know about dieting (the 'diet starts tomorrow' mentality). **Follow-up studies** have found that many people have an 'all-or-nothing' mentality to dieting — if they break the diet they tend to see it as immediate failure and so eat as much as they like.

Practice Questions

Q1 Explain why a fuller figure has traditionally been considered attractive in many cultures.

Q2 Suggest a reason why dieting might fail.

Q3 Describe a physiological effect of dieting.

Exam Question

Q1 Discuss the factors that affect eating behaviour and attitudes to food. [24 marks]

Eating behaviour — now that's the kind of study I'd volunteer for...

There's now such pressure on people, especially women, to look slim in order to feel attractive that it's hard to believe it's all just down to fashion. But from an evolutionary point of view the old-fashioned preference for a curvier figure makes more sense. This showed you had the physical resources to grow and provide for a baby successfully.

Biological Explanations of Eating Behaviour

As the title suggests, there are biological reasons for why you feel hungry or full at different times. And here they are...

Neural Mechanisms Control Eating and Satiation

Satiation just means feeling full.

1) The **hypothalamus** is a gland in the brain responsible for **homeostasis** (keeping conditions in the body constant).
2) It helps to **regulate** things like temperature, circadian rhythms and intake of food and drink.
3) The **ventromedial nucleus (VMN)** and the **lateral nucleus (LN)** are the parts of the hypothalamus that are thought to be involved in **food regulation**.

hypothalamus

The Ventromedial Nucleus is the Satiety Centre

The VMN is also called the ventromedial hypothalamus.

1) Satiety is the **unconscious physiological process** that **stops** you eating.
2) The **VMN** provides the signal to stop eating when it picks up **hormonal messages**. For example, when food is being digested the level of the hormone CCK in the bloodstream is high. This stimulates receptors in the VMN.
3) Experimental **electrical stimulation** of the VMN has been shown to **reduce food intake**.
4) Malfunctions in the VMN may cause **obesity**. This was demonstrated by Baylis et al (1996).

Baylis et al (1996) — VMN lesioning in rats

Method:	Two **symmetrical lesions** (injuries) were made in the VMN of eight male and five female rats. Their body weight was later compared with **age-matched controls**.
Results:	The rats with lesions in their VMN had become **obese**, while the control rats had not.
Conclusion:	Lesions in the VMN cause **hyperphagia** (overeating) and obesity, so the VMN must play a role in satiation.
Evaluation:	This was a very **small sample** using only one breed of rat, so the findings can't be generalised. Also, **other tissues** surrounding the VMN might have been damaged when the lesions were created, so it might not necessarily just be the VMN that is involved.

The Lateral Nucleus is the Hunger Centre

1) When the body's blood sugar level drops, homeostatic responses kick in to help restore the **equilibrium**.
2) **Receptors** in the LN detect the drop in blood sugar. This then causes neurons to fire that create the sensation of hunger.
3) The person is driven to eat and blood glucose levels increase. Receptors then send a hormonal message to the **VMN** to give the sensation of fullness (see above).

The LN is also called the lateral hypothalamus.

Damage to the LN can reduce food intake. For example, chemical lesions are known to produce **aphagia** (failure to eat). However, as with VMN studies, there may be **methodological problems** muddying the water.

Winn et al (1990) — LN lesioning in rats

Method:	The toxin **NMDA** was used to make **lesions** in the LN of rats. A small dose (lesions in **LN only**) and a large dose (lesions spread to **adjacent areas**) condition was used, and there was also a **control group**.
Results:	Rats that had the small dose of NMDA showed **no changes** in their eating behaviour after a brief recovery period. However, rats that had the large dose showed **long-term deficits** in their eating behaviour.
Conclusion:	Damage to the **hypothalamus** impairs feeding responses, but the LN may **not** have as much of an effect as previously thought.
Evaluation:	This research is useful as it shows that the localisation of brain function is **more complex** than originally thought. However, this was an **exploratory study** to test whether NMDA was an effective toxin for use on the hypothalamus and wasn't originally intended to investigate hunger. Therefore, all the relevant variables may not have been controlled, reducing the **reliability** of the results.

Biological Explanations of Eating Behaviour

There Are **Evolutionary** Reasons For **Food Preferences**

People need food to **survive** and throughout history it's been a driving force for **evolution**. This can help explain why so many people would rather have a chocolate eclair than a slice of grapefruit.

Why we like sweet stuff...

- **Harris (1987)** found that **newborn babies** have a preference for sweet things and dislike bitter things.
- These preferences and dislikes are **universal**, suggesting a **genetic** (therefore evolutionary) explanation.
- Early mammals were **frugivores** (ate mainly fruit). Sweet food now triggers the release of the pleasure-inducing brain chemical **dopamine** which acts as a reinforcer.
- Most **poisons** have a strong bitter taste — so our dislike of this type of taste could be a **survival reflex**.

Why we prefer food that's bad for us...

- **Burnham and Phelan (2000)** suggest that a preference for **fatty foods** would have helped our ancestors survive in times of **food scarcity** — these foods are full of energy-giving **calories**.
- Even though food is no longer scarce, we're still programmed to stuff ourselves with burgers and cakes when they're available in order to **build up fat reserves** in case there's ever a shortage. Again, **dopamine** may act as a reinforcing reward.

Why we like our meat spicy...

- **Sherman and Hash (2001)** analysed almost 7000 recipes from 36 countries and found that **meat** dishes contained far more **spices** than **vegetable** dishes. They hypothesised that this was because spices have **antimicrobial** properties — meat is more vulnerable to being infested with bacteria and fungi than vegetables are.
- This may also explain why people in **hot climates** tend to eat **more** spicy food — microbes grow faster in warmer conditions.

For the ultimate dopamine hit Jessie liked to take her sugar neat.

Why we won't eat green bananas or mouldy bread...

We've learned to avoid food that seems **unripe** or **mouldy**. Knowledge passed on from other people as well as our own experiences tell us that good food means life and bad food means death (or at least a dodgy tummy and wasted energy).

Practice Questions

Q1 Describe the function of the hypothalamus in eating behaviour.

Q2 How do Burnham and Phelan (2000) explain our preference for fatty foods?

Q3 Explain how Darwin's theory of natural selection can be applied to food preferences.

Exam Question

Q1 Describe and evaluate research studies into hunger and satiation and explain what they tell us about the neural mechanisms involved. [24 marks]

I can't help it — I've evolved to eat cheesecake...

This explains the mystery of why people seem to love chips, kebabs and anything bad, and shudder at the thought of broccoli and spinach. Our ancestors would be surviving on plants and thinking themselves lucky, and now and again having a big blow-out on a dead mammoth to keep them going through the lean times. Mmmm, barbecued mammoth. My favourite.

Anorexia Nervosa

Lots of people are worried about their weight, but for some this preoccupation leads to really serious health problems. Eating disorders like anorexia nervosa have become increasingly common over the past couple of decades.

Anorexia Nervosa Leads to Significant Weight Loss

Anorexia nervosa is one of the most common eating disorders in the UK. About **90%** of cases are **females** aged **13–18** years old. About **1 in 250 females** and **1 in 2000 males** in the UK between **15 and 30** suffer from anorexia. It involves a dramatic reduction in the amount of food eaten, leading to significant **weight loss**.

Eating disorders involve abnormal patterns of eating that are harmful to the affected person.

The **DSM-IV** (the main diagnostic manual for mental disorders) describes four main characteristics of anorexia:

See page 67 for more about the DSM.

Low weight — anorexia is characterised by a refusal to maintain a normal body weight. This is usually classified as consistently weighing **less than 85%** of the expected weight for their build, age and height.

Body-image distortion — people with anorexia have **distorted self-perception**. They believe they're overweight even when very thin, judge themselves based largely on their weight and refuse to accept the seriousness of their condition.

Anxiety — anorexics are very **fearful** of gaining weight or getting fat even when they're seriously underweight.

Amenorrhoea — females usually **stop menstruating** due to their low body weight. Missing **three consecutive periods** is a clinical characteristic of the disorder.

There Are Biological Explanations For Anorexia Nervosa

Genetic Explanations Have Been Suggested

Holland et al (1988) — concordance rates in twins

Method:	**Concordance rates** (extent to which twins share the same traits) were studied in 45 pairs of twins. At least one twin of each pair had been diagnosed as having anorexia nervosa — the study examined how often the other twin also suffered from the disorder.
Results:	The concordance rate was **56%** for **identical** (MZ) twins and only **5%** for **non-identical** (DZ) twins.
Conclusion:	Anorexia has a **genetic basis**.
Evaluation:	Identical twins share 100% of their genetic material, so **other factors** must also be involved in causing anorexia nervosa as the concordance rate was only **56%**. The higher concordance in MZ twins could be due to **environmental** rather than genetic factors, as looking the same may lead to more shared experiences.

Neural Causes Have Also Been Investigated

1) Researchers have suggested that anorexia nervosa may be due to **damage to the hypothalamus**, specifically the **lateral nucleus** (the area of the brain responsible for controlling hunger, see page 32). Lesion studies show that damage to this area can produce **aphagia** (a failure to eat) in animals, and recent research suggests that anorexics have **reduced blood flow** to this area. But it hasn't yet been proven whether this is a **cause** or an **effect** of the disorder.

2) Anorexics often also have **abnormally high levels** of the neurotransmitter **serotonin** and this causes abnormally high levels of **anxiety**. Serotonin production is stimulated by biological components (amino acids) in **food**, so starvation may actually make anorexics feel better. But again, it's not clear whether these serotonin levels are a **cause** or an **effect** of the disorder.

Anorexia Nervosa

The **Psychodynamic Approach** Suggests **Unconscious** Motivations

1) **Anorexia nervosa may be a reaction to sexual abuse.**

   If a person's sexually abused they may then **loathe their body** for appearing attractive to an abuser — anorexia nervosa is a way to help **destroy the body** and so make it less attractive to others.

2) **Anorexia nervosa may reflect a reluctance to take on adult responsibilities.**

   Anorexia nervosa prevents females developing **breasts or hips** — instead of gaining a womanly shape they **remain physically childlike** and so are able to remain **dependent** on their parents for longer.

3) **Anorexia nervosa may reflect low self-esteem.**

   Very low self-esteem may cause a person to believe their needs (in this case food) to be **wrong** in some way, or that they're **not worthy** of having food. They then **deny themselves** food.

4) **Anorexia nervosa may be a battle against controlling parents.**

   Bruch (1973) found that parents of anorexics tend to be **domineering**. Anorexia might be an attempt to regain some **control** by manipulating the one thing they have control of — their body.

Remember though — it's hard to find **empirical evidence** for theories like these, and there are many **counter arguments**, e.g. not everyone with anorexia nervosa has experienced sexual abuse or has controlling parents.

The **Behavioural Approach** Suggests **Conditioning** May Be the Cause

Classical conditioning

Leitenberg et al (1968) claimed that anorexia nervosa could be a result of someone learning to associate **eating** with **anxiety** — often to **phobic proportions**. Losing weight helps to **reduce** that anxiety.

Operant conditioning

Praise and admiration for initial weight loss acts as **positive reinforcement** for more extreme food avoidance. A constant feeling of **hunger** then acts as a **reward** in itself. **Gilbert (1986)** reported that anorexics experience pleasure and pride as a result of not eating. The **guilt** associated with eating is lessened (**negative reinforcement**), as well as the fear that their weight will attract negative attention (**punishment**).

Practice Questions

Q1 Outline the clinical characteristics of anorexia nervosa.

Q2 Explain how Holland et al's (1988) study provides evidence for a genetic explanation of anorexia nervosa.

Q3 Describe two psychodynamic explanations of the possible causes of anorexia nervosa.

Q4 Explain how operant conditioning may play a role in the development of anorexia nervosa.

Exam Question

Q1 a) Describe one biological explanation for anorexia nervosa. [4 marks]

b) Outline and evaluate psychological explanations for anorexia nervosa. [20 marks]

Anorexia nervosa isn't as recent a problem as you might think...

...in fact, it was first diagnosed in 1868 by William Gull. And although it's most common in teenage girls, it can affect all kinds of different people from all walks of life. It's probably caused by a mixture of the factors listed on these pages and each individual case will be different. Sufferers are often just as confused by their motivation as everyone else.

Bulimia Nervosa

Bulimia nervosa is another type of eating disorder that's common in the UK. It's a different condition from anorexia — sufferers don't starve themselves — but they can still have really serious health problems due to the condition.

Bulimia Nervosa Follows a Pattern of Binge Eating and Purging

Bulimia nervosa involves a pattern of binge eating followed by some kind of purge so that weight isn't gained — for example by inducing vomiting, doing excessive exercise or using laxatives. So, the person's weight fluctuates but stays within a normal range.

The **DSM-IV** (the main diagnostic manual for mental disorders, see p.67) describes five main characteristics of bulimia:

Bingeing — eating a large quantity of food in a short time frame. During a binge the person feels **out of control**, i.e. they can't stop themselves from eating.

Eating disorders involve abnormal patterns of eating that are harmful to the affected person.

Purging — after **bingeing** the person tries to **prevent weight gain**. This may involve vomiting, using laxatives, not eating for a long period of time or excessive exercise.

Frequent bingeing and purging — the binge-purge cycle needs to have been repeated about **twice a week** for at least **3 months** before a diagnosis of bulimia is given.

Distorted self-evaluation — people suffering from bulimia judge themselves based largely on their **body shape** and **weight**.

Separate condition to anorexia — bulimia isn't just a feature of anorexia, it can exist as a condition **on its own**.

There Are Biological Explanations For Bulimia Nervosa

Genetic Explanations Have Been Suggested

Concordance rates are the extent to which twins share the same trait.

Kendler et al (1991) studied over 1000 pairs of twins where at least one twin had bulimia nervosa and found **concordance rates** of **23%** in **identical** twins and **9%** in **non-identical** twins. Although this suggests **genetics** may play a part in bulimia nervosa, it can't be the full story. As identical twins share all of their genetic material, a concordance rate of 100% would be expected if genetics were the only factor.

Neural Causes Have Also Been Investigated

	Kissileff et al (1996) — The role of cholecystokinin (CCK)
Method:	25 people with bulimia nervosa and 18 **controls** were asked to binge eat (i.e. eat as much as they could in one sitting).
Results:	The participants with bulimia nervosa consumed an average of **3500 calories** whereas the controls only managed **1500 calories** on average. The participants with bulimia nervosa were also found to have **depressed levels of CCK** (a hormone related to satiety, see page 32).
Conclusion:	Depleted levels of CCK allowed bulimic patients to carry on eating without feeling full.
Evaluation:	This would seem to fit with the **enhanced appetite** that many bulimics report and their pattern of overeating. However, a lot of the research into the effects of CCK on satiety is based on **animal models**, so there's no guarantee that the same findings apply to humans. The study also used a fairly **small sample size**, so it might not be valid to generalise the results to the whole population.

It's also been found that bulimics often have **abnormally low levels** of the neurotransmitter **serotonin** leading to bouts of abnormally **low mood**. Serotonin production is stimulated by biological components (amino acids) in **food**, and so overeating may actually make bulimics feel temporarily better — although it later leads to guilt and purging.

Bulimia Nervosa

The **Psychodynamic Approach** Says Bulimia is a **Defence Mechanism**

1) **Bulimia nervosa may be a reaction to sexual abuse.**

   The binge-purge cycle helps to express **self-disgust** for attracting an abuser by punishing the body. **Wonderlich et al (1996)** interviewed 1099 American women and found a **correlation** between childhood sexual abuse, dissatisfaction with appearance and bulimia. 16-33% of cases of significant bulimia could be attributed to sexual abuse in childhood.

2) **Bulimia nervosa may be a result of emotional damage caused by poor relationships with parents.**

   According to **Halmi (1995)**, bulimics often **mistake** their emotions for **hunger**, as poor parental relationships stunted their ability to **distinguish** between internal **needs** and **feelings**.

3) **Bulimia nervosa may be a defence mechanism to help guard against trauma.**

   Bulimia is often **triggered** by a specific **traumatic event**, e.g. a divorce or long-term illness. Bulimics may try to **block out** unhappy feelings by indulging in overeating.

Theories from the psychodynamic approach are difficult to find **empirical evidence** for, and there are many **counter arguments.** For example, not everyone with bulimia has experienced sexual abuse or suffered a trauma that could be pinpointed as a trigger.

The **Behavioural Approach** Suggests Bulimia is **Learned**

Operant conditioning

Bulimics often have **poor eating habits** before they develop the disorder fully, e.g. they often reduce their food intake as part of a diet, then overeat to compensate for their deprivation. Both of these behaviours would bring about **positive reinforcement** — praise for weight loss and satisfaction from indulgence. However, overeating may lead to **anxiety** (a **punishment**) which is then reduced by purging (**negative reinforcement**). This makes the purging behaviour more likely to happen again.

Social learning theory

Hamilton and Waller (1993) found that bulimics **overestimated** their own size and shape after seeing **fashion magazine photos**. **Rodin (1991)** found that they often had **mothers** who also had the disorder, or who constantly dieted. This would suggest that exposure to **models** who are positively reinforced for their weight loss may lead to **imitation**.

Practice Questions

Q1 Outline the clinical characteristics of bulimia nervosa.

Q2 Explain why Kendler et al's (1991) study does not offer a complete explanation of bulimia nervosa.

Q3 How does social learning theory explain why some people suffer from bulimia nervosa?

Exam Question

Q1 Outline and evaluate one biological and one psychological explanation of bulimia nervosa. [24 marks]

Bulimia nervosa was only recognised as a condition in 1979...

...but it can have really serious health effects — for example, those who purge by vomiting (which accounts for 75% of people with the condition) can get peptic ulcers, become dehydrated and suffer from electrolyte imbalances. Electrolyte imbalances are especially worrying as they can lead to an irregular heartbeat that can prove fatal. Not good at all.

Obesity

It might seem odd to include obesity in a section on eating disorders — but overeating to the point of being clinically obese certainly counts as an abnormal eating pattern that's harmful to the person affected. And that's why it's in here.

Obesity is When Someone Has an Abnormally High Body Mass Index

1) A person is classed as obese if they have a **BMI** (body mass index) of **30 kg/m² or higher**. This is about 20% above normal for their height and body frame, i.e. they're carrying too much adipose (fatty) tissue.

2) Obesity is generally caused by a person **taking in more calories** (food) than they **burn off** (by exercise), but there are some genetic conditions and medications that can increase the risk of obesity.

3) It's estimated that by 2050 over half of the people in the UK will be obese. This is pretty worrying when you consider that it's already one of the leading **preventable** causes of death worldwide — it increases the risk of **illnesses** like heart disease, diabetes and cancer.

4) The most effective way to treat obesity is with a **sensible diet and plenty of exercise**. However, increasingly people are turning to quick fixes — 'miracle' pills or surgery such as stomach stapling, gastric band fitting or gastric bypass surgery.

Body mass index is a measurement of height relative to weight. A normal BMI is between 18.5 and 25.

Exercise is the best way to combat obesity, but that still didn't excuse Kristy's outfit.

Obesity Can Have Biological Explanations

Some studies have shown that there is a **genetic** element to obesity.

Stunkard et al (1986) — Adoption studies and obesity

Method:	The weight of 540 **adult adoptees** from Denmark was compared with that of both their **biological and adoptive parents**. The adoptees were split into 4 weight classes — thin, median, overweight and obese.
Results:	There was a **strong relationship** between the weight of the adoptees and that of their biological parents. There was **no relationship** between the weight of the adoptees and their adoptive parents in any of the weight classes.
Conclusion:	Genetic influences have an important role in determining adult weight, whereas **environment** seems to have **little effect**.
Evaluation:	This finding is **supported** by other biological versus adoptive relative research and even by some **twin studies**. However, it's probably too **reductionist** to say that genetics alone are responsible for obesity. Also, the participants were all from Denmark, so the results **can't be generalised** to the whole population.

In some cases obesity is caused by a **chemical** problem.

Montague et al (1997) — Leptin's role in obesity

Method:	Two severely obese children (male and female cousins) were studied — a large proportion of their total body weight was made up of **adipose (fatty) tissue**.
Results:	A **mutation** on the part of their DNA responsible for controlling their supply of **leptin** was found — they didn't produce enough leptin. Leptin is a protein produced by adipose tissue to signal that **fat reserves** in the body are **full**.
Conclusion:	Their leptin deficiency had caused the children's obesity. They did not have enough of this chemical to **suppress appetite** in the normal way.
Evaluation:	A number of trials in which obese patients were given doses of leptin have had **very little success**. Research now suggests that most people with obesity in fact have **high levels** of leptin — they're just **resistant** to its effects. This was a **case study** of only two children, so although it revealed a lot about their particular situation, the findings **weren't relevant** to the majority of obese people.

Obesity

The *Psychodynamic Approach* Links Obesity With *Emotional Conflict*

1) **Obesity may be the result of an oral fixation.**

   It's been suggested that obese people experienced trauma at the **oral stage** of psychosexual development and so developed a fixation there. This means that they derive **pleasure from food** and are **unable to delay gratification**, as they're ruled primarily by the **id** (the pleasure principle).

2) **Obesity may reflect a lack of coping skills.**

   Lots of people binge eat as a result of **stress** — it's a form of **denial** used to escape negative feelings that the person **can't cope** with.

3) **Obesity may be due to our thanatos instinct (death drive).**

   Psychodynamic psychologists believe that attempting to eat ourselves to death reflects the unconscious human **desire for self-destruction**.

4) **Parental overfeeding may be a reaction to trauma.**

   Parents who have experienced the **death of a child** are sometimes prone to **overfeeding** remaining or subsequent children to the point of morbid obesity. They feel **unable to deprive** the child of anything.

Psychodynamic theories are difficult to find **empirical evidence** for. Also, there are many **counter arguments**. For example, not everyone who is obese has parents who experienced a trauma.

The *Behavioural Approach* Suggests Obesity is *Conditioned*

Children learn from an early age to **associate** eating with happiness (i.e. classical conditioning) for several reasons:

1) Parents or teachers may use food to **reinforce good behaviour**, e.g. sweets as **rewards**.
2) Parents may **praise** children for clearing their plate or **punish** them for wasting food at mealtimes.
3) Advertisers use **brightly coloured** packaging, friendly **characters** and **free gift** giveaways.
4) **Celebrations** are always accompanied by food, e.g. birthday parties.

As adults they may then overeat to try to recapture these happy emotions (**positive reinforcement**) or to remove a negative state such as sadness, anger or boredom (**negative reinforcement**). So, operant conditioning is also in effect.

Practice Questions

Q1 Outline the clinical characteristics of obesity.
Q2 Why did Stunkard et al (1986) reject environmental factors as causes of obesity?
Q3 What did Montague et al's (1997) study suggest as a possible cause of obesity?
Q4 Explain why parents may overfeed children.
Q5 Describe how operant conditioning can cause obesity.

Exam Question

Q1 a) Outline one or more biological explanation(s) for obesity. [8 marks]

   b) Evaluate one or more psychological theories of obesity. [16 marks]

So it could be your genes stopping you fitting into your jeans...

Hmmm, this chapter has given me some food for thought and no mistake. In fact, my thoughts have been full of nothing but food. Too little, too much, too much rapidly followed by too little — eating can be a complicated business and trying to explain it isn't straightforward either. As usual, a single, simple explanation just won't cut it. Terribly sorry about that.

Psychological Influences on Gender

You'd think gender would be straightforward — you're either masculine or feminine. But that would make for some insultingly easy exam questions. And no-one likes to be insulted. So there's a bit more to it. I knew you'd be pleased.

Cognitive Developmental Theory *Suggests Ideas on Gender* Change *With* Age

1) **Gender** is the way someone acts and identifies themselves — the behavioural characteristics that make a person **masculine** or **feminine**.

2) **Cognitive developmental theory** was first proposed by Piaget. It suggests that children's thoughts and views on the world **change** as they develop.

3) Many theories use Piaget's ideas to explain how ideas about **gender** change with age.

For more on Piaget's cognitive developmental theory see p.52.

Kohlberg (1966) *Developed a* Theory of Gender Consistency

1) **Kohlberg's** (**1966**) theory of **gender consistency** is part of his wider cognitive developmental theory. It identifies **three stages** of gender development:

- **Gender identity** — the child is aware that they're **male** or **female**, but think their gender might **change** (e.g. by wearing opposite sex clothes). This stage usually occurs between the ages of 2 and 3½ years old.

- **Gender stability** — the child realises that their gender will remain **fixed** over **time** (e.g. boys will become men). However, they may think that gender can **change** in **different situations** (e.g. when doing an 'opposite-sex activity'). This stage usually occurs between the ages of 3½ and 4½.

- **Gender consistency** — the child is aware that gender remains fixed in **different situations** (e.g. cross dressing doesn't change gender). This usually occurs between the ages of 4½ and 7.

2) There is some evidence for Kohlberg's theory. For example, **McConaghy's** (**1979**) study showed that children in Kohlberg's **gender stability** stage determined the gender of dolls by their **clothing** rather than their genitals. This suggests they believe that when the situation (e.g. clothing) changes, gender does too.

3) Munroe et al's (1984) study found the same stages in children from **different cultures**.

4) However, Kohlberg's theory has been criticised for ignoring the effects of **social influences** and **conditioning**. Also, it describes what happens, but doesn't explain **why**.

Martin *and* Halverson (1981) *Developed the* Gender Schema Theory

1) Martin and Halverson's gender schema theory **combines** cognitive developmental theory and social learning theory to suggest how **gender stereotyping** helps children learn what is and what isn't appropriate for their gender.

2) It proposes that, by the age of **three**, children have developed a **basic gender identity**. They also have a **gender schema** which contains the child's ideas about **gender appropriate behaviour**.

3) Through **observation**, children continue to learn gender appropriate behaviours and **add** them to their schema.

4) A child's gender schema is based on the concept of an **in-group** and an **out-group**:

- Activities, objects and behaviours associated with their **own sex** are seen as **in-group**. Those associated with the **opposite sex** are **out-group**.

- So, for example, a boy might **label objects** such as cars and trousers as in-group and objects like dolls and skirts as out-group.

- Through reference to their **in-group/out-group schema**, children will show a **bias** towards **in-group** behaviours.

5) Having a gender schema can help children to manage all the information that they're exposed to. They can focus on **processing** information related to their **in-group** and **filter out** information related to their **out-group**.

6) However, there are also **disadvantages** — reinforcing stereotypical gender roles can discourage children from showing interest in things related to their out-group. This can limit their opportunities and lead to **discrimination**.

7) There is some evidence to support gender schema theory. For example, **Bradbard et al** (**1986**) gave children unfamiliar toys and found they were more likely to play with them (and remember them) if they were described as being for their **own gender** rather than the other.

8) As children get older they are capable of **more complex cognition** and understand that their gender doesn't limit them rigidly to in-group objects and behaviours.

Psychological Influences on Gender

People Who Don't Fit Gender Stereotypes Show Psychological Androgyny

1) **Bem (1974)** developed a self report questionnaire known as the **Sex Role Inventory**. It aimed to measure the mix of stereotypically masculine and feminine traits present in an individual.

2) Individuals rate how likely they are to display certain **character traits**, e.g. shyness. Those who score highly for both masculine and feminine traits are said to be **psychologically androgynous**.

3) Bem suggests that androgyny is **advantageous** in society as it means people have the traits needed to cope with a **range of situations**. Those who score highly on only one scale have a more limited range of skills.

4) Several studies suggest that **environmental factors** are the cause of psychological androgyny. For example:

   - Weisner and Wilson-Mitchell (1990) compared children raised in families that put an **emphasis** on traditional gender roles with children raised in families that actively **downplayed** traditional gender roles.
   - They found that androgyny was **higher** in children who had been encouraged to **ignore** traditional gender roles.

Gender Dysphoria is Also Known as Gender Identity Disorder

1) **Gender dysphoria** is a mental disorder which causes a person to feel that they're **biologically** one gender but **psychologically** the other — they feel that they're trapped in the wrong body.

2) For example, a boy may behave **effeminately**, want to wear **female clothes** and have a **baby**.

3) Some studies have indicated that gender dysphoria could be caused by **parental psychiatric problems** or **absent fathers**. For example, Rekers and Kilgus (1997) studied families where offspring had gender dysphoria and found that:

   - **80%** of the gender dysphoria sufferers had **mothers** with **mental health problems**.
   - **45%** had **fathers** with **mental health problems**.
   - **37%** of sufferers had **absent fathers** (or no male role model).

4) However **not all** children who experience these problems during childhood go on to develop gender dysphoria — so there must be **other explanations**.

Practice Questions

Q1 Give the three stages of gender development outlined in Kohlberg's (1966) theory of gender consistency.

Q2 According to Martin and Halverson's (1981) gender schema theory, what is an in-group?

Q3 Why did Bem consider psychological androgyny to be advantageous?

Exam Question

Q1 a) Outline Kohlberg's cognitive developmental theory of gender development. [8 marks]

b) Discuss Martin and Halverson's (1981) gender schema theory. [16 marks]

In-group, out-group, shake-it-all-about group...

Told you there was more to it — but it shouldn't be too bad to learn. It's just Kohlberg's theory (which is pretty simple) and gender schema theory (which there's a bit more to, but nothing to make your head spin). Then psychological androgyny (which could be good for you) and gender dysphoria (a.k.a. gender identity disorder). And then you're done (yay).

Biological Influences on Gender

Biological factors influence gender. No surprises there — the title gives that one away. You need to know what these factors are and how they influence gender. Luckily, these two pages are here to help you out. I'm too kind to you.

Gender Development is Affected by Genes and Hormones

Males and Females Have Different Sex Chromosomes

1) **Females** have a **pair of X** chromosomes — XX. So all ova contain an X chromosome.

2) **Males** have **one X** chromosome and **one Y** chromosome — XY. This means sperm may contain either an X chromosome or a Y chromosome. It's the **Y chromosome** that leads to **male development**.

3) If an ovum is fertilised by a Y carrying sperm, the offspring will be **XY** (**male**). If an ovum is fertilised by an X carrying sperm the offspring will be **XX** (**female**). Which sperm fertilises the ova is determined by chance.

4) Some humans are born with **variations** in the standard sex chromosome pattern. Studies of people with such variations indicate that **gender differences** can be caused by **different sex chromosomes** in males and females.

Sperm and ova only contain one sex chromosome.

> For example, in **Klinefelter's syndrome** males are born with **XXY sex chromosomes** — they have an **extra X chromosome**. Males with this syndrome are **sterile** and tend to be **less muscular** and have **less facial and body hair**. They can have problems using **language** to express themselves and may have trouble with **social interaction**.

Males and Females Have Different Hormone Levels

1) The major male and female hormones are **androgens** and **oestrogens**.

2) Both types of hormone are present in males and females, but in very **different amounts**.

3) **Men** produce more **testosterone** (an androgen) each day than females, and **females** produce more **oestrogens** than males.

4) However, some humans produce **smaller** or **larger** quantities of these hormones than normal.

> For example, sometimes people are born with much more **testosterone** than normal — a particular form of a syndrome called **CAH**.
>
> 1) This form of CAH can cause **early sexual development** in males, but doesn't have much of an effect otherwise.
>
> 2) The **behaviour** of **girls** with this type of CAH tends to be **masculinised** — they have a preference for playing with boys' toys and enjoy 'tomboyish' activities.
>
> 3) **Physically**, girls tend to look more **masculine**. Their **growth** is fast and **puberty** can happen early.
>
> 4) CAH can also cause **physical abnormalities** such as **ambiguous genitalia**. This can make it difficult to tell whether someone is **male** or **female** at birth.

5) Case studies of conditions like this suggest that the effect of **testosterone** on the **developing brain** is responsible for the **differences in gender behaviour**.

There are Evolutionary Explanations For Differences in Gender Roles

Gender roles are the behaviours seen as **appropriate** for one sex and not the other. For example, traditional gender roles would include men being the breadwinner and women staying at home to bring up the children. Many psychologists believe that gender roles originally developed through **evolution**. For example:

1) **Shields** (**1975**) suggests that men and women evolved to have roles that **complemented** each other — dividing the behaviours necessary for survival.

2) **Buss** (**1995**) suggested that the different behaviours shown by men and women are the result of different **reproduction strategies**. For example, Trivers (1972) suggests that women invest more in offspring than men do and so discriminate more when choosing a mate. This could lead to some stereotypically female behaviours, e.g. coyness. In contrast, men have to compete for mates so demonstrate more aggressive behaviours.

Timmy hoped his dad would give up on traditional gender roles soon — he was taking a pounding.

Biological Influences on Gender

The *Biosocial Approach* Can Explain *Gender Development*

The **biosocial approach** explains gender development as a result of both **biological** and **social factors**. **Money and Ehrhardt's (1972)** biosocial theory of gender has two main aspects:

1) During **foetal development**, **genetics** and **physiological changes** (such as the inheritance of an X or Y chromosome and the presence of hormones like testosterone) lead to the development of male or female **physical characteristics**.

2) Once the baby is **born** people **react differently** to it depending on its **gender** — it's given a **social label**. This labelling means that males and females are treated differently from birth and learn different attitudes and behaviours as a result — they are **socialised** in different ways.

Money and Ehrhardt suggest that the **social labelling** of infants and children has a **greater influence** on their behaviour than physiological differences do.

Smith and Lloyd (1978) investigated differences in behaviour towards male and female babies:

Smith and Lloyd (1978) — Behaviour towards male and female babies

Method: A sample of women were asked to play with an **unfamiliar baby**. A variety of toys were available for them to use. A number of babies were used in the experiment — some were **male** and some were **female**.

Results: Participants were likely to offer **gender stereotyped toys** to the baby they played with. They also used **different verbal communication styles** depending on the given gender of the child. Boys were given encouragement for **motor activity**, girls were more likely to be spoken to **calmly** and in a **soothing manner**.

Conclusion: People's behaviour towards babies alters depending on the babies' **gender**.

Evaluation: This study supports the **biosocial theory**, showing that people react differently to boys and girls. This imposes different ideas of what it is to be a boy or a girl on the baby, i.e. they are **socialised differently** and so learn to behave according to a particular gender role. However, the participants might have shown **demand characteristics** — they could have worked out the purpose of the experiment and acted to fit in with it.

Gender Dysphoria Could have a *Biological Influence*

1) Although **gender dysphoria** (see p.41) is currently classed as a **psychiatric condition**, recent studies have suggested a **biological cause**. For example, one study showed a link between male-female gender dysphoria and low **testosterone levels** in the **developing brain**. This could cause the development of a **female gender identity**.

2) The **biosocial approach** to gender development can be used to explain **gender dysphoria**. For example, a child might **biologically** be female, but be treated **socially** as a male. This could happen if parents were desperate to have a son but gave birth to a daughter. This could lead to the child feeling **confused** about their **gender identity**.

Practice Questions

Q1 Which chromosome leads to development of male features? And which are the major male hormones?
Q2 Explain what is meant by gender roles.

Exam Question

Q1 a) Outline the roles of hormones and genes in gender development. [8 marks]

b) Discuss the biosocial approach to gender development. [16 marks]

So, your gender is influenced by biology — never saw that one coming...

Ah, hormones. They're always popping up as reasons for this, that or the other. Maybe they're why you're feeling so restless and depressed now. No... wait... that would be the revision. Anyway, biological influences on gender — get learning.

Social Influences on Gender

Like most things in psychology, gender is influenced by social factors. These factors include the way that family and friends behave, the media you're exposed to, the school you go to and the culture you grow up in. Read on...

Parents and Peers Can Influence Gender Roles

1) **Social learning theory** suggests that we learn by **observing** and **copying** the behaviour of people around us.

2) This learning can be **passive** (when the behaviour is simply watched and copied) or it can be **active** (when the behaviour is reinforced by rewards or discouraged by punishments).

3) **Gender typical behaviours** can be learnt this way, with males copying the behaviour of other males and females copying behaviour of other females. For example, girls may imitate the behaviour of their mothers — the behaviour becomes part of their idea of the female gender role.

4) There's also evidence that parents and peers **react differently** to children depending on their gender:

Parents

- Rubin et al (1974) found that fathers used words like '**soft**' and '**beautiful**' to describe newborn **daughters** and '**strong**' and '**firm**' to describe **sons**.
- Culp et al (1983) found that women treated babies differently according to how they were dressed — **talking** more to those dressed as **girls** and **smiling** more at those dressed as **boys**.
- Hron-Stewart's (1988) study found that adults were **quicker** to comfort a crying baby **girl** than a crying baby boy, expecting boys to be hardier and braver. Also, mothers were more likely to help a **daughter** complete a task than a son.

Peers

- Maccoby and Jacklin (1987) found that children as young as three prefer **same-sex playmates**. Maccoby (1990) found that when children organise their own activities they tend to segregate themselves according to their **gender**.
- Serbin et al (1984) suggest that girls try and influence situations by **polite suggestion** whilst boys use **direct commands**.
- Lamb and Roopnarine's (1979) study of nursery behaviours found that children **encouraged** gender appropriate behaviour and **criticised** gender inappropriate behaviour.

5) The different behaviours that girls and boys observe and experience can lead to development of gender roles.

The Media Can Also Influence Gender Roles...

TV, **films**, **magazines** and **computer games** usually show **gender stereotypical behaviour**. Several studies have shown that the behaviour displayed in these media can influence gender roles. For example:

1) Some studies have shown that the **more TV** a child watches the **more stereotypical** their views on gender are.

2) Williams (1986) carried out a two year **natural experiment** in Canada. He looked at the effect of introducing TV to a town (Notel), by comparing it to a nearby town that already had TV (Multitel). At the start of the experiment, gender stereotyping was much greater in Multitel than Notel. Williams found that gender stereotypes of Notel children **increased** and became more like those of Multitel children after the introduction of TV.

...and So Can Schools

1) The attitude of **schools** and **teachers** can influence gender roles.

2) For example, if teachers hold gender stereotypes this may influence their beliefs about the **abilities** and **preferences** of girls and boys.

3) Bigler (1995) compared students in classes that were **divided by gender** with students in classes where gender **wasn't emphasised**. Students divided by gender were more likely to have **stronger gender stereotypes** and a stronger belief that all males are similar and all females are similar.

Boris tried not to conform to the stereotype of the 'cute baby'. Everyone agreed it was a great effort.

Social Influences on Gender

There's Been Cross-Cultural Research Into Gender Roles

1) **Cross-cultural research** has been carried out to identify how gender roles differ between cultures.

2) Cross-cultural research can also help us to understand the **causes** of gender roles — if roles are **similar** in different cultures it suggests a **biological** explanation. However, if they **vary** between cultures a **social** explanation of gender roles is more likely.

- Whiting and Edwards (1988) observed the behaviour of children in the USA, Mexico, Japan, India, the Philippines and Kenya.
- They found that gender behaviour was very **similar to Western stereotypes** and that there were clear differences between **male** and **female** behaviour.
- For example, girls were more **caring** than boys, and boys were more **aggressive** than girls.
- In societies where children were expected to work to contribute towards the family, there were further gender differences. Girls were more likely to look after **younger siblings** and do **domestic work**, whilst boys were more likely to look after **animals** and were less likely to work within the home.

Responsibility for Childcare May Determine Gender Roles

1) Katz and Konner (1981) looked at **80 different cultures** — they found that in **90%** of them **women** had the main responsibility for child rearing.

2) This **gender division** has implications for men and women in terms of **occupation**, **finance** and **mobility**.

3) D'Andrade (1966) looked at information from **224 societies** to investigate what **types of tasks** and jobs were performed by males and females. He found that:

- Men were more likely to **travel further** from the home, and be involved in **weapon making**, **metal work** and **hunting**.
- Women were more likely to **make** and **repair clothes**, **prepare** and **cook food**, and **make objects** for use in the **home**.

Max was slightly hurt by his sisters' reaction to his offer of looking after the baby

4) Segal (1983) suggested that the differences in **activities** associated with gender roles are related to the differences in **involvement in childcare**.

Practice Questions

Q1 What did Rubin et al (1974) discover about the way fathers describe their newborn children?

Q2 What did Maccoby and Jacklin (1987) find from their study on the type of playmates children prefer?

Q3 Which students in Bigler's (1995) study had the strongest gender role stereotypes?

Q4 How can cross-cultural research help us to understand the causes of gender roles?

Q5 Outline the activities associated with males and females in the D'Andrade (1996) study.

Exam Question

Q1 a) Discuss how parents and peers may influence gender roles.   [8 marks]

b) Describe and discuss cross-cultural research into gender roles.   [16 marks]

A whole town with no TV. Not a single one. In Canada. In 1986. Scary.

It seems everyone's plotting to force us into gender roles and turn us into stereotypes — parents, friends, teachers and the media. There's no getting away from it. I say we fight back. We could start off by getting rid of TVs. We'll just chuck 'em out — it's proven to work and then we'll be free. Life with no TV, it'll be great. Hmmm... maybe gender roles aren't so bad...

Theories of Intelligence

You might have thought intelligence was pretty straightforward — if you do well in your exams you're smart, if you don't you're not. Turns out it's not that simple — there are several theories of intelligence and you need to know them all...

The **Learning Approach** Suggests Intelligence is Developed by **Reinforcement**

1) The **learning approach** to intelligence suggests intelligent behaviours are developed through **conditioning**.

2) For this to happen there needs to be an initial **change in behaviour** that's then **rewarded**. This is known as **reinforcement** and encourages the person to **repeat** the behaviour.

3) For example, Skinner taught pigeons to play ping-pong by providing **positive reinforcement** in stages — for standing on the court, then for touching the ball, then for hitting it correctly, etc.

4) Intelligent human behaviours, e.g. **driving a car** or **writing**, can be learnt in the same way.

> **Comments**
> - This approach has been criticised for being **reductionist** — it ignores other aspects of intelligence, e.g. the biological approach.
> - More understanding is needed of what **cognitive abilities** are involved in intelligence and what **biological** and **environmental factors** influence individual differences in intelligence.

The **Psychometric Approach** Focuses on **Intelligence Testing**

1) The **psychometric approach** involves measuring intelligence to produce an **intelligence quotient** (**IQ**) **score**.

2) This is done through **intelligence tests** that are focused on mathematical ability and abstract, logical reasoning.

3) Spearman (1904) found that people who did well on **one** kind of test, e.g. arithmetic, usually did well in **other** kinds of tests, e.g. spatial reasoning. In other words, their test scores showed a **positive correlation**.

4) So, he proposed that everyone has a **general intelligence** that's **genetically determined** and **unchangeable**. He termed this '**g**'. He also suggested that people develop **specific abilities**, '**s**', which are influenced by **learning**. This can explain why, for example, some people are better at maths than at English.

> **Comments**
> - Thurstone (1938) argued **against** the concept of g, claiming that there are **7 independent groups** of primary mental abilities (e.g. numerical, verbal, spatial) rather than one general intelligence.
> - There are many issues with the use of IQ tests. Many things, e.g. musical ability, are **difficult to measure**. Also, tests may be biased towards one culture.
> - **Developmental factors** are not considered by the psychometric approach — g may be influenced by **education** and **nutrition**, which could promote or impair the development of intelligence.

The **Information Processing Approach** Focuses on **Cognitive Processes**

1) The **information processing approach** to intelligence focuses on the use of a **set** of **cognitive processes**.

2) **Sternberg** (**1985**) suggested that these underlie intelligence and can be split into **three components**:
   - **Metacomponents** — planning and control processes used in problem solving and decision making.
   - **Performance components** — processes that allow us to carry out actions, e.g. memorising, calculating, etc.
   - **Knowledge acquisition components** — processes used to learn new information.

3) Sternberg proposed that these three components are **universal** and apply to **three aspects of intelligence**:
   - **Analytical intelligence** — the ability to solve problems, see solutions, monitor and plan.
   - **Creative intelligence** — the ability to react to stimuli and develop ideas, either new or familiar.
   - **Practical intelligence** — the ability to adjust to different environments and contexts.

   These three kinds of intelligence make up **Sternberg's triarchic model of intelligence**.

> **Comments**
> - Sternberg's model allows for the influence of both **internal** and **external factors** on intelligence.
> - It also addresses intelligence in relation to **practical**, **real-life scenarios** rather than just academic contexts.
> - However, Gottfredson (2003) argues that Sternberg's concept of practical intelligence is **faulty** — it simply represents a set of skills developed to cope with a particular environment, rather than a kind of intelligence.

Theories of Intelligence

Gardner's (1985) Theory Identifies Seven Kinds of Intelligence

1) Traditionally, intelligence has been seen as a **single concept**, emphasising verbal, logical and mathematical skills.
2) Gardner's theory of **multiple intelligences** suggests that we have **several different kinds** of intelligence. These each involve different cognitive structures so are **independent** of each other, although they do interact.
3) So, a person could have a **high level** of ability in **some areas** of intelligence, but a **low level** in **other areas**.
4) Gardner identified **seven** kinds of intelligence:

- **Logical-mathematical** — ability in mathematics and logical and abstract reasoning.
- **Verbal-linguistic** — speaking, reading, writing and the ability to learn languages.
- **Visual-spatial** — ability in mental visualisation and art.
- **Musical** — abilities relating to sound, rhythm and tone.
- **Bodily kinaesthetic** — use of body, e.g. athletic and dance ability.
- **Intrapersonal** — associated with self-understanding, feelings, motivations and objectives.
- **Interpersonal** — social skills, empathy and ability to cooperate with others.

5) In 1997, Gardner added an **eighth** kind of intelligence to his model — **naturalistic intelligence**. People with high naturalistic intelligence are able to relate well to **nature** and **animals**.

Comments on Gardner's Theory

- Gardner's theory is based on a **range** of **research methods**, including psychometric tests and case studies of people who have low IQ scores but high ability in particular kinds of intelligence. For example, Horwitz et al (1965) found that some people who were considered to have low intelligence could rapidly calculate the day of the week that a particular date fell on.
- The concept of multiple intelligences can be **applied to education**. This would give a **broader approach** than the traditional emphasis on verbal and mathematical skills. It can also help teachers to understand the best ways for different students to **learn** things.
- The theory has been criticised because some aspects are **vague**, e.g. intrapersonal and musical intelligence are **difficult to define**. They're also **difficult to measure precisely**.
- Also, some people believe that some of the types of intelligence identified by Gardner are really just names for **talents** or **personality traits**, rather than a kind of intelligence.

Practice Questions

Q1 Give a problem associated with IQ tests.
Q2 In the psychometric approach to intelligence what does 'g' represent?
Q3 Give the three aspects of intelligence identified in Sternberg's (1985) theory.
Q4 Which of Gardner's multiple intelligences is associated with the ability to learn languages?
Q5 Give one criticism of Gardner's (1985) theory of multiple intelligences.

Exam Question

Q1 a) Outline the information processing approach to intelligence. [8 marks]

b) Describe and evaluate Gardner's (1985) theory of multiple intelligences. [16 marks]

Idle-slacker intelligence — the ability to do nothing, common in students...

Who'd have thought there were so many different kinds of intelligence. I wonder what they'll come up with next — maybe the ability to put together great outfits, or a high potential for buying exceedingly good birthday presents, or intelligence in the area of competitive eating perhaps. Tell you what is impressive though, those ping-pong playing pigeons. Marvellous.

Animal Learning and Intelligence

So, humans have varying levels of intelligence and are able to learn — even though it might not feel like much is going in sometimes. These pages look at whether the same applies to other animals or if us humans are a special case.

Classical Conditioning Involves Reflexive Responses

Classical conditioning occurs when a stimulus produces a response in an organism because it's become **associated** with **another** stimulus which normally produces that response. Animals can be classically conditioned.

> **Example**
>
> When dogs see food, they salivate. This is an automatic, unlearned response — a **reflex**. The food is an **unconditioned stimulus** (UCS) and salivation is an **unconditioned response** (UCR). **Pavlov (1927)** studied laboratory dogs that **always** received their food after a **bell** was rung. After a while the dogs would salivate when the bell was rung (before getting the food) as they **associated** the bell with food. The bell had become a **conditioned stimulus** (CS), and salivation had become a **conditioned response** (CR).

The principles of classical conditioning are:

1) **Generalisation** — when stimuli similar to the original CS (e.g. a bell with a different pitch) produce the CR (e.g. salivating).

2) **Discrimination** — when stimuli similar to the original CS don't produce the CR. This can be achieved by withholding the UCS (e.g. food) when the similar stimulus is used. The animal will begin to discriminate between the CS and the similar stimulus and will only respond to the CS.

3) **Extinction** — when the CR (e.g. salivating) isn't produced as a result of the CS (e.g. bell). This happens when the CS is repeatedly presented without the UCS (e.g. food) following it.

4) **Spontaneous recovery** — when a previously extinct CR is produced in response to the CS. This happens when the CS is presented again after a period of time during which it's not been used.

5) **Higher order conditioning** — when a new CS (e.g. a light) produces the CR because the animal associates it with the original CS. This can be achieved by consistently presenting the new CS before the original CS.

Operant Conditioning Involves Voluntary Behaviours

Operant conditioning occurs when organisms learn to associate **particular behaviours** with **particular consequences**. **Positive** consequences encourage them to **repeat** the behaviour, **negative** consequences discourage them from repeating the behaviour. Operant conditioning can involve **positive reinforcement**, **negative reinforcement** or **punishment**:

- **Positive reinforcement** — the behaviour produces a positive outcome, e.g. food, so the behaviour is reinforced.
- **Negative reinforcement** — the behaviour removes a negative stimulus, e.g. pain, so the behaviour is reinforced.
- **Punishment** — the behaviour is punished, e.g. electric shock, deterring the animal from repeating the behaviour.

Operant conditioning can be used to teach animals certain behaviours:

> **Example**
>
> Skinner (1938) studied laboratory rats to see if they could learn behaviour through operant conditioning. He placed the rats in boxes containing a lever. Pushing the lever provided the rat with food pellets — a **positive consequence**. Over time, the rats pushed the lever more frequently as they **associated** the behaviour with the reward of food.

> **Comments**
>
> 1) Most research into conditioning has involved **laboratory experiments**. This **reduces ecological validity** so the results can't be **generalised** to real-life. More **field research** would be useful.
>
> 2) Different **species** have different **capacities** for learning by conditioning. Some may also learn by simple observation, with no reinforcement involved.
>
> 3) **Genetics** seem to **influence** and **limit** what different species can learn by conditioning. For example, Breland and Breland (1951) gave food to pigs when they carried wooden coins (in their mouths) to a 'piggy bank'. However, they started to drop them on the floor and push them towards the bank with their snout (showing an **instinctive** foraging behaviour), so taking longer to get the food.

Animal Learning and Intelligence

Non-human Animals May Show Some Kinds of Intelligence

Self-recognition, social learning and **Machiavellian intelligence** are all seen as evidence of intelligence.

Self-recognition

Self-recognition may be assessed by the **mark test** — an animal is anaesthetised and red dye is put on its forehead. Later, the animal is placed in front of a mirror. If it touches the mark on its head it provides evidence that it **identifies** the image in the mirror as **itself**. A few animals, e.g. chimpanzees, have shown self-recognition. However, Heyes (1994) claims that this doesn't prove that they're self-aware in the same way that humans are.

Machiavellian Intelligence

Machiavellian intelligence is the ability to **manipulate social situations** to reach a goal. For an animal to do this it needs to have **theory of mind** — an ability to imagine the world from the perspective of **others**. Theory of mind allows animals to attribute behaviour to intentions, beliefs and feelings, and enables them to **deceive** others.

Woodruff and Premack's (1979) laboratory experiment

Method:	Chimpanzees watched as a trainer placed food under one of two containers, both of which were out of their reach. One of two trainers then entered. One trainer wore a green coat, the other a white coat. If the chimps were able to guide the **green-coated** trainer to where the food was, they were **given the food**. If they guided the **white-coated** trainer to the food, the trainer **kept the food**. However, if the white-coated trainer **did not** find the food, it would be given to the chimp.
Results:	After repeating the test several times, all of the chimps learned to guide the green-coated trainer to the food. Some of the chimps **intentionally deceived** the white-coated trainer, pointing to the opposite container to where the food was, whilst the rest **withheld information** about the location of the food.
Conclusion:	Chimps have **theory of mind** and are able to **deceive**.
Evaluation:	The chimps may have learnt to guide the green-coated trainer to the food through **conditioning** (with food acting as a **positive reinforcer**) rather than actively attempting to deceive the white-coated trainer. This doesn't require a theory of mind so wouldn't be an example of Machiavellian intelligence.

Social Learning

Social learning occurs when an animal **copies** behaviour that it sees another animal receive a **benefit** from. This is known as **vicarious reinforcement**. Kawai's (1965) **naturalistic observations** of macaque monkeys showed that one of them started to wash potatoes in the sea before eating them. Other monkeys soon seemed to **imitate** this. However, Nagell et al (1993) suggest that animals may just notice environmental features that others are **interacting** with, so also **explore** them and learn by **trial and error**.

Practice Questions

Q1 Outline Pavlov's (1927) experiment on classical conditioning in dogs.

Q2 What is spontaneous recovery?

Q3 What is Machiavellian intelligence?

Exam Question

Q1 a) Outline theories of simple learning in non-human animals. [8 marks]

b) Discuss evidence for intelligence in non-human animals. [16 marks]

I can't come out — I'm conditioning my hair...

So animals are able to learn things — nothing new there. After all, you can train parrots to talk and horses to jump, not to mention all the stuff that guide dogs learn. Don't know why everyone gets so excited about Pavlov's slobbery dogs.

Human Intelligence

Many animals are bigger, stronger or faster than humans but appear to be less intelligent. Many factors may explain why humans are more intelligent than other species, and why intelligence varies between individuals...

Evolutionary Factors May Have Affected the Development of Intelligence

1) **Darwin's** (1859) theory of **natural selection** suggests that characteristics that increase an animal's chances of **surviving** and **reproducing** are likely to be passed from one generation to the next.

2) If **intelligence** is **beneficial** to survival, the **most intelligent** members of a population are the **most likely** to **survive** and **reproduce**. This gives rise to **intelligent offspring**, who are also likely to survive and reproduce.

3) In this way the species **evolves** over time to become **more intelligent**.

4) Humans are a **highly intelligent species**. This suggests that intelligence is a characteristic that's been **beneficial** to the survival of humans and has **evolved** through **natural selection**.

5) **Several factors** may have contributed to the evolution of human intelligence. For example:

1 Ecological Demands

1) The **ecological demands** of the environment may have stimulated the development of intelligence.

2) For example, a hunter-gatherer or foraging lifestyle requires **memory** and **navigational skills**, so higher intelligence levels would be beneficial for survival.

2 Social Complexity

1) Humans are **social animals**. Living in **groups** could have contributed to the development of intelligence.

2) The **social complexity** of group living may help survival, e.g. by giving **protection** from predators and **cooperation** when hunting. However, social living also creates **competition** and **conflict**, e.g. for a mate.

3) Successful social living is more likely if animals are **intelligent** and have **theory of mind**, allowing them to understand others' intentions and feelings. This also allows for **Machiavellian intelligence** — where individuals and groups can deceive others for their own advantage.

4) There is some evidence that **social complexity** and **intelligence** are **linked**:

   • Other animals considered to be intelligent, e.g. **primates** and **dolphins**, also live in social groups.

   • Cosmides and Tooby (1992) found that people are better at solving logical problems if they are put in terms of **everyday social situations**, rather than presented in an abstract form. This suggests that intelligence may have evolved to deal with **social situations**. However, it's not clear which evolved first — intelligence or group living.

3 Brain Size

1) Jerison (1973), found a **positive correlation** between **body size** and **brain size** in animals. However, humans have brains **seven times larger** than expected for a mammal of our size.

2) Early hominids had a brain size of about 600 cubic centimetres. This remained relatively constant for 1.5 million years before **doubling** in size over the last 0.5 million years.

3) This is despite the fact that larger brains require **more energy** and make **childbirth** more **difficult** and **dangerous**.

4) However, these evolutionary costs are **balanced** by **increased intelligence**. Higher intelligence requires **more brain cells** and possibly **more specialised brain areas** — and so **bigger brains** evolved.

5) Research on brain size as a proportion of body size **supports** this theory. Willerman et al (1991) used MRI scanning to measure the brain size of college students. Those with **higher IQ scores** had **larger brains** (proportionate to body size). However, a limited, unrepresentative sample was used, meaning that it's hard to generalise the results. Also the type of IQ test may have had an effect on the results.

Human Intelligence

Intelligence Test Performance is Influenced by Genetics and the Environment

1) There's a lot of debate about the role **genetic** and **environmental factors** play in intelligence test scores.

2) Closely related people, e.g. siblings, tend to have more highly correlated IQ scores than less closely related people e.g. cousins.

3) Bouchard and McGue (1981) did a meta analysis of 111 studies and found that the people with the **highest** IQ correlations were **identical** twins reared **together**. They showed a correlation of **0.86** compared to **0.6** for **non-identical** twins reared together. This suggests that intelligence is influenced by **genetics**.

4) However, **environmental factors** must influence intelligence to some extent otherwise the identical twins would show a correlation of **1**.

5) Another way of testing for genetic influences is to **compare** the correlations **adopted children** show with their **biological** and **adoptive relatives**. A **higher correlation** with their **biological relatives** than with their adoptive relatives (whose environment they share) suggests a strong **genetic** link.

6) But Schiff et al (1978) found that children from lower socio-economic backgrounds who were adopted into families with higher socio-economic status showed **higher IQs** than their **biological relatives**. This suggests that intelligence is affected by **environmental factors**.

7) Also, Bouchard and McGue (1981) found that identical twins reared **apart** showed a **lower correlation** in IQ scores (0.72) than identical twins reared together. This supports the theory that environmental factors affect IQ.

8) So, genetics and environmental factors are **both important** in IQ test performance, and probably **interact**. For example, variations in intelligence caused by genetics could be **compounded** or **reduced** depending on the **environment** (e.g. quality of nutrition or education).

Comments

1) Different studies have used **different kinds of IQ test**, making **comparisons** difficult.

2) Closer relatives often share **more similar environments** (e.g. the same home) than more distantly related people. This makes it difficult to separate genetic influences from environmental influences.

Intelligence is Linked to Culture

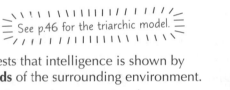
See p.46 for the triarchic model.

1) Sternberg's (1985) **triarchic model** of intelligence suggests that intelligence is shown by successfully adapting to the **physical** and **social demands** of the surrounding environment.

2) Sternberg et al 2001) found that some Kenyan children knew a huge amount about **herbal medicines** but didn't perform very well on normal **IQ tests**.

3) So intelligence must be understood in relation to the **culture** that a person lives in.

4) In some cultures the ability to **pass exams** could be seen as evidence of intelligent behaviour, whilst in others the ability to **hunt** has greater value.

5) Any **intelligence testing** that's carried out must take these differences into account.

Some behaviour isn't considered intelligent in any culture.

Practice Questions

Q1 List three evolutionary factors that may have contributed to the development of human intelligence.

Q2 How can group living help survival?

Q3 Give one piece of evidence that suggests that genetics influences intelligence.

Exam Question

Q1 a) Discuss the role of at least two evolutionary factors in the development of human intelligence. [16 marks]

b) Evaluate the roles of genetic and environmental factors associated with intelligence test performance. [8 marks]

Evolution of intelligence — feels like mine is going the other way...

That's the last pages on intelligence done — learn this stuff and you'll have this very clever topic wrapped up. The key things here are the development of human intelligence and the whole genetic vs environmental factors issue. Learn and enjoy...

Development of Thinking

This bright and shiny new section is all about thinking, and how your thinking develops as you get older. As you might be learning to expect by now, there are a lot of different theories about this. And I bet you want to know all about them. Well, as luck would have it, these pages are all about these theories. It's almost like they were designed just for you...

Piaget *Proposed That* Cognition *Progresses in* Stages

Cognition just means thinking.

Piaget said that we're all born with the **basics** to allow **cognitive progression** — reflexes and senses. He reckoned that more **complex** abilities become possible as children move through **stages of development** as they get older:

Sensorimotor stage (0–2 years)	The child's knowledge is limited to what their senses tell them when they're exploring their surroundings. This exploration brings about an understanding of the concept of object permanence (if you put a towel over a toy, the toy is still there).
Preoperational stage (2–7 years)	The child has some language now, but makes logic mistakes — e.g. cats have four legs, so everything with four legs must be a cat. They typically can't do the three mountains task (see below) or conservation tasks (see next page). Children at this stage show egocentrism, irreversibility and centration (see below).
Concrete operational stage (7–11 years)	The child's use of logic improves and they can do conservation tasks. They no longer show egocentrism, irreversibility and centration but can't yet use abstract reasoning (reasoning in their head).
Formal operational stage (11+ years)	The child is much more advanced now, and can use abstract reasoning in problem solving. They can also use hypotheses and theoretical principles, and deal with hypothetical situations.

1) Piaget used the idea of **schemas** a lot in his work. A schema contains all the information you **know** about an object, action or concept — e.g. the schema of a human face has two eyes, a mouth and a nose, and the schema of riding a bike contains all the movements you'd need to make.

2) Schemas help you to **organise** and **interpret** information — new experiences are taken into our schemas (**assimilated**) and are **accommodated** by them. Accommodation just involves altering existing schemas.

3) Piaget reckoned that children try to find a **balance** between assimilation and accommodation during cognitive development.

Piaget *Used the* Three Mountains Task (1956) *as Evidence for His Theory*

1) Piaget built a **3-D model** of **three mountains** (well, he was from Switzerland).

2) The mountains had different **landmarks** on them — e.g. one had a cross on it, and another had a house.

3) Piaget put a small doll on one of the mountains and then showed children photos of the mountains taken from **various angles**. The children were asked to pick the photo that matched what the **doll** could see.

4) He found that children at his **preoperational stage** (2–7 years old) picked the photo taken from their **own perspective**, rather than the one taken from the **doll's perspective**.

5) He concluded that children at this stage were unable to put themselves in the doll's shoes.

Piaget used this and other experiments as evidence that children at his preoperational stage have the following qualities:

1) **Egocentrism** — they can only view the world from their **own viewpoint**. They're not sensitive to the fact that others may have **different** views or thoughts (as demonstrated by the three mountains task).

2) **Irreversibility** — they don't understand that you can undo an action (e.g. that you can reform a sausage-shaped piece of clay into its original ball shape).

3) **Centration** — they focus on small aspects of a task, not the task as a whole.

Development of Thinking

Piaget Showed How *Other Skills* Develop in *Later Stages*

Understanding of conservation

1) **Conservation** is the understanding that a **set quantity** stays the **same**, even if it **looks** different. For example, if liquid is poured from a short, fat glass into a tall, thin glass, the amount of liquid is still the same. Another example is counters in a row — two rows of five counters both have the same number of counters, even if the counters in one row are spaced out so that it looks longer.

2) Children at the **concrete operational stage** can **correctly identify** that the amount of liquid or the number of counters stays the same even after they've been rearranged. But children at the **preoperational stage** will say that the spaced out row contains **more** counters or the tall glass **more** liquid.

3) However, **McGarrigle and Donaldson (1974)** found that if a puppet (Naughty Teddy) 'accidentally' knocked the counters so that the row looked longer, even younger children at the **preoperational stage** said that the number of counters was the **same**. This suggests that they **did** understand conservation.

The four beaker problem

1) **Piaget and Inhelder (1956)** gave children four beakers, each containing a colourless liquid. When two of the liquids were mixed the liquid turned yellow. Children had to work out the **right combination**.

2) Children at the **formal operational stage** used **systematic testing** of different mixtures to find the answer, whereas children at the **concrete operational stage** used a **random** approach.

3) However, some researchers have argued that **not everybody** gets to this stage of systematic hypothesis testing, so it might not be a **universal** stage of development.

There's Evidence *For* and *Against* Piaget's Stages of Cognitive Development

1) There's **cross-cultural similarity** in the stages — studies have suggested that children of all backgrounds progress through the stages in the same way, which provides **support** for Piaget's theory.

2) Piaget **underestimated abilities** at each age — for example, the experiment with Naughty Teddy showed that preoperational children **can** in fact understand the concept of conservation.

3) He said that **practice** and **teaching wouldn't** speed up progression through the stages but this isn't true — it's been found that teaching **can** help to move children on through the stages.

4) Piaget didn't think that **language** was important in cognitive development. He thought you needed **cognitive development first** in order to allow language to develop. But other theorists, such as **Vygotsky**, take a different view on this, as you'll find out on the next page...

Practice Questions

Q1 Name Piaget's four main stages of cognitive development.
Q2 How is the preoperational stage different from the concrete operational stage?
Q3 Did McGarrigle and Donaldson's (1974) experiment provide evidence for or against Piaget's theory?
Q4 Give two criticisms of Piaget's theory.

Exam Question

Q1 Describe and evaluate Piaget's theory of cognitive development. [24 marks]

Naughty Teddy! You've wrecked my theory...

Piaget's stages were an attempt to explain how children's understanding of the world changes as they develop, and the stages do help to show this. The trouble with any stage theory is that they tend to overestimate any differences between stages, and underestimate differences between individuals within the same stage. Oh well, nothing's perfect I suppose...

Development of Thinking

Some more highly interesting theories on cognitive development coming up — over to you, Vygotsky and Bruner.

Vygotsky Reckoned Culture Plays a Big Part in Cognitive Development

1) **Vygotsky** said there were two types of mental function — **elementary** and **higher**. Elementary functions can be thought of as **innate reflexes**, **sensory abilities** and certain types of **memory**. Higher functions include more complex tasks like **language comprehension** and **decision-making**.

2) **Social** and **cultural factors** play a necessary part in moving from one type of functioning to the other — it's the influence of **others** around you that drives cognitive development.

3) One of Vygotsky's ideas was the **zone of proximal development**. This is the difference between the problem solving a child can do on their **own** and the problem solving they can do with a **more able peer** or **adult**.

4) If your teacher has an idea of what your **potential** is, they can help you reach it by pushing and guiding. So it's **interaction** with the teacher that's important (unlike Piaget's idea that progression happens on its own).

5) Instruction is **social** and driven by the teacher using **language** and **cultural** influences. The intention is to help the child to be **self-regulated** and responsible for their own learning.

Language is Also Important in Cognitive Development

Vygotsky suggests that **language** is a **driving influence** on cognitive development:

1) Children first learn language as a means to **communicate** with caregivers. It's also a tool that allows adults to communicate **social** and **cultural information** to children.

2) As the child grows older they use language not only to communicate but also to **guide** their **behaviour** — they use **self-talk** (talking out loud) to **regulate** and **direct** themselves.

3) This self-talk eventually becomes **internalised** and becomes silent **inner speech**. At this point the child has developed two very different forms of language — **inner speech** and **external oral speech**.

4) **Oral speech** is used socially for **communication**, whilst **inner speech** is a **cognitive tool** that allows individuals to **direct** and **monitor** their **thoughts** and **behaviour**.

5) If someone finds a task difficult they may re-employ **self-talk** to exert greater **control** over their thoughts.

Vygotsky Also Came Up With Stages of Development

Vygotsky's stages **aren't as rigidly defined** as Piaget's — they're broader areas of development (without specified ages) giving an idea of the stages children go through as their thinking matures (**concept formation**). He came up with these 4 stages after studying how children of various ages went about solving a problem:

1) **Vague syncretic** — **trial and error** methods are used, with **no understanding** of the underlying concepts.
2) **Complex** — use of **strategies** begins but they're **not** used successfully.
3) **Potential concept** — successful strategies are used but only **one at a time**.
4) **Mature concept** — **lots** of strategies used at the same time. Thinking becomes **mature** and **developed**.

Vygotsky's Theory Has Strengths and Weaknesses

Vygotsky carried out **very few studies** whilst coming up with his theory. However, other people have carried out studies that have provided evidence that **supports** Vygotsky's theory:

1) **Gardner and Gardner (1969)** found that with **instruction** animals can reach **higher levels** of functioning. This is evidence for the role of **culture** in learning.
2) **Chi et al (1989)** showed that pretending to **talk to the author** as you read (self-explanation) can help increase understanding. This is evidence for the use of **speech in thought**.
3) **Berk (1994)** found that children who used **more self-talk** when solving maths problems did better over the following year. This is evidence for the use of **self-talk** in problem-solving.

Another strength is that the theory can be **successfully applied to education** (see page 56). However, a **major criticism** is that the theory over-emphasises social and cultural factors in intelligence and **ignores biological factors**.

Development of Thinking

Bruner's Theory Focuses on Representations of Knowledge

Bruner (1966) claimed that our brains use three **modes of representation** for knowledge:

1) **The Enactive Mode** — at first, knowledge is only in the form of **physical actions**, i.e. learning by doing. For example, a baby's knowledge of a rattle would involve how to hold and shake it. Later, this mode is used to represent knowledge such as how to swim. So, knowledge just involves '**muscle memory**'.

2) **The Iconic Mode** — at 2–6 years we begin to also store knowledge in the form of **mental images** involving different senses like vision, smell and touch. For example, our knowledge of what an apple is includes what it looks like and tastes like.

3) **The Symbolic Mode** — from about 7 years old we develop the ability to think in **symbolic ways** — we can store things as words and numbers. Language and thinking become strongly linked, e.g. we use language to talk about experiences. This allows us to **mentally manipulate** concepts and ideas, and to think in **abstract** ways.

Like Vygotsky, Bruner thought that **language** was very important for cognitive development. So, **language instruction** might help achieve understanding. However, **Sinclair-de-Zwart (1969)** found that although language appropriate for **conservation tasks** could be taught to children who couldn't conserve, most were still **unsuccessful** at the conservation tasks. Further development seems to be necessary before the next stage can be reached.

There is Some Evidence to Support Bruner's Theory

Bruner and Kenney (1996) — Iconic and symbolic thinking

Method: Children aged 5–7 were shown a grid with an arrangement of different sized glasses on it. These were removed and the children had to **replace** them as they had been (requiring **iconic thinking**), or **rearrange** them, e.g. in a mirror image (requiring **symbolic thinking**).

Results: All the children **replaced** the glasses correctly, but only the **older** children could **rearrange** them. Children without the appropriate language to talk through the problem were only able to do the **replacement task**.

Conclusion: Mental manipulation of ideas requires **symbolic representation**, and children must have progressed to the **symbolic mode** of cognitive development in order to think in this way. Language is important for more complex thinking.

Evaluation: This was a **laboratory experiment** so there was **good control over variables**. However, all the study really showed was that **older** children can manage more **complex tasks** — so, this could also be used as support for Piaget or Vygotsky's theory.

Practice Questions

Q1 According to Vygotsky, what is inner speech used for?

Q2 Give two pieces of evidence that support Vygotsky's theory of cognitive development.

Q3 What is the difference between iconic and symbolic representation?

Q4 What did Bruner and Kenney conclude from their 1996 experiment?

Exam Question

Q1 a) Outline one theory of cognitive development. [8 marks]

b) Evaluate the theory of cognitive development outlined in (a). [16 marks]

I like Bruner's theory best — he's the easiest to spell...

I wonder how many different spellings of Vygotsky's name crop up on exam papers... Quite a few, I imagine. If you're like me and struggle to remember how to spell your own name, it's worth taking the time to learn it now. Vygotsky, that is — not your name. If you really can't spell that by now I doubt you'll ever be able to. Sorry to be the one to break it to you.

Applying the Theories to Education

Psychologists don't spend their time carrying out experiments and coming up with theories just for fun, you know. Well, maybe some of them do, but even then the theories they develop can have practical applications, such as using ideas about cognitive development to improve education — which, funnily enough, is the next thing you need to learn...

Piaget's Theory Has Implications for Education

Piaget's theory suggests a **child-centred approach** to education, in which children can learn for themselves through their own experience. It can be applied to find ways to help children **learn** more effectively:

1) **Learning by discovery** — according to Piaget, when children encounter new experiences that their current **schemas** can't deal with adequately, they develop new schemas through the process of **accommodation** (see page 52). This implies that providing opportunities to **actively** experience new things in a stimulating classroom with lots of **different** resources will help promote cognitive development.

2) **Readiness** — Piaget claimed that development is limited by the process of **maturation**. So, children **can't** learn particular kinds of knowledge until they're **ready** to develop the necessary schemas. For example, a child at the **preoperational** stage isn't ready to understand conservation of volume.

3) **Appropriate materials** — teachers must provide **appropriate challenges**, e.g. **preoperational** children should be given **concrete examples** of new ideas to help their understanding. Teachers must also be sensitive to **developmental differences** between students, because some children mature and learn more quickly than others.

The Plowden Report (1967)

The Plowden Report reviewed **primary level** education and made **recommendations** for UK schools. The report included research and surveys. Some of the recommendations it made were based on **Piaget's theory**. For example, Piaget's ideas about **discovery learning**, **readiness** and a **set sequence** of developmental stages were used in the report. However, Piaget's theory **isn't** now as widely accepted as it once was. It's now known that children generally have **more abilities** than Piaget claimed, e.g. **operational** thinking may develop **earlier** than Piaget suggested.

Vygotsky's Theory Emphasises Social Interaction

Vygotsky's theory is a **teacher-guided approach** and suggests that **interactions** with others are important in learning. In other words, **other people** are needed to stimulate cognitive development. For example, **scaffolding** is an important concept developed from Vygotsky's theory where other people assist a child's cognitive development:

- **Scaffolding** is when a **teacher**, another **adult** or a **more cognitively advanced child** acts as an **expert** to guide the child.
- They do this by making suggestions or doing demonstrations to provide a **framework** by which the child learns to do a task.
- At first the child might need lots of help, but as they learn **less help** is needed and they can carry on learning **independently**.
- For scaffolding to work it needs to take place within the child's **zone of proximal development** (**ZPD**) (see page 54).

Prof. Telfer's trainee teachers suddenly realised he didn't know what he was talking about.

Wood et al (1976) studied scaffolding

Method:	**Thirty** children aged 3–5 were given the task of building a model and were **observed**. A **tutor** gave help to each child according to how well they were doing — the help was either in the form of showing or telling.
Results:	Scaffolding allowed the children to complete a task they **wouldn't** have been able to do alone. The **effectiveness** of the scaffolding was influenced by various factors, e.g. how the tutor **simplified** the task, and how they helped them **identify important steps**. **Showing** was used most when helping **younger** children, whilst **telling** was used more with the **older** children. Also, the **older** the child was the **less** scaffolding was needed for them to complete the task.
Conclusion:	Scaffolding **can** be helpful but consideration needs to be given to **maximise** its effectiveness.
Evaluation:	This study had fairly **good ecological validity**, but there was less control over variables, **reducing reliability**.

Applying the Theories to Education

Bruner Proposed a Spiral Curriculum

Bruner (1966) agreed with Vygotsky that **social interaction** is important for cognitive development, and he made some important suggestions for education:

1) **The Spiral Curriculum** — although a child's age and level of development will **limit** what they can learn, Bruner argued that even difficult concepts can be introduced at an appropriate level from an **early age**. As the child grows the concept can be **repeatedly revisited**, each time in more depth — this will achieve a more complete and in-depth understanding. In this way, children can **build up** their knowledge, and the earlier learning should make the later learning **easier**.

2) **Motivation** — Bruner argued that children are more motivated to learn if they have an **intrinsic interest** in what they're studying. This is **more of an incentive** than external motivations like getting good marks. So teachers should encourage an **active interest** in topics and aim to come up with engaging ways to teach them.

3) **Language** — by **discussions** in class, children can learn about **other perspectives**, and achieve **deeper understanding**.

4) **Discovery Learning** — Bruner emphasised that children should not just learn facts, but should learn by **exploring** and **discovering** facts. This also helps them to learn about the **process** of acquiring knowledge.

Bruner's ideas have been very influential — for example the use of a spiral curriculum is now quite common.

Application of Theories to Education May Need to Be Reviewed

1) Although theories of cognitive development have been **usefully applied** to education, there are often **practical difficulties** involved. For example, it can be very time-consuming to continually assess the ZPD of all the children in a class. Also, providing enough appropriate challenges and finding appropriate expert peer tutors can be a problem.

2) As **more research** is done and **theories develop**, the implications for education need to be regularly reviewed. For example, **Sylva (1987)** has suggested that Piaget's learning by discovery is **not** actually always the most effective approach and that his theory should not be relied on so heavily.

Archie suspected that his peer tutors were neither expert nor appropriate. He was no fool.

Practice Questions

Q1 What is meant by 'discovery learning'?
Q2 How is Vygotsky's approach to education different from Piaget's 'child-centred approach'?
Q3 What is involved in 'scaffolding'?
Q4 What is meant by a 'spiral curriculum'?
Q5 Why might applications of cognitive theories to education need to be regularly reviewed?

Exam Question

Q1 Outline and evaluate the application of theories of cognitive development to education. [24 marks]

A spiral curriculum — just going round and round in circles...

I'm pretty sure I experienced a spiral curriculum when I was at school. About twice a year in biology lessons they'd make us put a piece of pondweed in a beaker of water and count the bubbles. I never actually found out why though, so I'm guessing something went a bit wrong there. They should probably think about reviewing that approach, in my opinion.

SECTION EIGHT — COGNITION AND DEVELOPMENT

Development of Moral Understanding

Hmmm, moral development. Being good, being bad, it's not always simple and clear cut which is which. For example, would it be morally wrong to skip these pages and go watch TV instead? Well, you'll never know unless you read them...

Kohlberg *Thought That* Moral Understanding *Progresses in* Stages

1) Kohlberg argued that your **moral understanding increases** as you grow older because at each stage you take more and more of the **social** world into account.

2) He investigated this idea using a series of ten **moral dilemma** stories. An example of the type of dilemma he used is the **'Heinz dilemma'**. In the story, Heinz chose to break into a shop to steal expensive drugs to cure his dying wife.

3) The participants had to decide whether these actions were **justified**. Kohlberg was interested in the participants' **reasons** for their decision.

Fred had been waiting for help for hours. He wouldn't be volunteering for any more studies.

	Kohlberg (1963) — Study of moral understanding
Method:	A sample of **72 boys** aged 10, 13 and 16 were each **interviewed** for approximately 2 hours. Each child was asked to think about a selection of **moral dilemmas** and **comment** on the actions taken by the characters. They were then asked to **justify** their reasoning. Kohlberg **recorded** their answers.
Results:	Kohlberg classified the children's responses into three groups. He used these to come up with three levels of moral understanding — **preconventional morality**, **conventional morality** and **postconventional morality**. Each of these levels is made up of **two stages** (see below). The answers of the **younger** children tended to fit into the preconventional level, whereas the answers of the **older** children tended to reflect the conventional stage. Few participants showed postconventional morality. The participants appeared to be **consistent** in their thinking and presented similar answers to different moral dilemmas.
Conclusion:	Children **progress** from a state of preconventional morality into a state of conventional morality. Only **much later**, if at all, do they show postconventional morality.
Evaluation:	Participants had to come up with the responses themselves, rather than choosing from a list of possible responses. This meant that the responses were not influenced by any **pre-existing ideas** that Kohlberg may have had. However, in sorting the participants' responses into levels, Kohlberg may have shown some **investigator bias**. This study **lacked ecological validity** as the dilemmas were hypothetical, and showed **gender bias** as all the participants were boys. Also, the results of this study cannot be generalised to more **collectivist cultures** where the **rights of the individual** are more likely to come second to **social obligations**. Finally, as Kohlberg himself later pointed out, his study was **limited** as it did not allow for emotions such as **guilt** and **empathy**.

Kohlberg *Described* Three Levels *of* Moral Understanding

Kohlberg used his findings to come up with **three levels** of moral understanding — preconventional, conventional and postconventional. Each of these levels is made up of **two stages**.

Level 1 — *Preconventional Morality*

Stage 1 — Punishment and obedience orientation

Reasons for behaviour aren't taken into account. The only reason for not doing something is because you'll be **punished**. For example, Heinz shouldn't steal the drugs because he'll go to jail.

Stage 2 — Instrumental purpose orientation

Morality is based on meeting your **own interests** and getting what you **want**. For example, Heinz should steal the drugs because otherwise his wife will die and he'll be upset.

Development of Moral Understanding

Level 2 — Conventional Morality

Stage 3 — Morality of interpersonal cooperation

You try to live up to the **expectations** of people who are **important** to you. Behaviour that improves your relationship with these people is seen as moral. For example, Heinz should steal the drugs as his family and friends would expect him to do everything he can to save his wife.

Stage 4 — Social-order orientation

Moral behaviour is behaviour that fits in with **social norms**, **obligations** and **rules**, e.g. following the law. Morality is seen in the context of society as a whole. For example, Heinz shouldn't steal the drugs because it's against the law, and laws should always be followed.

Level 3 — Postconventional Morality

Stage 5 — Social-contract orientation

Laws are seen as **flexible** in certain situations, and not all of **equal importance**. Laws are only followed if they contribute towards the welfare of others. For example, Heinz should steal the drugs — although stealing is against the law, it's better to steal than to let his wife die.

Stage 6 — Universal ethical principles

You've developed your own set of **abstract moral principles** that you follow above those laid down by the law. For example, Heinz should steal the drugs as human life has a higher value than personal property.

Other Researchers Have Studied Kohlberg's Findings

Other researchers have reviewed and evaluated Kohlberg's work:

1) **Sobesky (1983)** found that using **different versions** of Heinz's dilemma (i.e. different consequences for Heinz and his wife of Heinz stealing or not stealing) **changes the response** of the reader. So an individual's response **isn't fixed** depending on the stage of moral development they're at, but changes according to the **situation**.

2) The theory is **sex-biased**. Most of Kohlberg's work was carried out on **US males**, so his findings may not apply to other groups. Gilligan claimed that the theory was **androcentric** and focused too much on male-oriented ideas about **justice** rather than also taking into account **other moral approaches** that might appeal more to women.

3) **Hart and Fegley (1995)** found that some morally-driven people are **not** motivated by duty or by right and wrong, as Kohlberg suggested — some people are motivated to behave morally because it makes them **feel good**.

Practice Questions

Q1 Give two problems with Kohlberg's (1963) study of moral understanding.

Q2 List Kohlberg's six stages of moral understanding.

Q3 What did Sobesky (1983) find when he studied Kohlberg's dilemmas?

Q4 What did Hart and Fegley (1995) discover about the motivation of morally-driven people?

Exam Question

Q1 a) Outline one theory of moral understanding. [8 marks]

b) Evaluate the theory of moral understanding outlined in (a). [16 marks]

The Heinz dilemma — baked beans or ketchup?

So the little kid who hangs around on the street corner nicking bikes can just blame it all on not having progressed through Kohlberg's different levels of moral understanding. Great. Anyway, whether you agree with it or not, you need to learn about Kohlberg's theory of moral understanding before you move on. Go on — you know it's the right thing to do...

Development of Social Cognition

Social cognition is about understanding about yourself and others, and being able to see things from other people's perspective. So, for example, I know that I'm awesome and that you're probably not having much fun right now...

A **Sense of Self** Develops During Childhood

Having a **sense of self** includes things like:

- being able to **distinguish** between self and others, and referring to each with **appropriate language**
- having knowledge of our **experiences**, **abilities**, **motivations**, etc.
- having ideas about **body image**

Important stages during development include:

1) **Existential self** — from about three months old we learn to **distinguish** self from non-self, and find out that we exist separately from other things. The development of **object permanence** (see p.52) may help this.

2) **Categorical self** — from about two years old we start to use language to **describe ourselves**, using culturally defined categories, e.g. age, male/female, tall/short, etc. We are also described by **other people** in this way, which can influence our idea of ourself. For example, describing a child as 'clever' or 'naughty' could influence their **self-esteem**.

3) **Identity crisis** — **Erikson (1968)** claimed that during **adolescence**, when going through body changes and starting to make plans for the future, we may **try out** different roles until we find our true identity.

Having a sense of self also involves being able to see yourself as **others** see you. This requires some understanding of the minds of others, and being able to see things from **their perspective**.

Theory of Mind (ToM) is About Understanding Other People's Minds

Humans have a unique ability to **cooperate** and carry out **complex interactions**. It's thought this is possible because we have a **theory of mind**. This involves **understanding that we and others have minds** with knowledge, feelings, beliefs, motivations, intentions, etc. We can **explain** and **predict** other people's behaviour by making inferences about their mental states. This includes the knowledge that others may have **false beliefs** about the world.

Baron-Cohen et al (1985) — theory of mind in autistic children

Method:	Three groups of children were studied — children with autism with an average age of 12 years, children with Down's Syndrome with an average age of 11 years, and 'normal' children with an average age of 4 years. The experiment used two dolls — Sally had a basket, Anne a box. Children were asked to name the dolls (the **naming question**). Then Sally was seen to hide a marble in her basket and leave the room. Anne took the marble and put it in her box. Sally returned and the child was asked, 'Where will Sally look for her marble?' (**belief question**). The correct response is to point to the basket, where Sally believes the marble to be. They were also asked, 'Where is the marble really?' (**reality question**) and 'Where was the marble in the beginning?' (**memory question**). Each child was tested twice, with the marble in a different place the second time.
Results:	**All** of the children got the **naming**, **reality** and **memory** questions correct. In the **belief** question, the children with Down's Syndrome scored **86%**, the 'normal' children **85%**, but the children with autism scored **20%**.
Conclusion:	The findings suggest that autistic children have an **under-developed theory of mind**, sometimes called **mind-blindness**. They seem unable to predict or understand the beliefs of others.
Evaluation:	Dolls were used throughout the study, causing it to lack **ecological validity**. Also, children with autism may in fact have a more highly developed theory of mind and understand that dolls don't have beliefs. Repeating the study by acting out the scenes with **humans** might show an increase in ability on the tasks. However, **Leslie and Frith (1988)** did a similar study with real people and not dolls and found the same pattern of results.

Most children develop ToM at around **four** years old. However, the kind of questions asked in Baron-Cohen et al's false belief task may be difficult for younger children to understand. It seems that **three-year-old** children can pass some versions of the test, so theory of mind may actually develop **earlier**.

There's also disagreement about the **development** of ToM. It may have an **innate** basis, but **nurture** and **experience** are also likely to be important in its development.

Development of Social Cognition

Understanding Others Involves *Perspective-taking*

One aspect of having a ToM is understanding that other people's **perspectives** can differ from your own. Children gradually become more skilful in their **perspective-taking ability**. **Selman (1980)** studied children's perspective-taking ability by analysing their responses to stories presenting dilemmas. For example:

> Selman told children a story about a girl who could rescue a friend's cat by climbing a tree. However, she'd promised her father that she wouldn't climb trees. Selman asked the children if she should be punished if she did climb the tree.

Like all little girls, Molly had perfected the "who, me?" look. She knew Daddy wouldn't mind about the tree.

From the children's answers, Selman identified **five** kinds of **perspective-taking**:

1) **Undifferentiated and Egocentric** — up to about six years of age, children can separate **self** and **other**, but in a physical sense only. They don't perceive any psychological differences, seeing the other person in the same way they see an object.

2) **Differentiated and Subjective** — from five to nine, children understand that other people have **different perspectives** because they have access to **different information** (i.e. know different things). However, only their own perspective is seen as important and they can't take the perspective of the other person.

3) **Second-Person and Reciprocal** — between seven and twelve, children can put themselves in someone else's shoes and view a situation from **another's perspective**. They also realise that other people can do the same.

4) **Third-Person and Mutual** — between ten and fifteen years old, children develop the ability to take the perspective of a **third impartial person** who's viewing an interaction between other people.

5) **In-Depth and Societal-Symbolic** — from about fourteen, children understand that **third-party perspectives** can be influenced by factors such as **social or cultural values**. They can see a situation from a variety of different perspectives, e.g. moral, legal, etc.

As children go through these stages they become better able to understand that other people have different perspectives, and can use information to put themselves in other people's shoes.

Selman's ideas about perspective-taking can have **practical applications** in **education**. For example, using **multi-cultural** materials and having **class discussions** can expose children to different perspectives. This may help to promote their perspective-taking ability.

Practice Questions

Q1 Explain what is meant by 'existential self', 'categorical self' and 'identity crisis'.

Q2 How does Baron-Cohen et al's false belief task show whether or not a child has a theory of mind?

Q3 How did Selman study perspective-taking ability?

Q4 Name Selman's five stages of perspective-taking.

Exam Question

Q1 a) Describe theories of the development of a child's sense of self. [8 marks]

b) Discuss the development of children's understanding of others, including perspective-taking. [16 marks]

Actually, I took the marble while your back was turned and swallowed it...

One of my friends at school definitely went through that identity crisis thing. He started out as an emo kid, suddenly went really sporty and obsessed with football, and then for a term or two he seemed to think he was a rapper. He also spent nearly a whole year dressing like a cowboy. I think he's settled down now though — last I heard he was an accountant.

The Mirror Neuron System

Here comes the science bit — all about the biological basis for social cognition. I knew you'd be thrilled. Enjoy.

Social Cognition Has a Biological Basis

1) **Neurons** (**cells**) in the cerebral cortex are organised into **four** main areas: the **frontal**, **temporal**, **parietal** and **occipital** lobes.

2) Different processes, such as **visual perception**, involve one or more of these lobes. Some areas of the brain seem to have very specialised roles in **cognition**.

3) It seems likely that many of our sophisticated **social** abilities, such as **theory of mind**, also involve complex brain mechanisms — these may have **evolved** as our brains and intelligence grew. Abilities like this could have been stimulated by our complex **social living** (see page 50).

4) Attempts have been made to **connect** findings from neuroscience and social psychology and combine them into more complete theories — this is known as **social neuroscience**.

Mirror Neurons Respond to the Actions of Others

Mirror neurons are brain cells that are involved in **performing** an action, such as holding a cup. However, they're **also** active when you **observe** someone else doing the same action. So, whether you're actually holding a cup, or only observing someone else holding a cup, particular mirror neurons will be **active**.

Di Pellegrino et al (1992) — recording neuron activity

Method:	**Electrodes** were inserted into individual neurons in the **premotor cortex** of macaque monkeys. When the monkeys reached for food, the **activity** in the neurons was recorded.
Results:	The neurons were **active** when the monkeys reached for food, but also, unexpectedly, active when they observed **someone else** reach for food.
Conclusion:	This was the **first** study to provide evidence for the existence of **mirror neurons**. Although the function of mirror neurons is not yet clear, they may help in understanding observed behaviour.
Evaluation:	The experiment was **not** designed to study mirror neurons, so the information gathered about them was **limited**. Also, this experiment involved inserting electrodes into animals' brains, which raises **ethical issues**.

It's hard to record the activity of individual neurons in the brains of **humans**. So, studies have been done using brain scanning techniques such as **functional Magnetic Resonance Imaging** (fMRI), which analyse **brain activity** during particular kinds of behaviours. For example, Iacoboni et al (1999) found that there are areas of the **frontal** and **parietal cortex** that are active when people carry out and observe actions.

Mirror Neurons May Be Important for Social Cognition

Neurons that are active both when **you** do something and when you see **other people** do the same thing may help you **understand** the behaviour of others.

Fogassi et al (2005) — Mirror neurons and intentions

Method:	The activity of **41 mirror neurons** in 2 macaque monkeys were recorded as they observed a person pick up an apple as if to eat it, or pick up the apple and place it in a cup.
Results:	**Different** groups of neurons responded to the two outcomes (eat or place). Also, some neurons fired after the apple was picked up but before the second action (eat or place) was carried out.
Conclusion:	Different patterns of response link with different **behavioural objectives** and some neurons seem to predict the **intention** of actions. So, mirror neurons may help to **understand** and **predict** the behaviour of others.
Evaluation:	Animals may behave differently under lab conditions, meaning the experiment has **low ecological validity**. Also, the experiment was carried out on monkeys so it's difficult to **generalise** the results to humans — neurons in humans may not respond in the same way.

Experiments with **humans** using **fMRI** show that brain areas that are active when we feel particular emotions (e.g. happiness or pain) are also active when we see others feel the same emotion. This supports suggestions that mirror neurons may be involved in **empathy**.

The Mirror Neuron System

There's a Lot of Debate About the Role of Mirror Neurons

1) The **function** and **importance** of mirror neurons is not yet fully understood. For example, they may be involved in **imitation** — but macaque monkeys (which have mirror neurons) have a **limited ability** for imitation learning.

2) A connection between mirror neurons and **theory of mind** (**ToM**) has also been debated. However, mirror neurons are found in monkeys that **don't** seem to have ToM in the same way that humans do. Also, **fMRI research** shows that ToM tests activate brain regions that **aren't** generally thought to be part of the mirror neuron system. It may be that mirror neurons can be involved in **learning by imitation**, but that the development of ToM involves **more** than this.

3) More needs to be learnt about the **development** of mirror neurons. **Falck-Ytter (2006)** reckoned that mirror neurons start to develop during the **first year** of life. However, **Meltzoff and Moore (1977)** found that human infants can imitate facial expressions **soon after birth**. This could either suggest that mirror neurons have an **innate** basis, or else that imitation **doesn't** necessarily involve mirror neurons.

Social Neuroscience Has Raised Important Issues

Jake knew what went on in those labs and was holding Dr. Anwar's dog hostage until Maeve was returned to him safely.

1) **Social neuroscience** is **inter-disciplinary** — it involves both **biological** and **social** concepts and theories. These different types of theories may **mutually inform** each other — biological research can help understand social processes better, and vice versa. This means we can understand behaviour at different levels of explanation.

2) This approach may bring important **insights** into human **social cognition** (e.g. the basis of **empathy**). Also, some conditions associated with developmental problems (e.g. **autism**) might be better understood.

3) Animal experiments involve invasive methods, e.g. inserting electrodes into the brain — this raises **ethical issues**.

Practice Questions

Q1 What are mirror neurons?

Q2 How have mirror neurons been studied in animals and in humans?

Q3 Who first identified mirror neurons?

Q4 Outline a piece of evidence supporting the idea that mirror neurons may be involved in empathy.

Q5 Why is social neuroscience a particularly valuable new field of research?

Exam Questions

Q1 Discuss the development of social cognition, including the role of the mirror neuron system. [24 marks]

Q2 Outline and evaluate research on the role of the mirror neuron system. [24 marks]

OK, he's picking up the cup — ready neurons... aim... and fire...

This is an interesting little topic to end the section with — it's all fresh and new and nobody knows quite what's going on. There are new ideas springing up and being shot down all over the place. And to think, if a monkey hadn't happened to look over and see someone picking up some food, these pages might never have existed. What a loss that would've been.

Clinical Psychology

This section is quite a nice one really — clinical psychology is all about diagnosing mental disorders and then treating them, so the researchers here are actually trying to help people. Almost brings a tear to your eye, doesn't it...

Clinical Psychologists Explain and Treat Mental Illness

1) Clinical psychology focuses on studying, explaining and treating **emotional** or **behavioural disorders**.

2) Clinical psychologists assess patients using **interviews**, **observations** and **psychological tests**. They then help patients work through their problems, e.g. using talk therapies.

3) Researchers gather **primary** and **secondary data** to improve understanding of mental disorders. Clinicians then apply this to **individual cases** to help them establish a clear **diagnosis** and decide upon the correct **treatment** for each individual.

> • **Primary data** — information collected during the researcher's direct observations of a patient, e.g. test results, answers to questionnaires, observation notes.
>
> • **Secondary data** — information collected from other studies. This data can be used to check the validity of studies, or used to prove or disprove a new theory.

Clinical Psychology Uses Twin Studies

1) **Twin studies** are used to find out if **genetic factors** influence the development of mental disorders.

2) They involve looking at **concordance rates** — the **chance** that both twins will develop the mental disorder.

3) **Identical (MZ)** twins share all their genetic material, and **non-identical (DZ)** twins share around half. So, if both MZ twins are **more likely** to develop schizophrenia (a higher concordance rate) than both DZ twins, it can be assumed that schizophrenia has a **genetic** cause. However, it can't be the full story unless concordance rates are **100%** in MZ twins.

There's more on schizophrenia and twin studies on p.68.

Gottesman and Shields (1966) — schizophrenia in twins

Method:	Hospital records for the previous 16 years were examined to identify people with schizophrenia who had a **twin**. Around 40 sets of twins agreed to take part in the study, which was a **natural experiment** using **independent measures**.
Results:	The concordance rate was about **48%** for **MZ** twins and about **17%** for **DZ** twins. The exact figures vary depending on the type of schizophrenia, but overall, MZ twins had a much higher concordance rate than DZ twins.
Conclusion:	As the results for MZ twins are much higher, this suggests a **genetic cause** for schizophrenia.
Evaluation:	The results for MZ twins don't show 100% concordance, which means that there must be **other important factors** that influence schizophrenia. Although the researchers had a large amount of data covering a long period of time, it's unlikely the study could be **replicated** until new data existed.

Twin Studies Have Strengths and Weaknesses

Strengths
• **Rich data** — researchers have the opportunity to study **rare phenomena** in a lot of **detail**.
• **Unique cases** — existing theories can be challenged, and ideas for future research can be suggested.
• **High ecological validity** — the variables aren't manipulated so the findings should be **true to real life**.

Weaknesses
• **Causal relationships** — the researcher **doesn't** have much **control** over the variables, so the findings could be the result of an extraneous variable. This means that it's **difficult** to establish **cause and effect**.
• **Generalisation** — only using a **single case** means it's difficult to generalise the results to other people.
• **Ethics** — it can be difficult to get **informed consent** if the subjects have a **mental disorder**.
• **Opportunities** — identical twins are quite **rare**, so there aren't very many research opportunities, and sample sizes are usually pretty small.

Clinical Psychology

Clinical Psychology Uses Animal Studies

Animal studies are used in clinical psychology because they allow researchers to carry out tests that couldn't be done on humans. However, using animals for research raises ethical issues.

	Lipska et al (1993) — schizophrenia in rats
Method:	This was a **laboratory experiment** that involved making lesions in rats' brains to see if they developed schizophrenia-like symptoms. Areas of the hippocampus associated with schizophrenia were damaged using an injection of ibotenic acid a week after the rats were born.
Results:	The rats with a damaged hippocampus developed schizophrenia-like symptoms as their brains matured, e.g. hyperactivity, memory problems and a lack of response to rewards.
Conclusion:	Damage to the hippocampus can lead to the onset of schizophrenia-like symptoms, which suggests that the hippocampus plays a role in the development of schizophrenia.
Evaluation:	The variables in this experiment were tightly controlled, which means that it should be possible to establish **cause and effect** — the rats wouldn't have developed these symptoms if their brains hadn't been damaged. However, it's difficult to know how many symptoms of schizophrenia the rats were actually experiencing, because you can't establish whether they were having hallucinations or delusions.

Animal Studies Have Strengths and Weaknesses

Strengths

- **Ethics** — researchers can conduct experiments on animals that they **couldn't** do on **humans** because of **ethical restraints**, e.g. lesion studies. This means that clinical psychologists can investigate the **causes** of **mental disorders**, e.g. the effects of particular chemicals or social deprivation. They also don't need to get the animal's informed consent or worry about deception.
- **Speed of reproduction** — most animals reproduce much more **quickly** than humans, so it's quicker and easier to carry out **longitudinal studies** of **genetic influence**, e.g. to see whether schizophrenia has a genetic cause.
- **Detachment** — it's easier for researchers to be **impartial** with animal participants than with humans, so the results are more likely to be **objective**.

Weaknesses

- **Qualitative differences** — humans and animals are qualitatively different, so there are **problems** with **generalising** the results from animal studies to humans. Substances can have different effects on different animals, e.g. **morphine** has a calming effect on humans, but it causes manic behaviour in cats.
- **Language** — animals don't have **language**, which is a vital part of human behaviour. In clinical psychology this means that animals **can't describe** their **symptoms**, so it's difficult to know whether they're experiencing any mental abnormalities.

Practice Questions

Q1 Outline the aims of clinical psychology.

Q2 What's the difference between primary and secondary data?

Q3 Outline one advantage of twin studies.

Exam Question

Q1 a) Describe two research methods used in clinical psychology. [8 marks]

    b) Evaluate the research methods outlined in (a). [16 marks]

Twin study — like a normal study but with two desks...

Just when you thought there couldn't possibly be any more different types of psychology, clinical psychology had to go and rear its ugly head. Woe is you. Although, to be honest, I've got limited sympathy. If you really thought that there weren't any other types of psychology then you obviously haven't been paying much attention. And we can't have that, can we...

Schizophrenia

*A lot of people think that schizophrenia involves having multiple personalities, but it **really really doesn't**, so don't make this mistake in the exam else you'll look like a right plum duff. And nobody wants to look like a right plum duff.*

Schizophrenia Disrupts *the* Mind's Ability *to* Function

'Schizophrenia' literally means 'split mind'.

1) **Schizophrenia** is a **thought process disorder**. It's characterised by **disruption** to a person's **perceptions**, **emotions** and **beliefs**.

2) The onset of schizophrenia can be **acute** (a **sudden** onset, where behaviour changes within a few days), or **chronic** (a **gradual** deterioration in mental health that develops slowly over time).

3) **Males** and **females** are **equally** affected. In **males** schizophrenia usually develops in their **late teens** or **early 20s**, while **females** tend to develop it 4 or 5 years **later**. Overall, **0.5%** of the population is affected.

4) It's thought that schizophrenia **isn't** a **single disorder** but that there are various **subtypes** — however, there still **isn't** an agreed **definition**.

Schizophrenia *has* Lots of Different Clinical Characteristics

People with schizophrenia can experience a **range** of possible **symptoms**:

1 Perceptual symptoms
- Auditory hallucinations — **hearing** things that **aren't there**. People often hear **voices** saying **abusive** or **critical** things.
- Sometimes people **see**, **smell** or **taste** things that aren't there.

2 Social symptoms
- **Social withdrawal** — not **taking part** in or **enjoying** social situations.
- People might be **aloof** or **avoid eye contact**.

3 Cognitive symptoms
- **Delusions** — **believing** things that **aren't true**. People can have **delusions** of **grandeur** (where they believe they're more **important** than they are, e.g. that they're the king) or of **paranoia** and **persecution** (where they believe people are out to **get them**). Some schizophrenics also experience **delusions** of **control** — they believe that their **behaviour** is being **controlled** by **somebody else**.
- **Thought control** — believing that your **thoughts** are being **controlled**. For example, **thought insertion** is when people feel that someone's putting thoughts into their heads. **Withdrawal** is when they believe that someone is **removing** their thoughts. They might also believe that **people** can **read** their thoughts — this is **broadcasting**.
- **Language impairments** — **irrelevant** and **incoherent speech**. People often show signs of **cognitive distractibility**, where they **can't maintain** a **train** of **thought**. They might also **repeat sounds** (**echolalia**), **jumble** their **words** (**word salad**), make **nonsensical rhymes** (**clang associations**) and **invent words** (**neologisms**).

4 Affective / emotional symptoms
- **Depressive symptoms** — a **lack** of **energy** and **interest** in things, especially in **personal care** and **hygiene**.
- **Lack of emotion** — **not reacting** to typically emotional situations. This is also called **emotional blunting**.
- **Inappropriate emotions** — **reacting** in an **inappropriate** way, e.g. laughing at bad news.

5 Behavioural symptoms
- **Stereotyped behaviours** — continuously **repeating** actions, which are often **strange** and **don't** have a **purpose**.
- **Psychomotor disturbance** — **not** having **control** of your **muscles**. People may experience **catatonia**, where they sit in an **awkward position** for a **long time**. In this state people will sometimes **stay** in whatever position they're **put** in (so if you lift their arm over their head it'll stay like that **until** you move it **back**).
- **Catatonic stupor** — lying **rigidly** and **not moving** for **long** periods of **time**. People are **conscious** during these episodes and can **remember** what was going on **around** them, although they **don't** seem **aware** of it at the **time**.

Symptoms *Can be* Categorised *into* Two Types

The **symptoms** of schizophrenia are sometimes categorised as **Type 1** or **Type 2**:

1) **Type 1** symptoms are **positive** symptoms. This is where people **experience** something, feel that something is **happening** to them, or **display** certain **behaviours** — e.g. hallucinations, delusions, jumbled speech.

2) **Type 2** symptoms are **negative** symptoms. This is where people **don't** display 'normal' behaviours — e.g. they're withdrawn, unresponsive and show a lack of emotion.

Schizophrenia

The DSM-IV Classifies Mental Disorders

1) The **DSM-IV** is the fourth edition of the American Psychiatric Association's Diagnostic and Statistical Manual of Mental Disorders.

2) It contains a list of **mental health disorders**. Individuals are rated on **multiple axes / dimensions** and diagnostic **categories** are used, e.g. personality disorders and psychosocial problems.

3) It aims to give diagnosis of mental disorders **reliability** and **validity**:

> For a person to be diagnosed as schizophrenic, the DSM-IV states that their symptoms must significantly impair reality testing — the ability to function in the real world. The symptoms have to have been present for at least six months.

Reliability is how far the classification system produces the **same diagnosis** for a particular set of symptoms. In order for a classification system to be reliable the **same diagnosis** should be made **each time** it's used. This means that **different clinicians** should reach the **same diagnosis**.

Validity is whether the classification system is actually measuring what it **aims to measure**.
- **Descriptive validity** — how similar individuals diagnosed with the disorder are.
- **Aetiological validity** — how similar the cause of the disorder is for each sufferer.
- **Predictive validity** — how useful the diagnostic categories are for predicting the right treatment.

There can be Problems with the Reliability and Validity of Diagnoses

Problems with reliability

1) Schizophrenia diagnosis may be affected by **cultural bias**. For example, **Harrison et al (1984)** showed that there was an **over-diagnosis** of schizophrenia in **West Indian** psychiatric patients in Bristol.

2) No research has found any cause for this, so it suggests that the **symptoms** of **ethnic minority** patients are **misinterpreted**.

3) This questions the **reliability** of the diagnosis of schizophrenia — it suggests that patients can display the **same symptoms** but receive **different diagnoses** because of their ethnic background.

Problems with validity

1) **Rosenhan (1973)** conducted a study where people with no mental health problem got themselves admitted into a **psychiatric unit** by saying they heard voices — they became **pseudopatients**.

2) Once they'd been admitted they behaved 'normally'. However, their behaviour was still seen as a **symptom** of their **disorder** by the staff in the unit. For example, one pseudopatient who wrote in a diary was recorded as displaying 'writing behaviour'.

3) This questions the **validity** of the **diagnosis** of mental disorders — once people are **labelled** as having a disorder, all of their behaviour can be **interpreted** as being **caused** by the **disorder**.

Practice Questions

Q1 What are the differences between positive and negative symptoms of schizophrenia?
Q2 What is the DSM-IV?
Q3 Outline the clinical characteristics of schizophrenia.

Exam Question

Q1 Discuss the issues surrounding the classification and diagnosis of schizophrenia. [24 marks]

Word salad — like crunchy alphabet spaghetti...

Like so many things in psychology, schizophrenia is incredibly hard to define. People can show a variety of symptoms, which can be classified in different ways. Learning this is a bit of a pain now, but at least it means you should have loads to say in the exam, and you can't really ask for more than that. Well, apart from a holiday in the Caribbean, private jet, yacht...

Explanations of Schizophrenia

Different people have different ideas about what causes schizophrenia. This was mostly a sneaky little ploy dreamt up by psychologists and examiners to make your revision harder. OK, that's not strictly true, but it does feel like it sometimes.

Schizophrenia Could be Caused by Biological Factors

> Concordance rates are the chance that someone will develop a disorder if they're related to someone who has it.

1) *Genetic Factors (Inherited Tendencies)*

Being **genetically related** to someone with schizophrenia can significantly **increase** a person's **chances** of developing it. **Family** and **twin** studies have looked at **concordance rates**:

> **Gottesman (1991)** reviewed about 40 twin studies and found that with **identical (MZ) twins** there was about a **48%** chance of **both** being schizophrenic. With **non-identical (DZ) twins** there was about a **17%** chance.

Evidence for...

1) **Shields (1962)** found that **MZ twins** raised in **different families** still showed around **50%** concordance.
2) **Adoption studies** have found that when children are **adopted** because one or both of their **biological parents** has schizophrenia, the **chance** of them developing it is still the **same**. This suggests that **genetics** are more significant than the **environment**.

Evidence against...

1) No study has found a **100%** concordance rate, so schizophrenia **can't** just be caused by **genes**. **Shared environment** may cause higher concordance rates in **family** studies because children **imitate** 'schizophrenic' **behaviours** from their relatives.
2) This means **other factors** need to be considered, e.g. biochemical or psychological factors.

2) *Biochemical Factors*

Post-mortems and **PET scans** have shown that schizophrenics have abnormally high levels of the neurotransmitter **dopamine**. These findings led to the development of the **dopamine hypothesis**, which states that **synapses** that use **dopamine** as a **neurotransmitter** are **overactive** in the brains of people with schizophrenia.

Evidence for...

1) **Antipsychotic** drugs **reduce** the **symptoms** of schizophrenia by **blocking** dopamine receptors. This suggests that it's the **overactive** dopamine receptors **causing** the symptoms.
2) Drugs like **amphetamines**, which **increase dopamine function**, can sometimes cause **schizophrenia-like** symptoms in people without schizophrenia.

Evidence against...

1) **Antipsychotic** drugs only work on the **positive symptoms** of schizophrenia, e.g. hallucinations. This means that increased dopamine function **doesn't** explain **negative symptoms** like social withdrawal.
2) The **link** with dopamine is **correlational**, so it doesn't show **cause and effect**. It may be that increased dopamine function is a **symptom** of schizophrenia, rather than a cause of it.

3) *Neurological Factors*

Abnormal brain structure, caused by **abnormal development**, could be the cause of schizophrenia.

Evidence for...

1) **Johnstone et al (1976)** compared the **size** of the **ventricles** (hollow areas) in schizophrenics' brains with non-schizophrenics' brains. They found that the people with schizophrenia had **enlarged ventricles**, which suggests that **schizophrenia is linked** to a **loss** of **brain tissue**.
2) **Buchsbaum (1990)** carried out **MRI scans** on schizophrenics' brains and found **abnormalities** in the **prefrontal cortex**.

Evidence against...

1) **Non-schizophrenics** can also have **enlarged ventricles**, which goes against **Johnstone's** evidence.
2) These findings are **correlational**, so they don't show **cause and effect**. It may be that abnormal brain structure is a **symptom** of schizophrenia, rather than a cause of it.

Explanations of Schizophrenia

Schizophrenia Could be Caused by Psychological Factors

1) Behavioural Factors

Behaviourists argue that schizophrenia is **learnt** through **operant conditioning**. Someone may do something that gets a **positive reaction** or **reward** from others. This **encourages** the person to **repeat** the behaviour — it **reinforces** it.

Evidence for...   **Token economies**, which use **reinforcement** to encourage '**normal**' **behaviours**, can help **treat** schizophrenia (see next page). This suggests that some of the behaviour could be **learnt**.

Evidence against... **Biological and psychological research** suggests that schizophrenia **isn't** just a **learnt behaviour**.

2) Psychodynamic Theory

Freud claimed that schizophrenia is caused by over-whelming **anxiety**. It's a **defence mechanism** involving **regression** into an **early stage** of **development**. **Hallucinations** are the **ego's** attempt to **restore contact** with **reality**.

Evidence for... Laing (1967) also argued that schizophrenics lose contact with **reality** as a way of **coping** with social pressure. He claimed that it was wrong to encourage schizophrenics to conform.

Evidence against... There **isn't** any **research evidence** to **support** Freud's theory. **Psychoanalysis isn't** an **effective treatment**, which suggests that psychodynamic theory **doesn't** explain what **causes** schizophrenia.

3) Socio-cultural Factors

The **social causation hypothesis** states that people with **low social status** are more likely to suffer from schizophrenia than people with higher social status. It's thought that factors like **poverty** and **discrimination** cause **high stress levels**, and that this can cause schizophrenia.

Evidence for... **Harrison et al (2001)** found that people who were born in **deprived areas** were more likely to develop schizophrenia. This suggests that factors like **poverty**, **unemployment** and **crowding** have an **impact** on schizophrenia.

Evidence against... These results are **correlational**, so they **don't** show **cause and effect**. The **social drift hypothesis** suggests that there are more people with schizophrenia in deprived areas because having schizophrenia gives them a **lower social status**, e.g. because they might be unemployed.

4) Cognitive Factors

Cognitive psychologists argue that schizophrenia is caused by **faulty information processing**. This leads to **delusions, thought interference, language impairment** and **memory problems**.

Evidence for...   **Neufeld (1978)** compared the cognitive processes of people with schizophrenia with a **control** group. The participants with schizophrenia took **longer to encode stimuli** and showed **short-term memory problems**. This suggests that their ability to process information was impaired.

Evidence against... **Biochemical** research suggests that **cognitive** problems are **caused by increased dopamine function**, rather than faulty information processing.

Practice Questions

Q1 Outline the role that biochemical factors might have in causing schizophrenia.

Q2 Outline the socio-cultural factors that could explain schizophrenia.

Exam Question

Q1 Outline and evaluate explanations of schizophrenia   [24 marks]

Explain schizophrenia — I can barely even spell it...

So there isn't just one definite idea about what causes schizophrenia — surprise surprise. At least these pages are quite useful though. When you're evaluating one explanation of schizophrenia, you can use all the other explanations as evidence against it — so you could use the evidence for social theory as evidence against genetic factors, or whatever. Not bad eh?

Treating Schizophrenia

There are a number of different treatments for schizophrenia, and most people benefit from having a combination of a few of them. After all, why just have one when you can have them all — the more the merrier I say...

Schizophrenia Can be Treated Using Biological Therapy

Therapy using drugs is also called chemotherapy.

1) The **biological** approach to treating schizophrenia involves **drug therapy**.

2) Treatment is based on the **dopamine hypothesis** (p.68) — the theory that schizophrenia is linked to increased dopamine activity in the brain. **Antipsychotic drugs** (**neuroleptics**) work by **blocking dopamine receptors**.

Advantages

- Drug therapy is effective at reducing **positive symptoms**, e.g. hallucinations.
- It's **successful** for a large number of schizophrenia patients, meaning that more people can live in the **community** rather than being institutionalised.
- It's the most **widely-used** and **effective** form of treatment for schizophrenia. Almost all other treatments are used **alongside** drug therapy.

When you're evaluating a treatment for schizophrenia, you can use the advantages of another treatment as a disadvantage of the one you're evaluating.

Disadvantages

- Drug therapy **isn't** very effective for treating **negative symptoms** like social withdrawal.
- It treats the **symptoms** of schizophrenia but **not** the **cause**. Symptoms often **come back** if people stop taking antipsychotic drugs. This leads to the '**revolving door phenomenon**', where patients are constantly being discharged and re-admitted to hospital.
- There are **ethical issues** surrounding the use of drug therapy. Some people argue that drug treatment is a '**chemical straitjacket**' — it **doesn't** really **help** the patient, it just **controls** their **behaviour** to make it more socially acceptable and easier to manage.
- Most people will experience some **short-term side effects** when taking antipsychotic drugs, e.g. drowsiness, blurred vision, dry mouth, constipation and weight gain.
- **Long-term side effects** include increased risk of **diabetes** and **tardive dyskinesia** (involuntary repetitive movements that continue even after they've stopped taking the medication).
- **Clinical trials** have shown that as many as **two-thirds** of people stop taking antipsychotic drugs because of the side-effects. However, **newer** antipsychotic drugs seem to have **fewer long-term side effects** than the **older** ones.

Schizophrenia Can be Treated Using Psychological Therapies

① Behavioural Therapy

1) **Behavioural** treatment for schizophrenia is based on **operant conditioning** — learning through **reinforcement**.

2) **Token economies** can help encourage people in **psychiatric institutions** to perform **socially desirable behaviours**, e.g. getting dressed and making their beds. Patients are given **tokens** which reinforce these behaviours — they can then **exchange** these for something they want, like sweets or cigarettes.

Advantages
- Token economy programmes can produce **significant improvements** in **self care** and **desirable behaviour**, even with **chronic institutionalised schizophrenics**.
- For example, **Ayllon and Azrin (1968)** set up a token economy with schizophrenic patients in a **psychiatric institution**. They found that the amount of socially desirable behaviour **increased** — patients went from performing an average of **5** chores a day to around **40**.

Disadvantages
- Token economies don't have high **ecological validity** — they don't **transfer** into the **real world**. Once people are away from institutions they often don't continue showing desirable behaviour, because there's **nothing** to **reinforce** it.
- The patients' behaviour might be **superficial** — they might only produce desirable behaviour if they're going to receive a token.
- There are **ethical issues** surrounding the use of **behavioural therapy**. It could be argued that it **doesn't** really **help** the patient, it just makes their behaviour more acceptable to other people.

Treating Schizophrenia

(2) Cognitive Behavioural Therapy

1) Cognitive behavioural therapy (CBT) is based on the assumption that patients can be helped by **identifying** and **changing** their 'faulty cognitions'.

2) Schizophrenic patients are encouraged to **reality-test** their **hallucinations** and **delusions**, e.g. to question and try to control the voices they hear.

3) They do **role-play exercises** and **homework** to test out their 'faulty thinking' and are helped to see the **consequences** of thinking differently. Through this they can gradually realise where the 'faults' in their thought patterns are, and can begin to change them.

Advantages
- **Sensky et al (2000)** found that CBT was **effective** in treating schizophrenic patients who **hadn't responded** to **drug treatment**. It was helpful with **positive** and **negative** symptoms, and patients **continued** to **improve** 9 months after treatment had ended.
- CBT puts patients **in charge** of their own treatment by teaching them **self-help strategies**. This means there are **fewer ethical issues** than with other therapies (e.g. drug therapy).

Disadvantages
- CBT only treats the **symptoms** of schizophrenia — it **doesn't address** the **cause** of the disorder.
- It's difficult to **measure** the effectiveness of CBT because it relies on **self-report** from the patient, and the **therapist's opinions**. This makes it **less objective**.
- Patients can become **dependent** on their therapist.

(3) Psychotherapy

1) Psychotherapy aims to identify the **underlying cause** of the mental disorder.

2) This is done using different therapeutic techniques, e.g. **dream analysis** and **free association**.

3) When the **unconscious conflicts** that are causing the problems are made **conscious**, the therapist and patient can discuss and try to resolve them. This will hopefully lead to the disorder being cured.

Advantages
- It aims to treat the **cause** of the disorder, not just the **symptoms**.
- Patients have **more control** over their treatment than with other therapies, e.g. drug therapy.

Disadvantages
- Other forms of treatment (e.g. CBT) have been found to be more **effective**.
- It's **difficult to prove** the effectiveness of psychotherapy — it's based on **subjective data** and the **unconscious mind**. There's also a risk that patients will develop **false memories**, e.g. of childhood abuse.

Practice Questions

Q1 Outline some disadvantages of drug therapy in the treatment of schizophrenia.
Q2 How can token economies benefit schizophrenia patients?
Q3 Outline one advantage of CBT in the treatment of schizophrenia.

Exam Question

Q1 Describe and evaluate treatments of schizophrenia. [24 marks]

Chemical straitjackets — might be a bit itchy...

Well, at least after reading about all the things that can go wrong with your brain it's nice to know there are some treatments. Not as nice as walks in the rain or cuddles or pink wafers, no, but quite nice all the same. I'd love a cuddle right about now. If you're in a similar predicament then take a moment to hold this book close to you and have a little snuggle. Ahh...

Depression

Everyone feels sad sometimes — it can be because a bad thing happens, or just be something you can't quite put your finger on. This is normal and nothing to worry about. It only becomes a problem when these feelings won't go away.

Depression is a Mood Disorder

Mood disorders are characterised by **strong emotions**, which can influence a person's ability to **function normally**. A mood disorder can affect a person's **perceptions**, **thinking** and **behaviour**. **Depression** is one of the most **common** mood disorders. There are many types, including:

1) **Major depression** (**unipolar disorder**) — an **episode** of depression that can occur **suddenly**.

- Major depression can be **reactive** — caused by **external factors**, e.g. the death of a loved one.
- Or, it can be **endogenous** — caused by **internal factors**, e.g. neurological factors.

2) **Manic depression** (**bipolar disorder**) — **alternation** between two **mood extremes** (**mania** and **depression**).

- The change in mood often occurs in regular **cycles** of days or weeks.
- Episodes of **mania** involve **over-activity**, **rapid speech** and feeling extremely **happy** or **agitated**.
- Episodes of **depression** involve the symptoms covered below.

Depression has Lots of Clinical Characteristics

People with depression can experience a **range** of possible **symptoms**:

Physical / behavioural symptoms
- **Sleep disturbances** — **insomnia** (being unable to sleep) or **hypersomnia** (sleeping a lot more than usual).
- Change in **appetite** — people may eat **more** or **less** than **usual**, and gain or lose **weight**.
- **Pain** — especially **headaches**, **joint ache** and **muscle ache**.

Affective / emotional symptoms
- Extreme feelings of **sadness**, **hopelessness** and **despair**.
- **Diurnal mood variation** — changes in mood throughout the day, e.g. feeling worse in the morning.
- **Anhedonia** — no longer **enjoying** activities or hobbies that **used** to be **pleasurable**.

Cognitive symptoms
- Experiencing persistent **negative beliefs** about **themselves** and their **abilities**.
- **Suicidal** thoughts.
- **Slower** thought processes — **difficulty concentrating** and **making decisions**.

Social / motivational symptoms
- Lack of **activity** — **social withdrawal** and loss of **sex drive**.

The DSM-IV Classifies Mental Disorders

The **DSM-IV** is the fourth edition of the American Psychiatric Association's Diagnostic and Statistical Manual of Mental Disorders. It contains a list of **mental health disorders**. Individuals are rated on **multiple axes / dimensions** and diagnostic **categories** are used, e.g. personality disorders and psychosocial problems. It aims to give diagnosis of mental disorders **reliability** and **validity**:

Reliability is how far the classification system produces the **same diagnosis** for a particular set of symptoms. In order for a classification system to be reliable the **same diagnosis** should be made **each time** it's used. This means that **different clinicians** should reach the **same diagnosis**.

Validity is whether the classification system is actually measuring what it **aims to measure**.
- **Descriptive validity** — how similar individuals diagnosed with the disorder are.
- **Aetiological validity** — how similar the cause of the disorder is for each sufferer.
- **Predictive validity** — how useful the diagnostic categories are for predicting the right treatment.

Depression

There can be Problems with the Reliability of Diagnoses

1) For a person to be diagnosed with **major depression**, the DSM-IV states that at least **five symptoms** must have been present nearly every day for at least **two weeks**.

2) However, the diagnosis of depression isn't always **reliable** — people displaying the **same symptoms** don't always get the **same diagnosis**.

3) Also, women are **twice as likely** to be diagnosed with depression than men:

Both Dr. Jim and Dr. Bob would defend their diagnoses to the death.

- There don't seem to be any clear reasons for why **women** would be **more likely** to suffer from depression than **men**.

- Some researchers have claimed that it's to do with **hormonal differences** between men and women. Others have said it's because of **socio-cultural** factors — the different ways that males and females are **socialised** means they react differently to stressful life events.

- However, it could be that clinicians **expect** more women to suffer from depression than men, so are more likely to diagnose a **woman** with depression than a **man** who displays the **same symptoms**.

There Can be Problems With the Validity of Diagnoses

Rosenhan (1973) conducted a classic study that questioned the **validity** of the diagnosis of mental disorders. He believed that psychiatrists **couldn't tell the difference** between **sane** people and people with **mental disorders**.

1) People who didn't have any kind of mental health problem got themselves admitted into a **psychiatric unit** by claiming they heard voices — they became **pseudopatients**.

2) Once they'd been admitted they behaved 'normally'. However, their behaviour was still seen as a **symptom** of their **disorder** by the staff in the unit. For example, one pseudopatient who wrote in a diary was recorded as displaying 'writing behaviour'.

3) This questions the **validity** of the **diagnosis** of mental disorders — once people are **labelled** as having a disorder, all of their behaviour can be **interpreted** as being **caused** by the **disorder**.

Practice Questions

Q1 What's the difference between major depression and manic depression?

Q2 What is anhedonia?

Q3 Outline the cognitive symptoms of depression.

Q4 What is the DSM-IV?

Q5 What does validity mean in terms of the diagnosis of mental disorders?

Q6 Outline a study that demonstrates problems with the validity of diagnoses.

Exam Question

Q1 a) Outline the clinical characteristics of depression. [8 marks]

b) Discuss issues surrounding the classification and diagnosis of depression. [16 marks]

I've got reactive depression just from reading this...

Yes, these pages are a touch on the gloomy side, but depression affects a lot of people, so it's really worth knowing about. And it's also in the exam... Make sure you can describe the different types of depression, outline the major symptoms, say what the DSM-IV is and have a bit of a chat about reliability and validity. By then you'll have probably cheered right up...

Explanations of Depression

These pages cover the possible causes of depression. And no, having to spend all your time revising won't go down well with the examiners as a valid cause of depression. It'll get you neither sympathy nor marks. Here's the stuff that will...

Depression *Could be Caused by* Biological Factors

① Genetic *Factors (Inherited Tendencies)*

Being **biologically related** to someone who has depression seems to **increase** a person's **chance** of developing it.

Evidence for...

1) **McGuffin et al (1996)** found that if one **identical (MZ) twin** has **major depressive disorder**, then in about **46%** of cases their **twin** is **also** diagnosed with it. For **non-identical (DZ) twins** the **concordance rate** is about **20%**.

2) **Wender et al (1986)** studied the **biological parents** of **adopted** children who had **major depressive disorder**. The **biological** parents were **8 times** more likely to have depression than the children's **adoptive** parents.

Evidence against...

1) The **concordance rates** found in **family** and **twin** studies **aren't 100%**, so **genetics** can't be the whole story. **Environmental factors** could also play a role.

2) Genetic factors only seem to explain **endogenous depression** (depression caused by internal factors) — **psychological** factors seem to have more **influence** in the development of **reactive depression**.

② Biochemical *Factors*

Low levels of **serotonin** have been linked to depression. **Kety (1975)** developed the **permissive amine theory**, which states that **serotonin** controls the **levels** of the neurotransmitter **noradrenaline**. A **low level** of **serotonin** causes the level of **noradrenaline** to **fluctuate** — **low** levels of **noradrenaline** then cause **depression**, while **high** levels cause **mania**.

Evidence for...

1) **Anti-depressant** drugs work by **increasing** the **availability** of **serotonin** at the synapses by preventing its reuptake or breakdown. This suggests that it's the **low levels** of serotonin that **lead** to **depressive disorders**.

2) **Post-mortems** carried out on people who committed **suicide** have shown abnormally **low levels** of **serotonin**, suggesting that this may have **caused** their depression.

Evidence against...

1) Just because **antidepressants** relieve the **symptoms**, it **doesn't** mean they treat the **cause**.

2) Low levels of serotonin could be a **result** of depression, not the cause.

3) **Psychological** research has found **alternative explanations** for the cause of depression.

Depression *Could be Caused by* Psychological Factors

① Socio-cultural *Factors*

Social psychologists focus on how depression can be **triggered** by something **external**, e.g. a bereavement or divorce.

Evidence for...

Brown and Harris (1978) studied depression by **interviewing** housewives in London. They found that **61%** of the subjects **with depression** had recently experienced a **stressful life event**, compared with only **19%** of the **non-depressed** subjects. Of the subjects who had experienced a stressful event but had a **close friend**, only **10%** had depression. This can be compared with the **37%** of depressed subjects who **didn't** have a **close friend**. These results suggest that **depression** is **influenced** by **stressful life events** and a **lack** of **emotional support**.

Evidence against...

1) Brown and Harris's study just shows a **correlation**, so you can't prove **cause and effect**. It could actually be that depression makes some stressful life events **more likely** to happen, e.g. someone might be more likely to lose their job or get divorced as a result of their depression.

2) The effect of social factors **doesn't** explain why some people experience **endogenous depression** (sudden depression that occurs because of internal factors). Other approaches might have better explanations.

Explanations of Depression

(2) Behavioural Factors

Behaviourists reckon that depression develops when **stressors** (e.g. death of a loved one or being made redundant) lead to a **lack** of **positive reinforcement**. The attention that depressive behaviour then draws (e.g. sympathy from others) can then provide **positive reinforcement**, meaning the person **learns** to continue being depressed. It may also be influenced by **learned helplessness**. This occurs when people **learn not to try** because they believe they'll **never succeed**.

Seligman (1975) restrained dogs so that they **couldn't avoid** receiving **electric shocks**. Later when they **could** actually avoid the shocks they **didn't** even **try** — they displayed **learned helplessness**. This can be **generalised** to humans — when people **aren't** in **control** of **stressful events** they eventually **learn not to try** and improve them, causing them to become **depressed**.

Evidence against...

Behaviourist theory **ignores** the influence of **biological** factors. It also only explains **reactive depression** (depression caused by external events). It may be that biological factors are responsible for causing **endogenous depression**.

(3) Cognitive Factors

Abramson et al (1978) developed **Seligman's (1975)** theory of **learned helplessness** into a **cognitive theory**. They looked at people's **thought processes** in response to **failure** and stated that failure can be interpreted as:

1) **Internal** (the person's fault) or **external** (caused by something else).
2) **Global** (applies to all situations) or **specific** (just applies to this situation).
3) **Stable** (likely to continue) or **unstable** (could easily change). ➡

> Depressed people may see failure as **internal**, **global** and **stable** (it's their fault, happens in all situations and won't change).

This is just one example of a model of faulty cognitions — there are other models (see page 77).

Evidence for...
Beck et al (1979) found that depressed people had **negative** thought processes — they **exaggerated** their **weaknesses** and **played down** their **strengths**.

Evidence against...
This is just a **correlation** — it doesn't prove **cause and effect**. It may be that **negative thinking** is actually the **result** of depression, **not** the **cause** of it. Instead, **biological** or other **psychological** factors could be the cause.

(4) Psychodynamic Theory

Freud claimed that if a child feels **unloved** by its **parents** it becomes **angry**. This creates **guilt**, so the anger is **redirected** towards the **self**. These feelings are **repressed**, but may later **return** following a **stressful life event**, causing **depression**.

Evidence for...
Brown and Harris (1978) found that the women they interviewed were **more likely** to have depression if they experienced **disrupted** childhood attachments, especially if their **mother** had **died**.

Evidence against...
There **isn't** any **research evidence** to **support** Freud's theory, so it's **unfalsifiable** (impossible to prove right or wrong). It also **ignores** the significance of **other factors** in causing depression, e.g. biological factors.

Practice Questions

Q1 Outline research evidence that supports the theory that genetic factors can cause depression.

Q2 Outline the role that serotonin might have in causing depression.

Q3 What evidence is there to suggest that depression is caused by stressful life events?

Exam Question

Q1 a) Outline biological explanations for depression.   [8 marks]

    b) Outline and evaluate a psychological explanation for depression.   [16 marks]

Genes can make you depressed — especially if the fly comes undone...

It's the usual drill here — learn an explanation of depression, then learn another one so you can use it to tear the first one apart. It's a wonder the psychologists who come up with these theories don't get more depressed themselves. You'd think having thousands of A-level students telling them they're wrong would upset them a bit. But no, they're as happy as Larry.

Treating Depression

Depression is horrible, so you'll be pleased to know that there are loads of treatments available for it. You may be less pleased to know that you have to learn them all, but you shouldn't really be surprised, so try to keep your chin up.

Depression *Can be* Treated *Using* Biological Therapy

Therapy using drugs is also called chemotherapy.

1) The **biological** approach to treating depression involves **drug therapy**.
2) Treatment is based on altering the levels of **serotonin** and **noradrenaline** in the brain. These **neurotransmitters** regulate things like emotions, sleep patterns, sex drive and reaction to stress.
3) There are **four** main types of antidepressant drugs:

> • **Selective serotonin reuptake inhibitors (SSRIs)** increase the availability of **serotonin** by preventing its reuptake.
> • **Tricyclic antidepressants (TCAs)** increase the availability of **serotonin** and **noradrenaline** by preventing their reuptake.
> • **Monoamine oxidase inhibitors (MAOIs)** increase the availability of **serotonin** and **noradrenaline** by preventing their breakdown.
> • **Serotonin and noradrenaline reuptake inhibitors (SNRIs)** prevent the reuptake of **serotonin** and **noradrenaline**, so increase their availability.

Ashley and George's sleep patterns were perfectly in sync.

Advantages
• Studies have shown that antidepressants are successful in **reducing** the **symptoms** of depression for **more than half** of patients.
• It's the most **widely-used** and **effective** form of treatment for depression. Psychological treatments are often used **alongside** drug therapy because antidepressants can remove some of the **symptoms**, allowing **other therapies** to focus on the **cause** of the depression.

Disadvantages
• Antidepressants only treat the **symptoms** of depression. **Other therapies** are needed to try and tackle the **cause** of it.
• There are **ethical issues** surrounding the use of drug therapy. Some people argue that drug treatment is a '**chemical straitjacket**' — it **doesn't** really **help** the patient, it just **controls** their **behaviour** to make it more socially acceptable and easier to manage.
• Antidepressants can have **side effects**, e.g. drowsiness, dry mouth, indigestion and nausea.

Depression *Can be* Treated *using* Psychological Therapies

① Psychotherapy

1) Psychotherapy aims to identify the **underlying cause** of the mental disorder.
2) This is done using different therapeutic techniques, e.g. **dream analysis** and **free association**.
3) When the **unconscious conflicts** that are causing the problems are made **conscious**, the therapist and patient can discuss and try to resolve them. This will hopefully lead to the disorder being cured.

Advantages
• It aims to treat the **cause** of the disorder, not just the **symptoms**.
• Patients have **more control** over their treatment than with other therapies, e.g. drug therapy.

Disadvantages
• Psychotherapy can be **distressing** for people because they're encouraged to **recall traumatic events**. This can sometimes be more difficult to deal with than the original symptoms.
• It's **difficult to prove** the effectiveness of psychotherapy because it's based on **subjective data** and the **unconscious mind**. There's also a risk that patients will develop **false memories**.
• **Other forms** of treatment, e.g. cognitive behavioural therapies (see opposite page) and drug therapy have been found to be **more effective**.

Treating Depression

② Cognitive Behavioural Therapies

There are several models that explain how **faulty cognitions** can lead to depression. For example:

Ellis (1962) — The **ABC model** claims that disorders begin with an **activating event (A)** (e.g. a failed exam), leading to a **belief (B)** about why this happened. This may be rational (e.g. 'I didn't prepare well enough'), or irrational (e.g. 'I'm too stupid to pass exams'). The belief leads to a **consequence (C)**. Rational beliefs produce adaptive (appropriate) consequences (e.g. more revision). Irrational beliefs produce maladaptive (bad and inappropriate) consequences (e.g. getting depressed).

Beck (1963) — Beck identified a **cognitive triad** of negative, automatic thoughts linked to **depression**: negative views about **themselves** (e.g. that they can't succeed at anything), about the **world** (e.g. that they must be successful to be a good person) and about the **future** (e.g. that nothing will change).

Cognitive behavioural therapy (CBT) aims to **identify** and **change** the patient's **faulty cognitions**. This is generally what happens during CBT:

1) The therapist and client **identify** the client's **faulty cognitions**.

2) Therapists sometimes encourage their clients to keep a **diary** so they can record their thought patterns, feelings and actions.

3) The therapist tries to show that the cognitions **aren't true**, e.g. the client doesn't always fail at what they do.

4) Together, they set **goals** to think in more positive or adaptive ways, e.g. focusing on things the client has succeeded at and trying to build on them.

5) Although the client may occasionally need to look back to past experiences, the treatment mainly focuses on the **present situation**.

Advantages of CBT

- **Brandsma et al (1978)** found that **CBT** is particularly effective for people who put a lot of **pressure** on themselves and feel **guilty** about being **inadequate**.

- CBT **empowers** patients — it puts them in charge of their own treatment by teaching them **self-help strategies**. This means there are **fewer ethical issues** than with other therapies like drug therapy.

Disadvantages of CBT

- Faulty cognitions might be the **consequence** of a disorder rather than its cause. For example, depression may be caused by a chemical imbalance in the brain, which causes people to think very negatively.

- Cognitive therapies may take a long **time** and may be more effective when **combined** with other approaches, e.g. drug therapy.

Practice Questions

Q1 Outline the biological approach to the treatment of depression.

Q2 Give one advantage of drug therapy in the treatment of depression.

Q3 Outline what happens in cognitive behavioural therapy.

Exam Question

Q1 a) Outline one or more approaches to the treatment of depression. [16 marks]

b) Evaluate one approach to the treatment of depression. [8 marks]

This depression stuff is really getting me down...

...but not to worry, these are the last two pages on depression. And they are all about treatment — which is surely the least depressing aspect of depression. Anyway, best learn these pages pretty sharpish, before you sink into a murky mire of miserableness. Then you can move on to the much more cheerful topic of... phobic disorders. Well, it's a bit more cheerful...

Phobic Disorders

Anxiety isn't always a problem — it can help to motivate you to perform your best. Like to revise before an exam, for example. It's only when you start feeling anxious all the time, or about slightly odd things, that it becomes a disorder.

A **Phobia** is an **Irrational Fear**

1) A phobia is an example of an **anxiety disorder**.
2) A phobia is an **extreme**, **irrational fear** of a particular **object** or **situation**.
3) There are **three** types of phobia classified by the **DSM-IV**:

1 Specific phobias

This is a fear of specific **objects** or **situations**. There are **five** subtypes:
1) **Animal** type (also called **zoophobia**, e.g. fear of spiders)
2) **Environmental dangers** type (e.g. fear of water)
3) **Blood-injection-injury** type (e.g. fear of needles)
4) **Situational** type (e.g. fear of enclosed spaces or heights)
5) **'Other'** (any phobia that isn't covered in the categories above)

2 Social phobia

This is the fear of **being** in **social situations** (e.g. eating in public or talking in front of a group of people). It's usually down to the possibility of being **judged** or being **embarrassed**.

3 Agoraphobia

1) This is a fear of **open spaces**.
2) It's specifically linked to the **fear** of having a **panic attack** in a public place and **not** being able to **get away**.
3) It often develops as a **result** of **other phobias**, because the sufferer's afraid that they'll come across the **source** of their **fear** if they leave the house.

Phobias have Several **Clinical Characteristics**

The different types of phobia all have very **similar** clinical characteristics.

Cognitive symptoms	**Irrational beliefs** about the **stimulus** that causes fear. People often find it **hard** to **concentrate** because they're **preoccupied** by **anxious thoughts**.
Social symptoms	**Avoiding** social situations because they cause **anxiety**. This happens especially if someone has **social phobia** or **agoraphobia**.
Behavioural symptoms	Altering behaviour to **avoid** the feared object or situation, and trying to **escape** if it's encountered. People are often generally **restless** and **easily startled**.
Physical symptoms	Activation of the **fight or flight** response when the feared object or situation is encountered or thought about. This involves release of **adrenaline**, **increased heart rate** and **breathing**, and **muscle tension**.
Emotional symptoms	**Anxiety** and a feeling of **dread**.

There are Various **Diagnostic Criteria** for **Phobias**

The **DSM-IV** (see next page) classifies a fear as a phobia if you can put a tick next to these criteria:
1) There's **significant prolonged fear** of an object or situation.
2) People experience an **anxiety response** (e.g. increased heart rate) if they're exposed to the phobic stimulus.
3) Sufferers **realise** that their phobia is **irrational** and **out of proportion** to any actual danger. They may try to **hide** their phobia from other people, which can cause more anxiety.
4) Sufferers go out of their way to **avoid** the phobic stimulus.
5) The phobia **disrupts** their lives, e.g. they avoid social situations.

Sophie did everything she could to hide her parrotophobia.

Phobic Disorders

The DSM-IV Classifies Mental Disorders

1) The **DSM-IV** is the fourth edition of the American Psychiatric Association's Diagnostic and Statistical Manual of Mental Disorders.

2) It contains a **list** of **mental health disorders**. Individuals are rated on **multiple axes / dimensions** and diagnostic **categories** are used, e.g. personality disorders and psychosocial problems.

3) It aims to give diagnosis of mental disorders **reliability** and **validity**:

Dr. Bale could pretend to read the DSM-IV all he liked — everyone knew he kept a comic inside it.

Reliability Reliability is how far the classification system produces the **same diagnosis** for a particular set of symptoms. In order for a classification system to be reliable the **same diagnosis** should be made **each time** it's used. This means that **different clinicians** should reach the **same diagnosis**.

Validity Validity is whether the classification system is actually measuring what it **aims to measure**.
- **Descriptive validity** — how similar individuals diagnosed with the disorder are.
- **Aetiological validity** — how similar the cause of the disorder is for each sufferer.
- **Predictive validity** — how useful the diagnostic categories are for predicting the right treatment.

There can be Problems with the Validity and Reliability of Diagnoses

Problems with validity

1) **Rosenhan (1973)** conducted a study where people who didn't have any kind of mental health problem got themselves admitted into a **psychiatric unit** — they became **pseudopatients**.

2) Once they'd been admitted they behaved 'normally'. However, their behaviour was still seen as a **symptom** of their **disorder** by the staff in the unit. For example, one pseudopatient who wrote in a diary was recorded as displaying 'writing behaviour'.

3) This questions the **validity** of the **diagnosis** of mental disorders — once people are **labelled** as having a disorder, all of their behaviour can be **interpreted** as being **caused** by the **disorder**.

Problems with reliability

1) Clinicians can show **bias** when they're diagnosing mental disorders.

2) For example, **Johnstone (1989)** found that patients from **lower social classes** tended to be given more **serious diagnoses** than patients from **higher social classes**.

3) This questions the **reliability** of the diagnosis of mental disorders — it suggests that patients can display the **same symptoms** but receive **different diagnoses** because of their social background.

Practice Questions

Q1 What are the five subtypes of specific phobias?
Q2 List some of the physical symptoms of phobias.
Q3 Outline the diagnostic criteria for phobias.

Exam Question

Q1 a) Outline the clinical characteristics of phobias. [8 marks]

 b) Discuss the issues of validity and reliability in the diagnosis of phobias. [16 marks]

Keep calm keep calm keep calm keep calm keep calm keep calm...

These pages don't exactly make for relaxing bedtime reading do they — anyone else got a sweat on? On a lighter note, writing out 'keep calm' so many times has meant I've got that weird thing where the words have lost all their meaning and look really strange. It looks more like 'keep clam' now, which I suppose is actually quite sound advice...

Explanations of Phobias

There are lots of possible causes of phobias, and they won't learn themselves. 'Tis a pity, but that lovely job is left to you.

Phobias *Could be Caused by* Biological Factors...

1 Genetic *Factors (Inherited Tendencies)*

1) Some phobias are much more **common** than others, and many of these are of things that can be **dangerous** to humans, e.g. snakes, spiders, heights.

2) This suggests that humans have **evolved** a **genetic predisposition** to fear these things because it has **survival value**. This is **preparedness theory**.

3) The assumption is that phobias have a **genetic** cause, so they should run in families, or be shared by identical twins who will have the same genes.

Mark's fear of heights was manageable, as long as Julie kept holding the bridge up.

Evidence for...	Using a family interview method, **Reich and Yates (1988)** found a **higher** rate of social phobias amongst **relatives** than other disorders. **6.6%** of those with phobias had a relative with it too, compared to **0.4%** of those with panic disorders.

Evidence against...	**Torgerson (1983)** found that identical (MZ) twins **don't** always share phobias. This suggests that **other factors** are also involved in causing phobias, e.g. psychological factors.

2 Neurological *Factors*

Biological theories explain why people can develop phobias without having had an associated bad experience.

Evidence for...

1) **Gray (1982)** identified the **behavioural inhibition system** — a circuit in the **limbic system** in the brain that's linked to **anxiety**. When something unexpected and possibly dangerous happens, signals are sent to this area from the **cortex**. This causes **anxiety** which may make the person 'freeze'. How **susceptible** someone is to anxiety and panic may depend on how **sensitive** this circuit is.

2) **Johnson et al (2000)** did a **longitudinal study** showing that adolescents who **smoked** were **15** times more likely to develop **anxiety disorders** later in life, especially if they were heavy smokers. This may be due to the effects of **nicotine**, which may make areas of the **brain** more **sensitive**.

Evidence against...

1) **Johnson et al's (2000)** research is **correlational** — it doesn't prove that smoking **caused** the anxiety.

2) This research **doesn't** take other factors into account. For example, **behavioural** research has shown that some phobias, especially specific phobias, can be **learnt**.

...or Psychological Factors *(surprise surprise)*

1 Behavioural *Factors*

Behaviourists believe that phobias are **learnt** through **classical** or **operant conditioning**.

Classical conditioning — This especially explains **specific phobias**. A previously **neutral** thing starts to trigger anxiety because it becomes **associated** with something **frightening**. **Watson and Rayner (1920)** conducted a study on an 11-month-old boy called **Little Albert**. A loud noise was made every time he played with a **white rat**. He then began to **associate** the **rat** with the **frightening noise**, and showed fear when he saw it.	**Operant conditioning** — This especially explains **social phobia** and **agoraphobia**. A person's fear goes when they **get away from** the situation that causes **fear**. This is **negative reinforcement** — they **learn** to avoid the stimulus that causes anxiety because they feel **better** when they **escape** it.

Evidence for...	Behavioural **therapies** are very **effective** at treating phobias by getting the person to **change** their **response** to the **stimulus** (see p.80). This suggests that they're treating the **cause** of the problem.
Evidence against...	**Davey (1992)** found that only 7% of spider phobics recalled having a **traumatic experience** with a spider. This suggests that there could be **other explanations**, e.g. biological factors. (But just because they couldn't remember the experience, this doesn't mean it didn't happen.)

Explanations of Phobias

② *Socio-cultural Factors*

It's thought that **upbringing** could affect the development of **phobias**.

Evidence for...
1) **Arrincell et al (1989)** reported that people with **social phobia** claimed that their parents were **controlling, over-protective** and **didn't** show much **affection**. This suggests that **upbringing** can cause social phobia.
2) **Social learning theory** states that behaviour is influenced by your **environment** and the people you grow up with. Children may see that a parent or older sibling is afraid of something and **imitate** their **response**.

Evidence against...
1) The research on upbringing is **correlational**, and it relies on people's **memory**, which can be **inaccurate**.
2) **Other factors** may be responsible, e.g. some people may have a biological pre-disposition that makes them more likely to develop phobias.

③ *Psychodynamic Theory*

Freud argued that phobias **hide** an **unconscious fear**. The real fear creates so much **anxiety** that it's **displaced** onto something less frightening or embarrassing.

Evidence for...
Freud used the case study of **Little Hans** to support his theory. Little Hans had a **fear** of **horses**, which Freud thought was caused by **Oedipal conflict**. Freud claimed that Hans was **attracted** to his mother and frightened that his father would **punish** him for being his rival. This fear created so much **anxiety** and guilt that it was **displaced** onto horses, which were like Hans' father because they wore bridles (which looked like his beard) and had big penises. Right...

Evidence against...
1) Freud's theories are **unfalsifiable** — they're **unscientific** because they can't be proved wrong.
2) Hans had been very frightened by seeing a horse fall down in the street. It could be that this produced a phobia of horses through **classical conditioning**.

④ *Cognitive Factors*

Beck and Emery (1985) proposed that interactions between an anxious person's **cognitive processes** and their belief in their **vulnerability** makes them more likely to interpret stimuli as being threatening.

Evidence for...
Hope et al (1990) showed participants words written in different colours. Participants with social phobia took **longer** to name the colour of **social threat words** (e.g. 'failure'). This suggests that they **processed** them in a different way.

Evidence against...
- This **doesn't** show **cause and effect** — it could be that feeling vulnerable is a **symptom** of anxiety, not the **cause** of it.
- Phobias could be caused by other factors, e.g. **biological factors**.

Practice Questions

Q1 Outline evidence to support the genetic explanation of phobias.
Q2 How can phobias be explained by classical conditioning?
Q3 Outline evidence against the Oedipus conflict being the cause of Little Hans' phobia.

Exam Question

Q1 Describe and evaluate psychological explanations for one anxiety disorder. [24 marks]

What was Little Hans' brother called? — Tiny Feet...

You've got to feel for Little Hans — somehow it's a bit more socially acceptable to be scared of horses than it is to be in love with your mum and scared of your dad's penis. In fact, these 'Little' chaps have had quite a raw deal overall — poor Little Albert's fear ended up being generalised to all white fluffy things, until he was afraid of Santa's white fluffy beard. Sob...

Treating Phobic Disorders

If, like me, you've completely lost concentration and started chewing your fingers off and staring at the wall, the ceiling or anything else in view, then these are just the pages to pick you up and give you a good shake. Just what you wanted.

Phobic Disorders *Can be* Treated *Using* Biological Therapy

Therapy using drugs is also called chemotherapy.

1) The **biological** approach to treating phobic disorders involves **drug therapy**.

2) **Anxiolytic drugs** (e.g. tranquillisers) such as benzodiazepines, **reduce anxiety** by increasing the activity of the neurotransmitter **GABA**. GABA produces a feeling of **calmness**.

Advantages
- **Benzodiazepines** take effect very **quickly**. This means that they're good for treating **phobias** in the **short term**, e.g. before stressful events like exams.
- **Davidson et al (1993)** compared the effects of **benzodiazepines** with a **placebo**, and found that benzodiazepines were **more effective** at reducing the symptoms of social phobia.

Disadvantages
- **Benzodiazepines** can cause side effects like **drowsiness**. They also cause physical and psychological **dependency**, so they **can't** be used **long-term**.
- The **symptoms** of phobias often **return** when people come off medication.
- Drug therapy only treats the **symptoms** of the disorder. Other therapies are needed to try and tackle the **cause** of it, e.g. behavioural therapies.

Phobic Disorders *Can be* Treated *Using* Psychological Therapies

1 Behavioural Therapies

Behavioural treatment for **specific phobias** is based on **classical conditioning** (learning through **association**). There are **two techniques** for treating specific phobias:

Systematic desensitisation — Wolpe (1958)

1) Systematic desensitisation works by using **counter-conditioning** so that the person learns to **associate** the **phobic stimulus** with **relaxation** rather than **fear**.

2) Patients **rank feared situations**, from the **least stressful** (e.g. saying the word *spider*) to the **most stressful** (e.g. holding a spider). They are then taught **relaxation techniques** like deep breathing.

3) The patient then **imagines** the anxiety-provoking situations, starting with the least stressful. They're encouraged to use the **relaxation techniques** and the process stops if they feel anxious.

4) Patients will gradually be able to work through the feared situations on the list without feeling **anxious**.

Exposure therapy

1) This involves exposing the patient to the phobic stimulus **straight away**, without any relaxation or gradual build-up. This can be done in **real life**, or the patient can be asked to **visualise** it. For example, someone who was afraid of heights might imagine standing on top of a skyscraper.

2) The patient is kept in this situation until the **anxiety** they feel at first has **warn off**. They realise that nothing bad has happened to them in this time, and their fear should be **extinguished**.

Advantages
- **Behavioural therapy** is very effective for treating **specific phobias**. **Zinbarg et al (1992)** found that **systematic desensitisation** was the **most effective** of the currently known methods for treating phobias.
- It works very **quickly**, e.g. **Ost et al (1991)** found that anxiety was reduced in **90%** of patients with a specific phobia after just **one session** of **therapy**.

Disadvantages
- There are **ethical issues** surrounding behavioural therapy — especially **exposure therapy**, as it causes patients a lot of anxiety. If patients **drop out** of the therapy **before** the fear has been extinguished, then it can end up causing **more anxiety** than before therapy started.
- **Behavioural therapy** only treats the **symptoms** of the disorder. **Other therapies** are needed to try and tackle the **cause** of it, e.g. cognitive behavioural therapy.

Treating Phobic Disorders

(2) Cognitive Behavioural Therapy

Cognitive behavioural therapy (CBT) helps patients by **identifying** and **changing** their **faulty cognitions**. For example, many people with **social phobia** assume that they'll **embarrass themselves** in social situations, so think it's best to avoid them. Here's what generally happens during CBT:

1) The therapist and client **identify** the client's **faulty cognitions**.

2) The therapist tries to show that the cognitions **aren't true**, e.g. the client doesn't always embarrass themselves.

3) Together, they set **goals** to think in more positive or adaptive ways, e.g. going to a party and talking to people they don't know. The aim is to prove to the client that their **negative thoughts** about what's going to happen are **wrong**, and so **reduce** their **anxiety**.

Advantages

- **CBT is effective** at treating phobias, e.g. **Thorpe and Salkovskis (1997)** found **reduced anxiety** in spider phobics after only **one session** of CBT.
- CBT **empowers** patients — it puts them in charge of their own treatment by teaching them **self-help strategies**. This means that it's a very **ethical** treatment.

Disadvantages

- Faulty cognitions might be the **consequence** of the disorder rather than its **cause**. For example, phobias may be caused by a chemical imbalance in the brain which leads to faulty thought processes.
- Patients can become **dependent** on their therapist.

Stuart's faulty cognition had led to a disastrous footwear decision.

(3) Psychotherapy

1) Psychotherapy aims to identify the **underlying cause** of the mental disorder.

2) This is done using different therapeutic techniques, e.g. **dream analysis** and **free association**.

3) When the **unconscious conflicts** that are causing the problems are made **conscious**, the therapist and patient can discuss and try to resolve them. This will hopefully lead to the disorder being cured.

Advantages

- It aims to treat the **cause** of the disorder, not just the **symptoms**.
- Patients have **more control** over their treatment than with other therapies, e.g. drug therapy.

Disadvantages

- Psychotherapy can be **distressing** for people because they're encouraged to **recall traumatic events**. This can sometimes be more difficult to deal with than the original symptoms.
- It's **difficult to prove** the effectiveness of psychotherapy — it's based on **subjective data** and the **unconscious mind**. There's also a risk that patients will develop **false memories**, e.g. of childhood abuse.

Practice Questions

Q1 Name a type of drug that can be used in the treatment of phobic disorders.

Q2 What is meant by exposure therapy?

Q3 Outline what happens in cognitive behavioural therapy.

Exam Question

Q1 Describe and evaluate one or more treatment for a phobic disorder. [24 marks]

I treat my phobic disorder really well...

Yesterday I took it to the pictures, then I bought it a choc ice and let it go on the swings for half an hour. You've got to show you care sometimes. And it doesn't have to be anything fancy, just a little token of your affection is often enough. The most important thing is to spend some quality time together, make each other laugh, and just show a little bit more love...

Obsessive-Compulsive Disorder

Obsessive-compulsive disorder (OCD) is a type of anxiety disorder. Most of us have the odd obsessive thought (like checking your phone's off ten times before the exam starts) — but in OCD it's taken to extremes and affects daily life.

OCD *is an* Anxiety Disorder *with* Two Parts

1) Obsessive-compulsive disorder is a type of **anxiety disorder** that has two parts — **obsessions** and **compulsions**. Most people with OCD experience obsessions and compulsions that are **linked** to each other. For example, excessive worrying about catching germs (an obsession) may lead to excessive hand washing (a compulsion).

2) Obsessive-compulsive disorder affects about **2%** of the world's population. Sufferers usually develop the disorder in their **late teens** or **early 20s**. The disorder occurs **equally in men and women** and in all **ethnic groups**.

Obsessions *are the* Cognitive Part *of the Disorder*

Obsessions are **intrusive** and **persistent thoughts**, **images** and **impulses**. They can range from worrying that you left the oven on to worrying that you might kill your parents. For thoughts like these to be **classified** as obsessions, the **DSM-IV** (see next page) states they must meet the following criteria:

- **Persistent** and **reoccurring** thoughts, images or impulses that are **unwanted** and cause **distress** to the person experiencing them. For example, imagining that you've left the door unlocked and burglars are rampaging through your house.

- The thoughts, images or impulses are **more serious** than just worrying too much. For example, continuing to focus mentally on the imaginary burglar, rather than dismissing it as an unlikely event.

- The person actively tries to **ignore** the thoughts, images or impulses but is **unable to**.

- The person is aware that the thoughts, images or impulses are **created by their own mind** and aren't the result of **thought insertion** (a symptom of some other disorders — see page 66).

Compulsions *are* Repetitive Actions

Compulsions are **physical** or **mental repetitive actions**. For example, **checking** the door is locked nine times or repeating a certain **phrase** or **prayer** to **neutralise** an unwanted thought. The problem is that the action only reduces the anxiety caused by an obsession for a **short time**, which means that the obsession starts up again. The **DSM-IV** uses the following diagnostic criteria:

1) The person **repeats physical behaviours** or **mental acts** that relate to an obsession. Sometimes the person has rules that they must follow strictly. For example, a rule that you must check the door is locked ten times before you can leave home.

2) The compulsions are meant to **reduce anxiety** or **prevent** a feared situation — in reality they're **excessive** or **wouldn't actually stop** a dreaded situation.

No matter how many times he checked, the doctor still couldn't prove who'd eaten his stash of lollipops.

The DSM-IV states that if the obsessions or compulsions last **more than an hour each day** this is an indication of a **clinical case** of OCD. An alternative indication of OCD is if the obsessions and compulsions **interfere** with a person's ability to maintain a relationship, hold down a job or take part in social activities.

There are Several Types *of* OCD Behaviours

There are several common types of OCD behaviours. Here are four:

1) **Checking** — includes checking that the lights are off or that you have your purse.
2) **Contamination** — this involves a fear of catching germs by, say, going to a restaurant, touching door handles, shaking hands or using public toilets.
3) **Hoarding** — keeping useless or worn-out objects, such as old newspapers or junk mail.
4) **Symmetry and orderliness** — getting objects lined up 'just right', such as having all the tins in your food cupboard facing forward in exactly the same way, or everything on your desk arranged in a neat order in the right places.

Obsessive-Compulsive Disorder

The **DSM-IV** Classifies Mental Disorders

1) The **DSM-IV** is the fourth edition of the American Psychiatric Association's Diagnostic and Statistical Manual of Mental Disorders.

2) It contains a list of **mental health disorders**. Individuals are rated on **multiple axes / dimensions** and diagnostic **categories** are used, e.g. personality disorders and psychosocial problems.

3) It aims to give diagnosis of mental disorders **reliability** and **validity**:

Bob didn't actually have OCD — he was just extremely adept at stationery management.

Reliability shows how far the classification system produces the **same diagnosis** for a particular set of symptoms. In order for a classification system to be reliable the **same diagnosis** should be made **each time** it's used. This means that **different clinicians** should reach the **same diagnosis**.

Validity is whether the classification system is actually measuring what it **aims to measure**.
- **Descriptive validity** — how similar individuals diagnosed with the disorder are.
- **Aetiological validity** — how similar the cause of the disorder is for each sufferer.
- **Predictive validity** — how useful the diagnostic categories are for predicting the right treatment.

There can be **Problems** with the **Validity** and **Reliability** of **Diagnoses**

Problems with validity

1) **Rosenhan (1973)** conducted a study where people who didn't have any kind of mental health problem got themselves admitted into a **psychiatric unit** — they became **pseudopatients**.

2) Once they'd been admitted they behaved 'normally'. However, their behaviour was still seen as a **symptom** of their **disorder** by the staff in the unit. For example, one pseudopatient who wrote in a diary was recorded as displaying 'writing behaviour'.

3) This questions the **validity** of the **diagnosis** of mental disorders — once people are **labelled** as having a disorder, all of their behaviour can be **interpreted** as being **caused** by the **disorder**.

Problems with reliability

1) The DSM criteria can cause **problems** in diagnosing OCD. How do you decide **objectively** when it is that worrying too much about something actually becomes an obsession? Is there a **clear point** when a physical behaviour or mental act becomes a compulsion?

2) People with **other disorders**, for example eating disorders, also experience obsessions and compulsions. This means that they could be **misdiagnosed** as having OCD.

Practice Questions

Q1 Give an example of an obsession.

Q2 Give an example of a compulsion.

Q3 List four common types of OCD behaviour.

Exam Question

Q1 a) Outline the clinical characteristics of OCD. [8 marks]

b) Discuss the issues surrounding the classification and diagnosis of OCD. [16 marks]

Doctor, Doctor, I'm having unwanted thoughts about revision...

OCD isn't always about checking and straightening rituals. Often the intrusive thoughts can be violent and upsetting. However, people suffering from OCD rarely act on these thoughts — but the thoughts do cause them considerable stress.

Explanations of OCD

There's more than one theory about what causes OCD and there's evidence for and against each of these theories.
So basically nobody is really sure — but don't go thinking that gives you an excuse not to read about it.

OCD Could be Caused by **Biological Factors**

\\\\\\\\\\\\\//
\ Concordance rates tell /
~ us how likely a person ~
− is to develop a disorder −
/ if their twin has it. ~
///////\\\\\\\

1 **Genetic** Factors (Inherited Tendencies)

Some researchers think that **genetics** plays a part in OCD. Studies have looked at **concordance rates** to see if being related to someone with OCD **significantly** increases your chances of developing the disorder.

Evidence for...

1) **Billet et al** (1998) did a **meta-analysis** of twin studies that had been carried out over a long period of time. They found that **identical (MZ) twins** had a concordance rate of **68%**, compared to **non-identical (DZ) twins** with a concordance rate of **31%**.

2) **Pauls et al** (2005) found that **10%** of people with an **immediate relative** (i.e. parents, offspring or siblings) with OCD also suffered from the disorder. This is compared to around **2%** of people in the general population.

Evidence against...

1) No study has found a **100%** concordance rate, so **genetics can't** be the full story in OCD. It's possible that children **imitate** the obsessive and compulsive behaviour of their relatives.

2) Concordance rates don't prove that OCD is **caused** by genetics. It may be that **general anxiety** is genetic and that going on to develop OCD itself has **other contributing factors**, e.g. biochemical or psychological factors.

2 **Biochemical** Factors

PET scans have shown that levels of the **neurotransmitter serotonin** are lower in OCD sufferers.

Evidence for...

1) **Insel** (1991) found that a class of drugs called **SSRIs**, which increase levels of serotonin, can reduce symptoms of OCD in **50 to 60%** of cases.

2) **Zohar et al** (1996) also found that **SSRIs alleviated symptoms** in **60%** of patients with OCD.

Evidence against...

1) **SSRIs** appear to offer some relief to sufferers of OCD. However, as this is **not** true in **100%** of cases, there must be **more** to understanding OCD.

2) The **link** with serotonin is **correlational**, so it doesn't show **cause and effect**. It may be that decreased serotonin levels are a **symptom** of OCD, rather than a cause of it.

3 **Neurological** Factors

Some research using **PET scans** has found that **abnormality** in the **basal ganglia** within the brain may be linked to OCD.

Evidence for...

1) **Max et al** (1995) found **increased rates** of OCD in people after **head injuries** that caused brain damage to the **basal ganglia**.

2) Other researchers have found **increased activity** in this area during OCD-related thoughts and behaviours.

3) OCD is often found in people with **other diseases** which involve the basal ganglia, e.g. **Parkinson's** and **Huntington's chorea**.

Evidence against...

1) **Aylward et al** (1996) didn't find a significant difference in **basal ganglia impairment** between OCD patients and controls.

2) Basal ganglia damage **hasn't** been found in **100%** of people with OCD, so it can't be the full story.

Explanations of OCD

OCD Could be Caused by Psychological Factors

1 Behavioural Factors

1) Behaviourists use both **classical** and **operant conditioning** (see page 48) to explain OCD.
2) A person might behave in a certain way **by chance** when they are feeling anxious.
   When the anxiety goes away they unconsciously learn to **associate** the action with the removal of the anxiety.
   It becomes a reflex response. This is **classical conditioning**. They then **repeat** the action when they next feel anxious because they've learnt that it removes anxiety. This is **operant conditioning**.

Evidence for...	**Baxter et al (1992)** and **Schwartz et al (1996)** found that **behavioural therapy** can reduce the **symptoms** of OCD and change the **biochemical factors** associated with it.
Evidence against...	Both these behaviourist explanations **only** explain the **compulsive behaviour** and **not** the **obsessional thoughts**, which are an important aspect of OCD.

2 Psychodynamic Theory

Freud claimed that **potty training** causes **conflict** and **anger** in the child when their parents teach them how to use a toilet properly. This is **repressed** because the parents are more powerful. In adulthood this **can resurface**, causing anxiety, which is **displaced** into obsessions and compulsions.

Evidence for...
- Research into **stress** supports the idea that feeling **unimportant** and **out of control** may increase the likelihood of developing a mental disorder.
- **Adler (1931)** suggested a **link** between developing OCD and having had **overbearing parents**. In adulthood, engaging in **ritualistic behaviours** gives the person an opportunity to be very good at something (like hand washing) and so feel an increased level of **control**.

Evidence against...
Milby and Weber (1991) found **no link** between potty training conflicts and developing OCD.

3 Cognitive Factors

1) The cognitive-behavioural approach to OCD was put forward by **Rachman and Hodgson** (1980). It suggests that people with OCD **process thoughts** differently. As a result they're **unable** to easily dismiss any unwanted thoughts and impulses. This can be made worse if they're feeling **stressed** or **depressed**.
2) These unwanted thoughts and impulses cause **anxiety**, and the sufferer uses compulsive behaviours to **remove** this. This is the **behavioural** part of the cognitive-behavioural approach.

Evidence for...	1) There is a **link** between **depression** and **OCD**. This supports **Rachman and Hodgson's** idea that feeling stressed or depressed may make people more vulnerable to OCD.
	2) **Salkovskis and Kirk (1997)** asked OCD sufferers to try to **suppress** their obsessional thoughts on some days and allow them to surface on others. They reported **more** distressing thoughts on the days they were deliberately trying to suppress them compared to the other days.
Evidence against...	The cognitive-behavioural explanation **describes** the difficulty OCD sufferers have in suppressing unwanted thoughts but it **doesn't really explain** why they have this difficulty.

Practice Questions

Q1 What differences in concordance rates for OCD did Billet et al (1998) find in MZ and DZ twins?
Q2 What were the findings of the Salkovskis and Kirk (1997) study?

Exam Question

Q1 Compare and contrast two or more explanations for OCD.
   Refer to psychological evidence in your answer. [24 marks]

That Freud was potty...

There's not a single bit of evidence for potty training disasters triggering OCD — but old Freud said it so it must be true... The other theories hold a bit more water though (sorry). Anyway, just make sure you know them really well.

Treating OCD

Choosing the right treatment can be difficult — one man's meat is another man's poison and all that. However, some treatments for OCD do appear to be more effective than others. Sadly we still haven't found the magic solution.

OCD Can be Treated Using Biological Therapy

Therapy using drugs is also called chemotherapy.

1) The **biological** approach to treating OCD involves **drug therapy**.

2) Drug treatments usually work by increasing levels of **serotonin** in the brain using **selective serotonin reuptake inhibitors (SSRIs)**. These are a type of **antidepressant** drug that **increase** the availability of **serotonin**.

3) SSRIs **prevent the reuptake** of serotonin in the gap between two neurons.
This allows the nervous system to get **more benefit** from the serotonin as it passes across.

Advantages

- Several researchers have found SSRIs to be **effective** in treating OCD. **Thoren et al** (1980) found that use of an SSRI was significantly better at **reducing obsessional thoughts** than a placebo.
- Research has found that using **other antidepressants** that don't affect serotonin levels is **ineffective** at reducing OCD symptoms.

Disadvantages

- Up to **50%** of patients with OCD **don't** experience any improvement in their symptoms when taking SSRIs. Out of those that do improve, up to **90%** have a **relapse** when they stop taking them.
- SSRIs have to be taken for **several weeks** before the patient experiences an improvement in their symptoms.
- **Side effects** of using these types of drugs include **nausea** and **headaches**, and sometimes increased levels of **anxiety**. This can cause people to **stop taking** their medication.

OCD Can be Treated Using Psychological Therapies

① Cognitive Behavioural Therapies

Cognitive behavioural therapy (CBT) can be used as a psychological treatment for OCD.

1) CBT **challenges the obsessions** by making the person **test** or **question** the accuracy of some of their unwanted thoughts. For example, if a person believes they have to check that their front door is locked 10 times, they could be encouraged to test this by only checking the door once and then going out. When they come back and see that they haven't been burgled, and that the door is still locked, they may **question their need** to check the door 10 times.

2) CBT also uses **thought stopping**, which means shouting "Stop!" when the patient indicates that they are having the **obsessional thoughts or impulses**. They then **refocus** their mind on a more appropriate thought. The idea is that over time the patient will be able to do this by themselves **without support**.

3) By giving the sufferer **information** to challenge their obsessions, CBT can help **prevent the compulsions**.

Advantages of CBT

- CBT can be used to treat both the **obsessions** and the **compulsions**.
- **Franklin et al** (2002) found that CBT can be **combined with ERP** (see next page) to create a treatment that's **more effective** than either on its own.
- The patient is more **active** if they use CBT than if they use drugs. Encouraging people to be active in their treatment might be a more **positive** way to treat patients.

Disadvantages of CBT

- CBT can be **very challenging** for patients — they have to be willing to cope with the **increased anxiety** that is caused by the treatment. This might be **too distressing** for some and so drug treatments might be a better option for these patients.

The mouse had shouted "Stop!" several times, but it didn't seem to have stopped the owl's obsessional thoughts about eating him.

Treating OCD

2) Behavioural Therapies

Exposure and response prevention (ERP) is commonly used as a behavioural treatment for OCD. Here's how it could go:

1) With support from a therapist the OCD patient **identifies** some **situations** that cause them anxiety. They then rank these situations in order of the anxiety they produce. For example, if the OCD is to do with germs the patient's list might include touching a doorknob, using a communal toilet and shaking hands.

2) The patient is then exposed to the **first situation** and encouraged **not to use the compulsions** they usually use in this situation (e.g. using elbows to operate a door handle). Although this causes an **increase in anxiety**, after a time the **anxiety drops** as it can't stay high for long periods of time.

3) At the same time the patient is taught to use **relaxation techniques**, is **reassured** and is encouraged to take part in **different behaviours**. Once this is successful they then move on to the **next exposure task** that they listed.

Advantages

- It's been found in studies that ERP was **effective** in treating around **75%** of patients with OCD.
- For people with **mild OCD** it's possible to use ERP **without a therapist** as a **self-help** technique.
- Behavioural therapies only take around **3 to 8 weeks**.

Disadvantages

- Behavioural treatment is much **less successful** in patients who have obsessional thoughts but **don't** carry out **compulsive behaviour**.
- The **distress** caused by **resisting** compulsions can cause patients to **drop out** of therapy.

3) Psychotherapy

1) Psychotherapy aims to identify the **underlying cause** of the mental disorder.

2) This is done using different therapeutic techniques, e.g. **dream analysis** and **free association**.

3) When the **unconscious conflicts** that are causing the problems are made **conscious**, the therapist and patient can discuss and try to resolve them. This will hopefully lead to the disorder being cured.

Advantages

- It aims to understand the **underlying cause** of the disorder, rather than just focusing on the **symptoms**.

Disadvantages

- Psychotherapy **ignores the biological cause** of OCD.
- There's **no controlled study** that supports the **effectiveness** of psychoanalysis in the treatment of OCD.
- **Other treatments** such as the use of drugs or ERP have much **higher success** rates.

Practice Questions

Q1   What does SSRI stand for?

Q2   What is meant by 'thought stopping', used in CBT?

Q3   Give an example of an exposure task for a person using ERP to treat OCD related to germs.

Q4   Give two therapeutic techniques used in psychotherapy.

Exam Questions

Q1   Compare and contrast at least two treatments for OCD. Refer to psychological evidence in your answer.   [24 marks]

Q2   Tony has been offered a choice of a drug prescription or a course of ERP to treat his OCD.
Give him advice and information based on psychological research.   [24 marks]

Exposure and response prevention — an end to the joys of skinny dipping...

No treatment is without its problems. Some ethical problems apply to any kind of mental health treatment. For example, patients should be able to withdraw from treatment at any time. However, health care professionals sometimes encourage them to continue even when the side effects of drugs are uncomfortable or the therapies are causing increases in anxiety.

The Influence of Media on Social Behaviour

Violent television shows and video games are all over the place these days and they get blamed for all kinds of problems — mostly for corrupting young people. Psychologists are interested in what effect they actually have on viewers...

The **Media** May Influence Our **Behaviour**

1) **Social learning theory** suggests that we **model** our behaviour on behaviour that we **observe** — whether it's anti-social or pro-social behaviour.

2) There's much **debate** about whether the media influences our behaviour in this way. A central point to this debate is the effect of observing violence in TV programmes and video games — particularly on children's behaviour.

3) **Bandura's Bobo Doll experiments** (1961) showed that children who'd watched an adult behaving aggressively towards a doll were **more likely** to behave **aggressively** than those who hadn't seen the aggressive behaviour.

4) If the observed behaviour has a **positive outcome** we are **more likely** to copy it than if the outcome is negative.

5) Social learning theory also claims that if the model is **high status** or **admired** they are **more influential**.

Violent Media May be Used as a **Justification** for **Anti-social Behaviour**

1) Aggressive behaviour falls **outside the social norm** — it's considered to be **anti-social**.

2) Knowing this and still displaying aggressive behaviour can cause someone to feel **psychologically uncomfortable**.

3) **Justification theory** suggests violent media can be used to **reduce** this psychological discomfort.

4) If someone watches violent programmes or plays violent video games, they will become used to seeing aggressive behaviour — they may begin to think that it's **normal** and **acceptable**.

5) This helps them **justify** their own anti-social behaviour and feel **less guilty** about it.

6) This justification of their anti-social behaviour means that they're **more likely** to behave that way **again**.

There Have Been Many **Studies** Into the Effect of **Television** on **Behaviour**

Loads of studies have examined the **link** between **violence on TV** and **aggression**.

> **Huesmann et al** (1984) conducted **longitudinal studies** which found a relationship between **exposure to TV violence** at a young age and the number of **criminal convictions** at the age of 30. They claimed it showed the development of anti-social behaviour and aggression.

> **Paik** and **Comstock** (1991) conducted a **meta-analysis** that summarised the findings of over a thousand studies examining the link between **TV violence** and **aggressive behaviour**. The results suggested a **strong link** between exposure to violent programmes and aggressive behaviour.

The results of these studies show a **correlation** between exposure to violent TV programmes and aggressive behaviour, but they don't show **cause and effect**. This means we can't say for sure that watching violence on TV causes aggressive behaviour — it could be that **aggressive** children are **more likely** to **watch violent programmes**.

There have also been studies examining the effect that observing **pro-social behaviour** on TV has on **behaviour**.

> **Sprafkin et al** (1975) showed 3 groups of children different TV programmes. Group 1 watched a programme where a boy **saves a puppy**. Group 2 watched a similar programme but with **no helping behaviour**. Group 3 watched a programme with **no interaction** between animals and humans. The children could hear the sounds of some distressed puppies and were placed in front of two buttons. They were told that each time they pressed one button they would be given **points** — the more points they got the bigger the prize they would be given. Pressing the other button wouldn't give them any points but it would alert someone to **help** the puppies. Group 1 children were the **most likely** to spend their time **calling for help** rather than collecting points.

Many studies **don't measure** whether pro-social behaviour is a **long-term** or **short-term effect** of exposure to such programmes. **Sagotsky et al** (1981) found that 6 and 8 year olds modelled cooperative behaviour **immediately after** they witnessed it. However, **7 weeks** later, **only the older children** were still showing the behavioural effects.

The Influence of Media on Social Behaviour

Video Games and Computers May Also Affect Behaviour

1) The popularity of **video games** has stimulated new research into the influence that media has on behaviour.

2) Like other media (e.g. films), games receive **age ratings** depending on their content. Ratings are determined by things like violence, sexual themes, drug use, criminal behaviour or bad language.

3) It's thought that games may have **greater potential** to **influence behaviour** than other types of media due to their **interactive nature**.

4) Some people believe that violent video games can be held **directly responsible** for influencing some specific crimes.

Example

> The use of violent video games by the **Columbine High School shooters** has been cited by some people as a reason for the 1999 massacre that killed 13 people and injured 24 others. The families of some of the victims took **legal action** against the companies that produced them but were **unsuccessful**.

5) However, many people **don't believe** that video games can be blamed for crimes. They point out that most people who use the games don't go on to imitate the violent behaviour that they see in them.

6) **Greitemeyer and Osswald** (2010) found that playing games with a **pro-social** theme (e.g. saving a city or fighting crime) leads to an **increase** in pro-social behaviours. Other research has found that playing **action** video games can help **improve speed**, **accuracy** and even the ability to see **contrast**.

A **meta-analysis** of early research by **Anderson and Bushman** (2001) suggests that playing violent video games does **increase aggression** and **decrease pro-social behaviour** in young people.

Studies have been carried out on the effect that violent video games have on the **emotions** of people playing them.

Anderson and Bushman (2002) — Video games and emotions

Method:	This study was a **lab experiment** involving 224 participants in **two independent groups**. Participants played either a violent or non-violent video game and were then asked to 'finish off' three stories from a variety of 'story stems', e.g. one started with a minor car accident. Each participant was asked to describe what the main character would do, say and feel.
Results:	Participants who had played the violent game described the main character as being **more aggressive** than those who'd played the non-violent game, e.g. shouting at, starting a fight with or stabbing the other driver.
Conclusion:	Playing video games produces **aggressive thoughts** and **emotions** in players.
Evaluation:	**Low ecological validity** may have led the participants to give responses which didn't reflect the way they would react in real life. Participants might have shown **demand characteristics** (see page 113) due to their recent exposure to violent scenarios. This was a lab study so there was good **control of variables** and the results are therefore **reliable**.

Practice Questions

Q1 What does justification theory say about violent media?

Q2 List two positive effects that some video games could have on the player.

Q3 Describe Anderson and Bushman's (2002) study.

Exam Question

Q1 a) Describe and evaluate at least one explanation of media influences on behaviour. [8 marks]

   b) "Violent video games have a more harmful effect than any other form of media." Discuss this statement. [16 marks]

You know what else is anti-social? Staying in to revise. Grrrrr.

Nothing to stress you out here — you do need to learn all the different studies though. General waffling that the media can affect behaviour won't cut any mustard in the exam. Funny saying that, why would you want to cut mustard...

Persuasion and Attitude Change

Love, hate, approval, disapproval... attitudes we hold on many different things. If attitudes predict behaviour it'd be pretty nifty to know how to shape the attitudes of other people. Pretty manipulative as well, but that's how things go.

Persuasion is the Art of Changing Someone's Attitude

Our **attitudes** are our feelings towards something — they can be **positive** or **negative** views.
Persuasion is **changing an attitude**, usually using **messages** about the object, person or concept in question.

① *The **Hovland-Yale Model** Identifies the **Key Elements** of Persuasion*

1) **Carl Hovland** researched **effective persuasion techniques** at Yale University.

2) Hovland argued that a person's change in attitude was a **sequential process**:

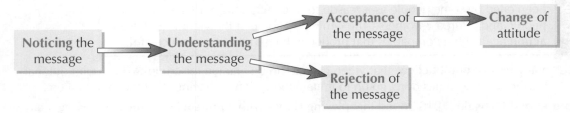

3) Hovland wanted to find out what factors affect the likelihood that a change in attitude will take place. To do this, his team took an **experimental approach** to studying persuasion, systematically **changing one variable** at a time.

4) The results of his research became known as the **Hovland-Yale model** (1953) and identified **four important components** of persuasion:

- **The source of the message** — e.g. the **trustworthiness**, **expertise** and **attractiveness** of the persuader.
- **The message content** — e.g. the **number**, **strength**, **order** and **emotional appeal** of the arguments.
- **The recipient** — e.g. the **age**, **IQ** and **personality traits** of the person being persuaded.
- **The situation** — e.g. whether given **formally** or **informally**, and whether the message is **relevant**.

5) The Hovland-Yale model suggests the key factors involved in creating a change in attitude but **doesn't address why** these factors are important.

6) The Hovland-Yale model assumes that we always carry out a **very careful thought process**. More recently, other psychologists have found evidence to suggest that we **don't** always carry out such a thorough process.

② *The **Elaboration-Likelihood Model** Identifies the **Processing Routes** of Persuasion*

1) **Petty and Cacioppo** (**1986**) agreed with Hovland that if you try and persuade someone about something, they **consider** the argument. However, they believed that people **don't always** consider all of the information available, such as the credibility of the source, as this takes up too much **cognitive effort**.

2) Petty and Cacioppo (1986) reckoned that a persuasion message can take effect through **two processing routes**:

- **The Peripheral Route** — low-level mechanisms such as **conditioning**, use of quick **decision-making rules** (e.g. 'experts are always right') and **attractiveness** of the message determine our attitudes. The peripheral route **doesn't involve much analysis** of the merits of the message itself.
- **The Central Route** — high-level mechanisms, such as **evaluation of the source** and **content** of the message, determine our attitudes. Persuasion via the central route occurs when someone has the **time**, **motivation** and **ability** to **analyse** the message. When this happens, the likelihood that they'll elaborate on the information that they have increases.

This is known as the **elaboration-likelihood model** (ELM).

3) The elaboration-likelihood model is comprehensive and can explain particular experimental findings, but it can't be used to predict them beforehand — it **lacks the predictive power** which a useful model should have.

Persuasion and Attitude Change

The *Media* are Pretty *Good* at *Persuading* Us

1) Both the **Hovland-Yale model** and the **ELM model** (see previous page) attempt to explain the process that can lead us to **change our attitude** about something. It's something that **advertisers** and the **media** are pretty keen to understand (for obvious reasons).

2) Television is used by **advertisers, political parties** and **health organisations** to persuade their audience.

3) TV is a really popular way of delivering a persuasion message because of the double whammy of **audio** and **visual information** which is delivered, and the potentially **huge audience**.

4) **Different techniques** based on models of persuasion are used to make TV persuasion as effective as possible. Here are a few to think about:

Martin knew those porridge adverts he watched were getting at something, but he just couldn't quite put his finger on it.

- **Pleasant associations** — products being sold are often teamed with things the audience will automatically feel positive about, such as **humour, success** and **sex**. Through **classical conditioning**, the product may become associated with these things — the audience may be persuaded through the **peripheral route** that they need to buy it.

- **Making the message bizarre** — many TV adverts are 'off the wall' and totally **unconnected** to the product they're advertising. This encourages **deep processing** of the persuasion message and accesses the **central route** of persuasion.

- **Using familiar figures** — **celebrities** are often used to advertise products and they're usually **matched up** to the product they're selling, e.g. models advertising beauty products. People delivering the message don't actually need to be famous — just **recognisable figures**. A man in a white coat spouting long words will give an image of scientific credibility, for example. In this way, advertisers can tap into the **peripheral or central route** of persuasion by activating **mental associations** with the personalities used, or increasing motivation to **process** the message more deeply.

- **Fear** — adverts often tap into the **emotion** of fear. For example, NHS **anti-smoking adverts** have shown children breathing out cigarette smoke to emphasise the **dangers** of passive smoking. Researchers like **Meyerowitz and Chaiken** (1987) have found that adverts like these, which arouse fear in the viewer, can act as a **peripheral cue** for persuasion. However, according to **Witte et al** (1998), if a message creates **too much fear**, there is a point at which the audience will just **switch off**.

- **Repetition** — most adverts are repeated more than once. One reason for this is that **peripheral emotional cues** (e.g. the Andrex puppy) only last as long as they are **memorable** — repetition makes them more memorable and eventually **automatic**. Repeating a message enough also leads to **familiarity** with it. Researchers have found that, more often than not, familiarity leads to **trust** and **persuasion**.

Practice Questions

Q1 List the four factors in persuasion identified by the Hovland-Yale model.

Q2 Explain the difference between the peripheral and central routes of persuasion.

Q3 Describe a technique used in TV for persuasion.

Exam Question

Q1 a) Describe and evaluate at least one model explaining how attitudes can be changed. [16 marks]

b) Discuss the effectiveness of television in persuasion. [8 marks]

The lots-of-revision model has one key element of persuasion — fear...

So there you have it — you should be able to persuade anyone of anything now. Just make sure that the source, content, recipient and situation of the model are correct, go at them via the peripheral and central routes, make them feel afraid (mwah ha ha) until they don't know what they think anymore — and do it all through their telly. You can't go wrong.

The Psychology of 'Celebrity'

"When I grow up, I wanna be famous" trill countless starry-eyed children. As an outcome of the relatively new mass media, we've only just begun to look for ways to explain 'celebrity', but there are already a few different theories...

Audiences Can Develop **Relationships** With **Celebrities**

1) The relationships that audiences develop with celebrities are very **different** from the relationships formed within **normal social networks**.

2) They are **one-sided**, with one person knowing lots and the other usually knowing nothing about the other party.

3) The term used to describe this type of relationship is **parasocial**.

4) The **study** of parasocial relationships between audiences and celebrities has become a branch of **social relationship research** in its own right.

5) As well as audiences developing relationships with celebrities, many people are **attracted** to the **concept of celebrity** and want to be one themselves.

Their relationship was distinctly one sided but that didn't discourage Molly.

The **Attraction** of Celebrity Can be Explained in an **Evolutionary Context**...

1) The **evolutionary explanation** for the attraction of celebrity is based on the idea that everyone has a basic selfish drive to ensure their **genes** have the best possible chance of being **passed on**.

2) Celebrity is seen as a way to achieve this and can be looked at from **two different perspectives**:

- **Becoming a celebrity makes a person more desirable.** In evolutionary terms, it may result in gaining **economic advantage**, which may make a person **more attractive** to others. This then increases their chances of **passing on their genes**.

- **Desirable people become celebrities.** Celebrities may be seen as individuals who are hugely popular due to their **personality traits**. So becoming famous acts as confirmation of having characteristics that others find attractive. **Hartup** (1992) researched the characteristics of people who became popular in their own social circles from an early age. The characteristics that were valued included **social dominance** and **athletic ability** in boys and **prettiness** in girls.

...or in a **Social Psychological Context**

1) Wann (1995) studied the **active role** that audiences play as **fans** — a **social psychological explanation** for the attraction of celebrity.

2) This has led to the creation of the term **fandom** — used to describe **a group of fans** of a particular celebrity. Fandom can provide individuals with:

- **Enhanced self-esteem.**
- **Escape, entertainment** and **excitement.**
- **Enhanced family** and **group affiliation.**

3) The extent to which fandom provides these **varies** between individuals and contributes to how **likely** someone is to be a fan. For example, someone whose self-esteem is greatly increased and who finds high levels of entertainment and escape in fandom is likely to find the concept of celebrity more attractive than someone whose self-esteem is only slightly enhanced.

4) Several aspects of fandom are **very social in nature**, providing a group of people with a **shared focus of interest**. Some people believe that 'being a fan' of something can play an important role in adolescence — it might help young people make the **transition** from **parental** to **peer attachments** by providing a **common source** of gossip.

The Psychology of 'Celebrity'

There are Three Stages of Fandom

Explanations of fandom suggest that celebrity worship can be a result of **normal instincts** and **motivations**. However, sometimes fandom can take on a **more intense form** and becomes something which is **pathological**. **Three stages of fandom** have been identified:

1) **Entertainment-Social** — where the relationship with the celebrity exists as a source of fun, shared with others in a social group.

2) **Intense-Personal** — obsessive thoughts begin to arise in relation to the celebrity, (e.g. "Justin Timberlake is my soul mate").

3) **Borderline-Pathological** — obsessive thoughts begin to give rise to fully-fledged fantasies (e.g. "Justin Timberlake is my boyfriend") and behaviours (e.g. sending love letters to Justin Timberlake). It is at this stage that stalking may begin, which involves a level of pursuit that is intimidating.

Stalkers Don't Always Conform to the Stereotypical Image

The word '**stalker**' immediately conjures up images of an unattractive and obsessive loner-type, whose walls are decorated with news clippings and photographs of the star who has become the object of their fixation. This image is largely created by the media and contains several **misconceptions**, which **Spitzberg** is largely credited with de-bunking:

1 Myth: Stalking mainly affects celebrities

Stalking involving a well-known person is more likely to be reported in the media than stalking involving a member of the public — so it's clear why this would be assumed. However, it's estimated that around **21% of the population** will be pursued at some point.

2 Myth: Stalkers are strangers

In fact, in most cases stalkers have been involved in an **intimate relationship** with the person they're pursuing.

3 Myth: Stalking ends in violence

News reporting usually focuses on cases where there has been some dramatic ending, and films which portray a sensational account of stalking draw the most attention. However, stalking **doesn't usually involve violence**.

Practice Questions

Q1 What is meant by a parasocial relationship?

Q2 What are the three stages of fandom?

Q3 Give two misconceptions about stalking.

Exam Question

Q1 a) Discuss research into intense fandom. [8 marks]

   b) Outline the social explanation of the attraction to celebrity. [16 marks]

Celeb worship is harmless. My fiancé Justin Timberlake totally agrees...

So in summary, it's normal to be interested in celebrities and what they do, unless you take it too far and become a stalker. But even if you do you'll still look normal, so no-one will know you're a stalker. Now just learn all the details and technical terms and you'll be all set for the exam. And whilst you do that I'll just nip out and grab my favourite glossy magazine...

Models of Addictive Behaviour

Alcohol, smoking, gambling, chocolate, shopping... examples of things people claim to be addicted to. So what is it that makes them all so darn irresistible? Guess what... no one's quite sure yet so there are several different theories.

Addiction often involves three stages — **initiation** (e.g. taking up smoking), **maintenance** (e.g. carrying on smoking even when you have to go outside in the rain) and **relapse** (e.g. having a cigarette when you'd given up). There are three models that attempt to explain addiction — biological, cognitive and learning.

Addictive Behaviour *Can be Explained by the* Biological Model *of Addiction...*

The **biological approach** includes **neurological** and **genetic explanations** for addictions.

1 The Neurological Approach

Both the highs and lows of addiction can be explained at the level of **neurons**...

1) The neurotransmitter **dopamine** is released at particular synapses in the brain and affects **motivation** and **pleasure** (amongst other things).

2) Some substances (e.g. food and addictive drugs), **increase the release** of dopamine or **prevent its reuptake** at synapses.

3) These both **increase dopamine levels** in the brain and so **dopamine receptors** on neurons are **stimulated** — this gives the person a feeling of pleasure or satisfaction.

4) Once the dopamine has been removed from the synapses (reuptake), this feeling **disappears**. In order to regain it, the person wants to take **more** of the substance.

5) If the substance is used **repeatedly**, the body becomes **used** to the **higher levels** of dopamine. The rate at which it's broken down increases and its **reuptake** also **increases**. This means that **more** of the substance is needed to produce the **same effect**. This is known as **tolerance**.

6) If the addict then **stops** taking the substance, they experience effects which are the **opposite** of the drug's effects. These are called **withdrawal symptoms** and can be removed by taking **more** of the substance.

2 The Genetic Approach

1) It's been suggested that some addictions are **inherited**.

2) A review of studies by Sayette and Hufford (1997) concluded that **identical (MZ) twins** showed a **higher rate of concordance** for **alcoholism** than **non-identical (DZ) twins**, suggesting that alcoholism is controlled to **some extent** by **genes**.

3) This can explain why, despite the fact that many people drink alcohol on a regular basis, only a **small proportion** develop an **addiction** to it.

4) However, there must be an **environmental aspect** to alcoholism as the MZ twins didn't show 100% concordance. It's also not clear whether the result is just **specific to alcoholism**, or can be generalised to addiction as a whole.

The true cost of his addiction only hit Andy when he was asked to settle his tab.

However, the biological model of addiction doesn't take **psychological** and **social influences** into account.

...by the Cognitive Model *of Addiction...*

The **cognitive approach** looks at the **thought processes** behind an addiction. These could be shaped by a person's...

1) **attitude towards the behaviour** — e.g. 'alcohol helps me to feel confident and relaxed'.

2) **perception of others' opinions** — e.g. 'I need to drink to fit in'.

3) **perception of their ability to control their own behaviour** — e.g. 'I can't cope in social situations if I don't drink'.

The cognitive model can be used in therapy sessions to **reduce addictive behaviour**. Cognitive therapists help the addict to **identify** the **thoughts** that **trigger** their addictive behaviour. They're then taught **strategies** to **change** their behaviour, e.g. avoiding certain situations, and practicing new thought patterns. Cognitive therapy usually contains a **behavioural component** which teaches the addict **new skills**, e.g. alternative relaxation techniques.

Models of Addictive Behaviour

...and by the **Learning Model** of Addiction

The **learning approach** explains addiction by looking at the role the **environment** plays in the **maintenance** and **relapse** of **addictive behaviour**.

1) **Repeatedly** using a substance, e.g. heroin, in the **same environment** will lead to **associations** forming between the substance and the **stimuli** in the environment, e.g. needles, other addicts.

2) When these stimuli are present the body **expects** to receive the substance and will **compensate in advance** for certain **effects** of the drug. For example, heroin addicts feel anxious without the drug, because their body anticipates the increased relaxation that will follow its use.

3) This is known as **classical conditioning**, and is one of the factors that leads to the **initiation** of addiction, tolerance and **withdrawal effects**.

- **Addiction** — The environmental stimuli lead to compensatory effects which are often the opposite of the drug effects. The user then wants the substance in order to remove these effects.
- **Tolerance** — Compensatory effects oppose the effect that the substance has on the body, so large quantities of the substance are needed to create the same effect.
- **Withdrawal symptoms** — If the body experiences compensatory effects but doesn't receive the substance, the person will feel the opposite of how they would if they took the substance.

There is research evidence for this model of addiction.

	Siegel et al (1982) — The effect of context on overdose likelihood
Method:	This was a **lab experiment** using **independent groups** of rats. Two groups of rats were given heroin until they developed a **tolerance** to it. After 30 days the heroin dose was **doubled**. For half of the rats, this dose was given in the **usual room**. For the other half, it was given in a **different room**.
Results:	32% of the rats that had the double dose in the usual room died, compared to 64% of the rats in the new room.
Conclusion:	**Tolerance** and **withdrawal symptoms** are a **conditioned response** to drug-related stimuli. When there's no familiar stimuli to allow anticipation of the drug, compensatory effects aren't triggered and the body is less prepared to deal with a larger quantity of the drug than usual. This increases the risk of death.
Evaluation:	This result can explain **unusual cases** of overdose where addicts have died after taking an amount of drugs which they had coped with in the past. Also, it can explain why many ex-addicts, having 'got clean', go back to taking drugs when they return home — there they are surrounded by stimuli that are **associated** with drugs. Studies like this have **real-life applications**. As a result of findings that drug-related stimuli can increase cravings, anti-drug campaigns no longer use posters which show drug paraphernalia, e.g. syringes and spoons.

Practice Questions

Q1 What is tolerance?

Q2 What are the three cognitive factors underlying addiction?

Q3 Describe the results of the study by Siegel et al (1982).

Exam Question

Q1 a) Outline and evaluate at least one biological explanation of addiction. [16 marks]

b) Discuss another explanation for the initiation, maintenance and relapse of addiction. [8 marks]

My tolerance for this topic is rapidly reducing...

There you have it — nice explanations for any sneaky little addictions you've got. I think the cognitive model explains my peanut butter on toast addiction pretty well — I can't get through the working day without it. But then again, it could be the dopamine hit that has me reaching for the toaster, or the sight of the toaster itself... which, now I think about it... mmm, toast.

Explaining Smoking and Gambling

As the pastimes of gangsters and cowboys, you can understand why so many people think that smoking and gambling must be cool. But they'd be wrong — addictions are so last century, and can cause a fair number of problems.

Many People Are **Addicted** to Smoking

The chemicals in cigarettes can cause diseases such as **cancer**, **emphysema** and **bronchitis**. Despite this, many people smoke and some continue to smoke after being diagnosed with one of these conditions — this is because smoking is **addictive**. Even though many smokers want to quit, the **success rate** of those who attempt it is **very low**.

Addiction to smoking can be explained in more than one way:

1) The **Biological Approach** Explains Smoking as an **Addiction to Nicotine**

1) There are many chemicals in cigarettes but it's the **nicotine** that causes **addiction**.

2) Nicotine stimulates the release of **dopamine**, increasing the level of dopamine in the brain and providing feelings of **pleasure** and **relaxation** (see page 96).

3) If nicotine's taken **regularly** the body **expects it** and **reduces** the amount of dopamine that's released naturally.

4) In order to maintain **normal dopamine levels** and the effect that they have on the body, nicotine needs to be taken regularly. This **reinforces smoking behaviour**, leading to more frequent smoking and **addiction**.

5) **Quitting** smoking is very difficult as the body becomes used to nicotine and **relies** on it to stimulate dopamine release. Quitting deprives the body of nicotine, leading to **low dopamine levels** until the body readjusts.

6) This causes unpleasant **withdrawal symptoms** such as anxiety, restlessness, sleep disturbance and weight gain.

2) The **Social Learning Approach** Explains Why People **Start** Smoking

1) **Social learning theory** states that new behaviour (in this case smoking), is learned through **observation**, or **modelling**. Whether the behaviour is imitated depends on the perceived **consequences**.

2) If smoking is **positively reinforced**, e.g. by **benefits** such as fitting in with peers, then it's likely to be **copied**. Seeing **role models** (e.g. parents or celebrities) smoking also encourages people to smoke.

3) Once someone has started smoking they will experience withdrawal symptoms if they stop. These encourage people to start smoking again (to remove the symptoms). This is known as **negative reinforcement**.

4) Often, smoking becomes **associated** with other activities and objects, e.g. alcohol — this is classical conditioning and it makes it difficult to not smoke in certain environments (see page 97).

	Akers and Lee (1996) — the effects of social learning over time
Method:	A five year **longitudinal study** of 454 secondary school students was conducted using **self-report questionnaire surveys**. These measured how frequently the students smoked and 'social learning variables'. These were things like whether friends smoked, how often friends smoked, and perceived attitudes of friends and parents towards smoking.
Results:	Significant **positive correlations** were found between the social learning variables and smoking.
Conclusion:	Social learning can partly account for whether smoking begins in adolescence.
Evaluation:	Methods relying on self report may be **unreliable**, and correlation doesn't prove that social learning causes smoking to begin. Also, the effect of social learning wasn't analysed to show the relative influence of different **variables**, e.g. gender or parental vs. peer influence.

There's Been **Debate** Over Whether Smoking is an **Addiction** or a **Habit**

For a long time cigarette companies claimed that people smoked for **psychological** reasons (smoking for pleasure, which becomes part of a routine), rather than **physiological** reasons (smoking to avoid the unpleasant withdrawal symptoms caused by changes in the brain). They argued that this meant smoking was a **habit** rather than an **addiction**. However, **both** the physiological and psychological aspects are important in smoking. The physiological impact of withdrawal symptoms are well documented but the effects of psychological dependence shouldn't be underestimated.

Explaining Smoking and Gambling

Gambling Doesn't Involve Any Substance Use But Can Still Be Addictive

Addiction to gambling can also be explained by many approaches:

1 The Biological Approach Explains Gambling as an Addiction to Adrenaline

1) The **stress** of awaiting the outcome of a bet triggers the release of the hormone **adrenaline**.
2) This induces an **adrenaline rush**, making the person more alert and experiencing a 'natural high'.
3) In order to regain this rush, gamblers will place **more bets** and a **physiological addiction** may develop.
4) **Repeated gambling** can cause the body to develop a **tolerance** to adrenaline. This can lead to more frequent gambling or bets involving more money in order to get the same rush.
5) **Other chemicals** triggered by stress could also be responsible for gambling addictions. There's some evidence that gambling releases **endorphins**, chemicals that block pain and negative effects of stress.

2 The Psychodynamic Approach Suggests Gambling is Driven By Masochism

1) **Bergler (1958)** proposed that gamblers gamble to **lose**, in order to **punish** themselves.
2) This **reduces the guilt** they feel from rebelling against their parents during childhood. He suggests that gamblers **identify** with the casino dealer or roulette wheel, etc. as **parental figures**.
3) Bergler presented **case studies** where treatment relevant to his theory was successful in curing some gamblers of their addiction but **scientific evidence** is still lacking at the moment.

3 The Cognitive Approach Suggests Gambling is Driven By Faulty Reasoning Mechanisms

1) **Decision making** can be based on **rational consideration** or **quick (sometimes faulty) rules**.
2) **Wagenaar (1988)** identified 16 rules that gamblers commonly use when making decisions. These include:

- **The illusion of control** — gamblers think of gambling as **skill-based**. This creates superficially high expectations when in reality the outcomes are often determined by chance alone.
- **Representative bias** — gamblers believe that **random events** should **look random**, e.g. 'tails' seems increasingly likely the longer a run of consecutive 'heads' lasts. Many gamblers believe that the longer a losing streak lasts the more likely a win will follow. This is known as the **gambler's fallacy**.
- **Illusory correlations** — gamblers have **superstitions** which they believe help them succeed, e.g. blowing the dice for a 6.
- **Fixation on the absolute frequency of successes** — gamblers can **recall many past wins**, just because they gamble so much. This creates a false image of how often they win.

Practice Questions

Q1 Describe the study by Akers and Lee (1996).

Q2 Define 'physiological' and 'psychological' dependence to smoking.

Q3 List the faulty reasoning mechanisms that can lead to gambling addiction.

Exam Question

Q1 a) Outline a biological explanation for addiction to smoking. [8 marks]

b) Outline an alternative approach to explaining this addiction. [8 marks]

c) Discuss the difference between smoking as a habit and as an addiction. [8 marks]

Exams = stress = adrenaline = addiction to exams. Something's not right...

There are a lot of people out there who think that smoking and gambling are evil addictions that ruin lives — and I'm one of them. If they didn't exist you wouldn't have to learn about them, the examiners couldn't ask you about them and we'd all be much happier. Unfortunately that's not the case, so you'd best get down to business and learn these pages. Enjoy.

Vulnerability to Addiction

Not everybody becomes an addict. Behaviours such as drinking and gambling remain controllable pastimes for many people, so there must be individual differences at work. And, surprise surprise, you need to know what they are.

Stress *Could be a Factor in the* Development of Addiction

1) **Sinha** (2007) used **brain imaging** to investigate the relationship between **stress** and **drug addiction**. She found that the **same part of the brain** was activated during stress as during drug craving.

2) Sinha suggests that stress makes people more **vulnerable** to reacting to **cues** associated with drugs. This could make them **more likely** to develop an addiction.

3) This research shows an **association** between stress and addiction — but it **doesn't explain** it. Drug use might cause altered brain function, or altered brain function might encourage drug use — or there may be **another cause**, and drug use and altered brain function are both results of this.

I'm stressed just looking at them — pass the chocolate.

4) **Operant conditioning** (learning through reinforcement — see page 48) could explain why stress might make people more vulnerable to addiction if the pleasurable effects of the substance **reduce the symptoms** of stress. For example, alcohol is a **depressant** so it can make a stressed person feel **more relaxed**. This acts as a **positive reinforcement** and so they're more likely to **repeat** the drinking behaviour.

Age *and* Peers *are Factors that Seem to be* Linked *in* Addiction

1) **Zucker** (2008) found that the **age of onset** of drinking was important. The **earlier** people start drinking the more likely they are to have drinking problems.

2) **Martino et al** (2006) carried out a **longitudinal study** to look at the social factors that affect the **drinking habits** of adolescents. They concluded that the norms for drinking behaviour are learned through **social observations** and **interactions**. The **perceived approval** or **use** of alcohol by **parents**, other important adults and **peers** **increased the likelihood** of future decisions to drink and get drunk.

3) Research has shown that although being **socially withdrawn** can be negative for other reasons, such as loneliness, it actually **protects** young people from the **influence** of their **peers** in relation to addiction:

   • **Fergusson and Horwood** (1999) found that children who were **socially isolated** from their peer group at the age of **10** because of **social anxiety** were **less likely** to use drugs or drink alcohol when they were **15**.

   • **Shedler and Block** (1990) found that **18-year-olds** who hadn't tried drugs were more likely to be **socially isolated**, **over-controlled** by others and **anxious**.

Younger People *are* More Affected *by* Peer Pressure

Sumter et al (2009) found that a person's **age** affects their ability to **resist peer pressure**.

	Sumter et al (2009) — age differences in resisting peer pressure
Method:	**464 children and adolescents** were given a questionnaire that assessed their ability to resist **pressure** from their **peer group**. The questionnaire was written in a **style** suitable for all ages and used hypothetical **everyday situations**.
Results:	The participants' answers showed that they were **more vulnerable** to being influenced by their friends when they were **younger**. The participants became **more resistant** as they got **older**.
Conclusion:	As adolescents become **more mature** they are **less influenced** by others. This could explain why early experiences with substances have **long-term effects**.
Evaluation:	This was a **cross-sectional study** so individual differences could have affected the results. Carrying out longitudinal research avoids this design flaw, but it takes longer to collect the data. Peer pressure can be both **positive** or **negative** when it comes to abusing substances. You're less likely to do it if your friends aren't — but more likely if they are.

Vulnerability to Addiction

Personality Can Affect Addictive Behaviour

1) **Eysenck and Eysenck (1976)** outlined three main personality dimensions:

- **P** for **psychoticism**, which includes being egocentric, aggressive and impulsive.
- **E** for **extroversion**, which includes being outgoing, happy and sociable.
- **N** for **neuroticism**, which includes being anxious, moody and irritable.

Eysenck suggested that some personality characteristics make a person **more prone** to addiction.

2) **Francis (1996)** found that people with nicotine, heroin and alcohol addictions scored **more highly** on N and P scales on psychometric tests compared to the E scales.

3) The exact relationship between addiction and personality is **unclear**. Being irritable and impulsive could mean you are **more likely to use** substances such as alcohol or drugs. Or it could be that these personality characteristics make you **less able to control** your use of the substances.

4) Alternatively it could be that **having an addiction** leads a person to be moody and impulsive, and makes them less likely to be happy and outgoing.

Some Personality Disorders are Associated with Substance Abuse

1) **Rounsaville et al (1998)** found that people diagnosed with **antisocial personality disorder** were more likely to be alcoholics compared to those without the disorder.

2) Other research suggests a link between **attention deficit disorder** and alcohol abuse.

3) Substance abuse is a problem for some people with **mental health problems** as they may use alcohol and drugs to **self-medicate**. This makes it difficult to work out where the **causal relationship** lies. A person with mental health problems might drink or use drugs to help them **cope**, or using these substances might make them more **vulnerable** to mental health problems. It's **difficult to test** this as ethics is a major issue in this area.

Practice Questions

Q1 What technique did Sinha use when investigating the relationship between stress and addiction?
Q2 What was concluded from Martino et al's (2006) study?
Q3 Identify the relationship that has been established between age and resistance to peer influence.
Q4 Give the personality characteristics that P, E and N stand for.
Q5 Give two personality disorders that are more common in people with alcohol addiction.

Exam Questions

Q1 Describe and discuss research into risk factors associated with the development of addiction. [24 marks]

Q2 "Some people are more likely to develop alcohol addiction than others."
Evaluate the accuracy of this statement and refer to psychological evidence in your answer. [24 marks]

We can blame our parents? That's a relief. I knew it wasn't my fault...

It looks like the great mystery of why some people never know when to grab some cheesy chips and call it a night remains unsolved for the moment. It's likely that a combination of factors including stress, peer influence, age and personality explain why some people are more at risk of developing addictions than others — but I'm just going to blame my parents.

Reducing Addictive Behaviour

The old adage is true, prevention certainly is better than cure. That's why health psychologists are trying to figure out how to stop addictive behaviour before it starts. And how to stop it once it has started, just in case.

The **Theory of Reasoned Action** Explains How We **Decide How We'll Behave**

1) **Fishbein** and **Ajzen** (1975) developed the **theory of reasoned action** (**TRA**) model of behaviour.

2) It states that an individual's behaviour, e.g. whether they will give up alcohol, can be **predicted** by their **intention** to perform it. Intention is determined by two factors:

- The person's **attitude to the behaviour** — this is shaped by their **beliefs** about the **outcome** of the behaviour, e.g. 'I'll save money', and their **judgement** of whether the outcome is **positive or negative**, **likely or unlikely**.
- **Subjective norms** — this describes their **expectations** of the **social consequences** of the behaviour, e.g. 'My friends will think I'm boring', and their **motivation** to **follow these norms**, e.g. 'I want to be popular'.

3) Sheppard et al (1988) carried out a meta-analysis and found that the TRA had a **strong predictive use** — it was pretty good at predicting intentions and behaviour. It's also a useful model for knowing how to **alter** an individual's intentions and behaviour. However, it's been criticised for **neglecting factors** such as **habits** and **emotional aspects**, which are also important when intentions are being formed.

The **Theory of Planned Behaviour** is a **Modification** of the **TRA**

1) **Ajzen** (1991) added a third factor to the TRA — a person's **perceived behavioural control**, e.g. 'I don't have the will power to give up alcohol'. This factor **increases** the model's **predictive power**.

2) This theory is known as the **theory of planned behaviour** (**TPB**). It suggests behaviour is influenced in two ways:

- **Indirectly** — if a person believes that the behaviour is **too difficult** they don't form the initial intention to carry out the behaviour.
- **Directly** — if the **perception** of their own level of control is **accurate**, e.g. they don't have sufficient willpower, they won't succeed.

3) In contrast to the TRA, the TPB takes into account the fact that people **don't always have complete control** over their behaviour, as there may be obstacles that stand in their way.

4) Norman et al's (1998) study found that **perceived behavioural control** was a strong predictor of binge-drinking. The TPB could therefore be used to develop **intervention strategies** and **prevention programmes**.

5) Both models ignore the fact that there may be **discrepancies** between **attitude** and **behaviour** and that a person's behaviour is not always a reflection of their **intentions**. People's actions aren't always rational and based on deliberate decision making processes. This is especially true for **addictive behaviour**, which is often **irrational**.

The **Health Belief Model** Can be Used To **Predict Behaviour**

1) The factors that the **health belief model** uses as predictors of behaviour include someone's:

- **Perception of susceptibility and severity** — their belief of how **likely** and **serious** the threat to their own health is if they don't carry out the preventative health behaviour, e.g. the danger of developing lung cancer as a result of smoking.
- **Perception of cost-benefit** — they weigh the **benefits** of the behaviour (e.g. reduces cancer risk) against its **costs** (e.g. suffering withdrawal symptoms).

2) The health belief model takes into account factors that **encourage** people to break their addictive behaviour. These factors are known as **cues to action** and include experiencing **symptoms** of health problems or exposure to **media campaigns**.

3) The model also considers the influence that **personal variables**, e.g. age, sex, social class and personality traits have on a person's perceptions.

4) The comprehensive nature of the model means that it's an ideal tool for designing **individual intervention strategies** and highlights the importance of **tailoring interventions** to an individual's personal profile.

Reducing Addictive Behaviour

A Range of *Interventions* Are Used to *Reduce Addictive Behaviours*

Biological Interventions

1) The biological approach to reducing drug and alcohol addictions involves a **gradual detox**, where the **quantity** of the substance used is **reduced over time**.

2) **Medication** may be prescribed to stop addictive behaviour, e.g. Antabuse® is prescribed to alcoholics. It causes nausea if it's combined with alcohol, discouraging alcoholics from drinking. The addict will form an **association** between drinking and nausea — this will continue even when they stop taking Antabuse®. This is known as **aversion therapy**.

> **Meyer and Chesser** (1970) carried out a **repeated measures experiment**. A group of alcoholics who were prescribed Antabuse® were compared to a **control group**. Around **50%** of those taking Antabuse® stayed **teetotal** for at least a year — significantly more than in the control group. From this study they concluded that an **unpleasant response** can be **conditioned** to an **addictive behaviour**.

3) However, any medication prescribed has to be **carefully controlled** so it doesn't become an addiction itself.

Psychological Interventions

1) The psychological approach consists of a range of therapies that aim to change the way an addict **behaves** by changing their thought processes.

2) **Cognitive behavioural therapy** identifies the thoughts that cause the behaviour, e.g. 'I can't cope without cigarettes', and then changes this thought process. This is known as **cognitive restructuring**.

3) Cognitive behavioural therapy has had some **success**, e.g. it has enhanced the effectiveness of nicotine replacement treatment for quitting smoking.

Public Health Interventions

1) Public health interventions address addictive behaviours on a **wide scale** to **reduce** their **impact on society**.

2) For example, to reduce smoking the government **banned adverts** for cigarettes. They also ran **anti-smoking campaigns**, placed **warning messages** on cigarette packs and **increased prices**. More recently, they've made it **illegal** to smoke in **enclosed public places**.

3) Some public health interventions **aren't** as **straightforward** as they sound. It was once proposed in America that the amount of **nicotine** in cigarettes could be **reduced gradually** until smokers were no longer addicted. However, in reality smokers might just end up **smoking more** to get the same effect. The measure would also meet with **opposition** from smokers.

4) It's **difficult** to prove the **efficacy** of public health interventions. One study found **5.1%** of smokers gave up smoking after asking their **GP** for advice — but there's no way of telling if they'd have done that without help.

Practice Questions

Q1 According to the theory of reasoned action, what factors determine attitudes to addictive behaviour?
Q2 Describe the main findings of the study by Meyer and Chesser (1970).
Q3 How has the government tried to reduce smoking?

Exam Question

Q1 a) Outline the theory of planned behaviour. [4 marks]

b) Discuss some different interventions used to reduce addictive behaviours. [20 marks]

I need an intervention to sort out my TRA — tremendous revision anger...

Phew, that's a whopping amount of information on reducing addictive behaviour. You need to learn all the models of prevention and all the types of intervention that are so carefully described for you on these two pages. Lovely jubbly.

Studying Anomalous Experience

It may make entertaining TV, but lots of people just aren't convinced that paranormal abilities like telepathy and out-of-body experiences really exist. And there's a very good reason for their doubt — a serious lack of evidence.

Anomalous Experiences Can't Currently be Explained by Science

1) Something that **can't be explained by science** is called an **anomalous experience**. There are many different types:

   - **Out-of-body experience** — a sensation of **floating** around **outside** of your own body.
   - **Near-death experience** — sensations experienced when you're **close to death**, often interpreted as a glimpse into the 'afterlife'.
   - **Spontaneous psychic ability (psi)** — **extra-sensory perception**, e.g. telepathy, clairvoyance or psychokinesis (altering an object, e.g. moving, bending or softening it using the mind).
   - **Past-life experience** — remembering events from a **previous existence**.
   - **Anomalous healing** — healing through **unexplainable methods**, e.g. by a spiritual healer or through prayer.

2) Anomalous experiences **can't just be immediately rejected** — many things that were once considered mysterious, e.g. thunder and lightning, can now be explained scientifically.

3) So it's important that all anomalous experiences are **investigated thoroughly** — they may one day be explainable, either by what we **already know** about human behaviour, or accepted as something **completely new**.

Pseudoscience and Fraud Can be Mistaken For Anomalous Experiences

Pseudoscience

Explanations based on evidence that's been collected through **faulty scientific processes** are known as **pseudoscience**. The results of many demonstrations of so-called anomalous experiences turn out to be caused by methodological issues such as **cognitive bias** and **experimenter effects**.

Cognitive biases

Spontaneous events, such as having a dream come true, are the main reasons why people believe in anomalous experiences. People who believe in such things have been shown to be **more susceptible** to the **illusion of control** than people who don't. The illusion of control is a **cognitive bias** (a faulty judgement) which causes people to believe that they're able to **control** or **influence** the outcome of an event over which, in reality, they have no control.

Experimenter effects

The **outcome** of any psychological experiment can be affected by the **expectations of the experimenter** and how this manifests itself in their **behaviour**. Certain researchers consistently find significant results using the same methods whilst others consistently fail. This is known as **experimenter effects**. As a result of this, it's been suggested that only people who **don't believe** in that particular anomalous experience should be allowed to replicate the experiments. Experimenter effects exist in **both directions** though, and the expectations of sceptics could affect the experiment **just as strongly** in the **other direction**.

Fraud

Research has also been blighted by cases of **fraud**, where scientists have **deliberately deceived people**, invalidating observations and results. Researchers who believe in the anomalous experience are **more likely** to **miss the tricks** of fraudsters as they are biased towards results that are **consistent with their existing beliefs**.

People claiming to have **psychic abilities** usually demonstrate them **most successfully** when they have some **control** over how they show them and the way they are observed. In order to reduce the chances of pseudoscience and fraud being passed off as anomalous experiences, **Wiseman and Morris** (1995) developed a set of **methodological guidelines** for research into this area. They include advice on issues such as **randomisation of stimuli** and **preventing 'sensory leakage'** (soundproofing rooms, etc.).

Studying Anomalous Experience

Studies into Psi Often Provoke Controversy

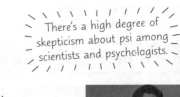

There's a high degree of skepticism about psi among scientists and psychologists.

1 Ganzfeld Studies Have Shown Mixed Results for ESP

1) **Ganzfeld studies** test participants for **extra-sensory perception (ESP)**.

2) One participant, known as the **receiver**, is in a state of mild sensory deprivation. This is usually done by covering their eyes with halved ping pong balls, playing white noise through headphones and sitting them in a soundproof room lit with red light.

3) A participant in another room, the **sender**, then concentrates on a visual stimulus in an attempt to transfer it to the receiver.

4) The receiver is then shown **four stimuli** — one is the stimulus the sender attempted to transfer by ESP. If the receiver correctly identifies this stimulus it's called a **hit**.

5) The results and interpretation of Ganzfeld experiments vary:

Suddenly the idea of sensory deprivation seemed a lot more appealing...

A review of 28 Ganzfeld studies by **Honorton** (1985) showed a **38% hit rate**, significantly above the 25% rate of chance. He claimed that this provided **evidence for ESP**. Hyman (1985) disagreed, **criticising** the studies for a **lack of randomised stimuli, inconsistent judging procedures** and **selective reporting**. After consideration, Honorton and Hyman jointly agreed on suitable conditions to address these flaws and **autoganzfeld studies** were designed to take these into account. The results of autoganzfeld studies **still produced significant results**.

A **meta-analysis** by **Milton and Wiseman** (1999) of 30 autoganzfeld studies showed **no significant evidence for ESP**. This analysis was criticised for including studies which **deviated** from the conventional technique. When the ten studies closest to the original technique were analysed by **Bem et al (2001)**, a **significant hit rate was found**.

2 Little Evidence Has Been Found for Psychokinetic Ability

1) Some people claim to have **psychokinetic ability**, which allows them to move objects using their mind alone.

2) Many people dispute these claims — they believe that **tricks** are used to make it appear that objects have been altered by psychokinesis. Several **magicians** have demonstrated how this can be done.

3) Belief in psychokinesis is often explained by cognitive biases such as the **illusion of control** (see opposite page).

4) To establish whether psychokinesis is possible researchers have searched for evidence in **laboratory conditions**:

One common method is to ask participants to **alter the outcome** of a computerised **random number generator**. This allows a lot of data to be collected in **controlled conditions**. Holger et al (2006) conducted a **meta-analysis** on the results of 380 such studies. They did find an effect but it was extremely small — it was probably only reported because of its **interesting** and **controversial nature**.

Practice Questions

Q1 What is pseudoscience?
Q2 Name two methodological issues which could explain so-called anomalous experiences.
Q3 Summarise the method used in Ganzfeld studies.

Exam Question

Q1 a) Explain the term anomalous experience, using examples. [8 marks]

b) Describe how pseudoscience can influence research into anomalous experiences. [8 marks]

c) Outline and evaluate the evidence for the existence of ESP. [8 marks]

I don't condone cheating — but telepathy would be a mighty useful skill...

This is all getting a bit odd now — what with past life and out-of-body experiences. If you're not too spooked out you need to learn about pseudoscience, fraud and the controversy around Ganzfeld studies. If you are too spooked out you need to learn about pseudoscience, fraud and the controversy around Ganzfeld studies as well. There's no getting away from it.

Explanations for Anomalous Experience

When it comes to the paranormal most people fall into one of two groups — skeptics and believers. Skeptics explain weird and untoward stuff as anything from a hoax to a misunderstanding, whereas believers, well, they believe...

Coincidence *Could Explain* Anomalous Experience

1) A **coincidence** is when events **appear to be linked** (e.g. dreaming about a car crash and then being involved in one) when in fact the two events are unconnected and occurred closely together purely by **chance**.

2) **Marks (2000)** suggests that coincidence can be explained by **subjective validation**.

> Subjective validation is a **cognitive bias** (an error of judgement caused by faulty thought processes) that means we are more likely to believe in and pay attention to information that has **personal relevance**. As we concentrate on this personally relevant information (e.g. a dream we had), we don't pay attention to information that **feels less relevant** to us but is actually more relevant (e.g. the fact that a car pulled out in front of us). So we only see evidence that **reinforces** our belief in a **psychic reason** for the coincidence.

Probability Judgements *Could Explain* Anomalous Experience

1) Making a **probability judgement** involves assessing **how likely** it is that something will happen. This is usually **subjective**, so the judgment may differ widely from the actual true statistical probability.

2) According to **Wiseman and Watt (2006)**, **probability misjudgements** mean that we may believe in a psychic reason for something happening rather than the real reason.

3) An example of this would be believing that destiny is at play just because you find out that you have the same birthday as the person you fancy. However, the **statistical likelihood** of them being born on that particular date is the same regardless of whether or not it has personal relevance to you.

Magical Thinking and Superstition *Involve* Cognitive Bias

1) A **superstition** is a belief that an object or action will affect outcomes when there is **no logical reason** for it to do so. For example, believing that wearing your lucky green underpants will mean you pass your driving test — even though passing this test is down to your driving skill and what you wear is irrelevant.

2) Superstitions are the result of **cognitive biases** such as the **illusion of control** (see page 104).

> - **Lorenz (1963)** suggests that superstition is a **response** we have adapted as a way to cope in some situations where we don't know or don't understand the **true causality**. It is better for us psychologically to believe in a false relationship rather than not to know what the relationship is at all.
>
> - **Vyse (2000)** suggests that in some situations (e.g. job interviews, weddings or sports events), even if people have prepared as much as they could have, there are still some aspects which are **out of their control**. This means it's difficult to predict the outcome. Using superstition allows people to **feel more in control** than they actually are.

Karl's flock of ducks worked like a lucky charm — he had yet to be hit whilst crossing the road.

3) Superstitions can be **negative** (e.g. believing that breaking a mirror brings bad luck) or **positive** (e.g. believing that lucky charms bring good luck).

4) Positive superstitions may promote **optimism** and **self-efficacy** (belief in your ability to do something). This increased belief may increase the chances of the person influencing the situation themselves. This is known as the **placebo effect**, and it **reinforces** the initial superstition.

5) However, positive superstitions can still have a **negative effect** if the person is very **dependent** on them. E.g. putting your red underpants on by mistake on the day of a test might cause **anxiety** that impairs performance.

6) **Magical thinking** is believing that if you **think** about something happening, or **say** that it will happen, it's **more likely** to actually happen. For example, you might think that wishing that you will win the lottery will make it more likely that you will win. This shows an **incorrect understanding of causality**. **Cognitive bias** means you **ignore** the actual cause (which is **pure chance**) and believe that your wish manipulates the outcome.

Explanations for Anomalous Experience

Some **Personality Factors** are Related to **Anomalous Experience**

1) **Ramakrishna (2001)** used students as participants in his research and tested them for their **extra-sensory perception (ESP)** ability.

2) He reported a **positive correlation** between scores in ESP tests and some personality traits, including being **relaxed**, **assertive**, **sociable** and **talkative**. He found a **negative correlation** between ESP scores and other personality traits, including being **withdrawn**, **suspicious** and **impatient**.

3) Ramakrishna's study is supported by **other research** that has found a similar relationship between personality and anomalous experience. However, we can't assume that certain personality factors make anomalous experience more likely (or vice versa. This research only suggests a relationship and **doesn't show causality** — other variables besides personality could also be involved.

Bob might not have scored highly on the ESP test but he still had a hunch that it was time to move house.

Extroversion Might Be Linked to ESP

Evidence for...

- **Honorton et al (1998)** did a meta-analysis of **38 studies** testing **ESP** and **extroversion**.
- The experiments included **Ganzfeld studies** that **limit** the choice of possible answers, and tests that allowed **free choice** in the answers. They found that overall extroverts scored more highly than introverts on ESP tests in **77%** of the studies.
- Other research also supports the possibility of a **causal relationship** between anomalous experiences and extroversion.

Evidence against...

- When ESP is tested in an **experimental setting** the situation is very **artificial**. Introverts may feel less comfortable and less able to focus on the task. Extroverts are **less likely** to feel uncomfortable and so their performance isn't affected. If this is true then the **anxiety** of taking part in an unfamiliar task could be an **extraneous variable** that affects **introverts** more than extroverts.
- **Haight (1979)** conducted **spontaneous ESP tests** in a social situation so that all participants would feel **relaxed** whatever their personality type. Introverts and extroverts **didn't score differently** on these tests

Practice Questions

Q1 What is a coincidence? Give an example.

Q2 What is a superstition? Give an example.

Q3 Describe the cognitive bias involved in magical thinking.

Q4 Outline the correlations found by Ramakrishna (2001) between performance in ESP tests and personality traits.

Q5 How many studies did Honorton et al (1998) use in their meta-analysis?

Exam Question

Q1 a) Outline the role of coincidence and probability judgements in anomalous experience. [8 marks]

b) Discuss explanations for superstitious behaviour. [8 marks]

c) Discuss the findings of research investigating personality and anomalous experience. [8 marks]

Magical thinking — an effective revision spell...

If you're a skeptic you're probably scoffing at all this anomalous experience malarkey by now. But chances are you've indulged in some superstitious behaviour in your time — touching wood, not walking under ladders, crossing your fingers — they all fall under paranormal belief. We've all dabbled in it, whether truly skeptical or out there giving the evil eye.

Research into Exceptional Experience

Whether you believe in anomalous experiences or not, the paranormal can't be dismissed as hokum unless it's been researched properly. The big problem with this is that paranormal experiences are really quite hard to study...

There's Been **Research** Into **Psychic Healing...**

Psychic healers claim they can treat illness and injury **without any physical intervention**. Instead, the healer moves their hands over the patient's body without making contact. The aim is to transfer a force and restore **balance** in the patient. Some studies have been done to try to determine whether psychic healing actually works.

Attevelt (1988) — Evidence for the psychic healing of asthma

Method:	In an **independent groups design**, 96 asthma patients were allocated to one of 3 groups — an **optimal group**, a **distance group** and a **control group**. Patients in the optimal group received treatment from a psychic healer in the usual way. The distance group patients were also treated by a healer, but this time from behind a screen. The control group didn't receive any treatment but the screen was present. Distance group and control group patients didn't know which group they belonged to as their physical experiences were the same. **Physical** and **subjective** measures of asthma symptoms were taken.
Results:	The **physical symptoms** of asthma (measured by peak flow) improved significantly in **all patients**. The **optimal group** improved significantly more than the other groups on **subjective measures** of well-being (i.e. they 'felt' an improvement).
Conclusion:	The lack of difference between **physical symptoms** of patients in the different groups shows that improvement was **not down to paranormal effects**. The **subjective improvement** in the optimal group patients but not distance group patients shows the influence of **psychological** rather than paranormal factors.
Evaluation:	Participants were **randomly allocated** to groups after being stratified (see page 112) according to the severity of their asthma. This prevented **bias** in the groups. The people who took the patients' peak flow measurements didn't know which group each patient belonged to. This also prevented **bias**. The use of a **control group** distinguished the psychological effects of visiting a healer from the physiological effects.

...Out-of-Body Experiences...

An **out-of-body experience** (**OBE**) is a sensation of floating **outside the body**, seeing the world from a different perspective. They're **spontaneous** and **rare** events so researching them is difficult. Most evidence is based on **case studies**.

Many people remain skeptical about OBEs and much of the research into them has been heavily criticised.

Tart (1968) — The Case of Miss Z

Method:	This **case study** was based on a young woman (Miss Z) who reported experiencing OBEs in her sleep since childhood. Tart brought her into a sleep lab for 4 nights to **compare** her reports of OBEs with **physiological data** collected from an EEG that monitored her brain activity. Also, numbers were written down and placed where they couldn't be seen from the bed (e.g. lying on top of high shelves). Miss Z was asked to find these target numbers during her OBE, whilst she was physically still in bed.
Results:	Miss Z's OBEs **correlated** with a particular pattern of non-dreaming, non-awake brain waves. On one occasion, she also correctly identified a 5 digit target number.
Conclusion:	OBEs have a **physiological** basis.
Evaluation:	The study had to rely on Miss Z's own reports of when and for how long she had left her body. These reports were **retrospective** and **subjective**. Tart couldn't be sure that Miss Z hadn't found out the target number conventionally, e.g. from seeing its reflection in the nearby clock face. This study isn't accepted as reliable psychological research by the wider scientific community.

Some recent studies have **induced** states similar to OBEs through brain stimulation of participants. This suggests that OBEs could be explained by **physiological mechanisms** causing a kind of 'waking dream'.

Research into Exceptional Experience

...Near-Death-Experiences...

Like OBEs, NDEs are hard to prove and many psychologists question whether they actually occur or not.

There are obviously **ethical issues** involved in creating states of near death for the purposes of studying **near-death-experiences (NDEs)**. So, like OBEs, most research has to be taken from **case studies**. From an accumulation of 102 case studies, Kenneth Ring (1980) determined that:

1) Individuals reporting NDEs **don't fit** a particular **gender**, **age**, or **religious profile**.

2) There also appears to be **no link** between the reporting of a NDE and a person's **attitude** towards the paranormal.

3) Individuals who came close to death or were clinically dead for a period of time report experiences such as moving through a tunnel towards a **light**, **OBEs**, **reuniting** with **dead loved ones** and feeling total **contentment**. These experiences were found even when the moments leading up to near-death were particularly nasty.

4) **Medication** at the time of death **did not predict** the experience of NDE.

5) Reports of NDEs are more **coherent** than reports of hallucinations.

6) Individuals who report experiencing a NDE also report **life-changing shifts of attitudes**, often developing a newly found appreciation of life and loved ones.

...And Psychic Mediumship

Psychic mediumship is the ability to **communicate with spirits** and transmit messages from the dead to the living. There are a range of methods with which mediums claim they can communicate with the dead, including **telepathy** and being **possessed by spirits** that then talk through them. Studies of psychic mediumship are usually based on **séances** — intentional attempts to communicate with spirits. One of the most famous studies into psychic mediumship is the **Scole Experiment**.

> The **Scole Experiment** took place in Norfolk between **1993** and **1998**. Researchers including Fontana, Ellison and Keen witnessed 37 séances in rooms that were thoroughly **searched** beforehand to try to **prevent any trickery**. A professional magician was also present to identify any attempts at **fraud**. During the séances a number of paranormal occurrences were reported. These included the **materialisation** of objects, **levitation**, patterns of **light**, **voices** and the appearance of **whole people** or **body parts**.

Some people believe that the Scole Experiment provides **evidence** of life after death and mediumship. No fraud was identified at any time during the experiment and the professional magician present confirmed that **no currently known trickery** could have produced the effects that were observed. However, the experiment has been **heavily criticised** and isn't widely accepted as evidence for mediumship. The **experimental conditions** were unreliable — to some extent they were controlled by the mediums. For example, the researchers wanted to use infra-red imaging (as most of the séances took place in darkness) but this was rejected by the mediums as they claimed it would distract them. Also, all the experimenters believed in the paranormal so may have shown **experimenter effects** (see p.112).

Practice Questions

Q1 Describe the findings of the study by Attevelt (1988).

Q2 Describe the case study of Miss Z.

Q3 Outline some typical features of a near-death-experience.

Exam Question

Q1 a) Outline the difficulties of studying paranormal experiences scientifically. [8 marks]

b) Discuss the effectiveness of psychic healing. [16 marks]

Revision — definitely a near death experience...

And that's the end of the section — yay. Once you've learnt these two pages that is. Then you'd best go back through the whole section to check you still remember all the fascinating stuff you've learnt on the way. Yep, back through the spooky bits, the addictions and the celeb worship, all the way to attitudes and persuasion. What a strange journey you've been on.

Is Psychology a Science?

Whether psychology is a science or not is a real slippery rogue of a topic. Before you can decide, you need to know what science is — and no-one seems to have quite agreed on that either. It's like they're trying to make life difficult...

Science is about Establishing Truths

1) Scientific research should be **objective** — independent of **beliefs** or **opinions**.

2) So, the methods used should be **empirical** — based on **experimental data**, not just theory. The best way to make sure of this is to carry out an experiment that collects **quantitative data** and has strictly **controlled variables**.

3) This means that you should be able to establish **cause** and **effect**.

However, it's **hard** to make an experiment completely **objective**. **Rosenthal and Fode (1963)** showed this in an experiment on psychology undergraduates. They were told to train some **rats** to run a maze, and that some of the rats were **genetically pre-disposed** to be **better** at **learning** than others. Actually there was **no difference** between any of the rats, but the students' **results** showed that the supposedly more **intelligent** rats did **better** in the maze task. This shows how researchers can bring their own **biases** and **expectations** to an experiment.

Scientific Theories Should Have Validity and Reliability

1) All scientific work must undergo **peer review** before it's published — it's sent to **experts** in the field (**peers**) so they can assess its **quality**.

2) Poor research **won't pass** peer review so it won't get published. This helps to **validate conclusions** — it means published theories, data and conclusions are more trustworthy.

3) Other scientists then read the published research, and try to **repeat** it. This tests whether the theory is **reliable**. If it is, then the results should be **replicated** every time the experiment is done — this shows that the findings **aren't affected** by **time** or **place**.

4) If the replica experiments provide evidence to back it up, the theory is thought of as scientific 'fact' (**for now**).

5) If **new evidence** comes to light that **conflicts** with the current evidence the theory is questioned again. More rounds of **testing** will be carried out to see which evidence, and so which theory, **prevails**.

There are Problems With Doing Research on Humans

Psychological research is very **different** to the research in **other sciences** — humans are **complex**, so it's **hard** to find **general laws** for their behaviour.

1) **Sampling** — scientists can't study every occurrence of something, so they need to use **samples** that **represent** what they're looking at. This is fine if it's something like carbon or gravity. The problem in psychology is that humans **vary** a lot, and in different ways — e.g. age, gender, culture or class could all be explanations for a person's behaviour. This makes it really **difficult** to **generalise** to the whole population from small samples.

2) **Operationalisation** — operationalising variables means **defining** them in **measurable** terms. However, **human behaviour** is often hard to define, so it's questionable whether things like **motivation** or **love** can be operationalised accurately. This means that human behaviour is a very **difficult variable** to **control**.

3) **Procedures** — experiments focus on just a few specific variables, so they're **simplistic** compared to real life. The lack of **ecological validity** means you might never see genuine behaviour in a controlled experiment.

4) **Participant variables** — people bring their past **learning** and **experiences** to experiments. They may try to figure out what the sexperiment's about and **change** their behaviour — **demand characteristics**. People's behaviour also changes if they know they're being watched — the **Hawthorne Effect**. **Social desirability bias** is when people change their behaviour to make themselves look better, e.g. more generous.

5) **Experimenter effects** — the experimenter can **influence** participants without meaning to, by giving out subtle **clues** about how they should behave. This means you can never know for sure if behaviour is genuine.

Is Psychology a Science?

Some Psychological Approaches are More Scientific than Others

Very scientific ↑

Biological

Empirical methods are used which get quantitative data, e.g. brain scans. This means results can be replicated and aren't affected by participant variables such as past experience. The theories are falsifiable.

Falsifiable means that they can be proved wrong.

Timmy wondered if giving the tortoise a push would prove that it could run.

Behaviourist

Only looks at observable behaviour, not thought processes or emotions, so the methods are empirical. E.g. animal studies get quantitative data and falsifiable theories. However, participant variables can have an impact on results.

Cognitive

Empirical methods are used, e.g. memory tests, so findings can be replicated and the theories are falsifiable. But, it's hard to isolate the variables because it's hard to separate cognitive processes. Also, participant variables can affect results.

Social

Some experimental methods are used which get quantitative data, e.g. Milgram's (1963) study. Other methods are based on observation and get qualitative data, e.g. studies that look at prejudice. This means the variables can be difficult to operationalise and control.

Not very scientific ↓

Psychodynamic

Psychodynamic theories are based on abstract concepts that can't be tested, e.g. the unconscious mind. This means they're non-falsifiable. The non-experimental research methods (e.g. dream analysis) produce qualitative data and are unreliable, so the findings can't be replicated or generalised.

Practice Questions

Q1 Describe the role of peer review in validating new knowledge.

Q2 Give three problems with doing research on humans.

Q3 Describe one psychological approach that can be said to be scientific.

Exam Question

Q1 Discuss the extent to which psychology is a science.   [24 marks]

Is psychology a science — it's a bit late in the book to bring this up...

So, you might have to answer the question of whether psychology is a science or not. Trouble is, the answer isn't a simple 'yes' or 'no'. Instead, you'd have to give a selection of arguments for and against, demonstrating how carefully you've revised this topic and how clever you are. So unless you've a particular desire to look like a plonker — I'd learn these pages.

Designing Psychological Investigations

Before you can study something, you need to design your investigation. In order to do this you need to have a clear idea about exactly what information you need to collect, and what the most appropriate method for this might be.

Research Takes **Samples** From a **Target Population**

It's really important that the sample is **representative** of the population. It should include the **variety of characteristics** that are found in the group, e.g. the group '**student**' includes both **males** and **females**. If the sample is **biased** in any way, it's hard to **generalise** any findings to the whole population.

There are many different ways to select a sample:

1) **Random sample** Everyone in the target group has an **equal chance** of being selected. Although this is **fair** and will probably provide a **good variety** of people, it doesn't guarantee that the sample will be **representative** — some subgroups could be **missed**.

2) **Systematic sample** Taking every *n*th name from a **sampling frame** (a record of all the names in a population), e.g. every 3rd name from a register, or every 50th name from a phone book. This is useful if there is a sampling frame available, but it isn't **truly random** or **representative**, and subgroups may be missed.

3) **Opportunity sample** Studying **whoever is available** at the time, e.g. students. This is **quick**, **easy** and **cheap**, but it's very unlikely that the sample will be **representative**.

4) **Self-selected sample** Participants **volunteer**, e.g. by responding to a newspaper advertisement. This can **save time** and there may be many replies, producing a **large sample**. However, it's unlikely to be representative as only certain types of people are likely to volunteer.

5) **Stratified sample** All of the **important subgroups** in the population (e.g. different age or ethnic groups) are identified and a **proportionate number** are **randomly obtained**. This can produce a fairly representative sample, but it takes a lot of **time/money** to do and subgroups may be **missed**.

Here's a reminder of some of the different **research methods** used for psychological studies, and their advantages and drawbacks. Most of this should be familiar to you from AS, but you can never have too much information...

Questionnaires — Face-to-Face, on the Phone, or via the Internet

Questionnaires are a **self-report** method.
Self-report methods involve asking participants about their feelings, beliefs and attitudes, etc.

Advantages **Practical** — can collect a large amount of information quickly and relatively cheaply.

Disadvantages
Bad questions — leading questions (questions that suggest a desired answer) or unclear questions can be a problem.
Biased samples — some people are more likely to respond to a questionnaire, which might make a sample unrepresentative.
Social desirability bias — people sometimes want to present themselves in a good light.
What they say and what they actually think could be different, making any results unreliable.
Ethics — confidentiality can be a problem, especially around sensitive issues which people might not want to discuss.

Other self-report methods include **interviews** and **case studies** (see page 124).
Self-report methods often provide **qualitative data**.

Correlational Research Looks for Relationships Between Variables

Correlation means that two variables appear to be **connected** — they rise and fall together, or one rises as the other falls.

BUT it **doesn't** always mean that one variable **causes** a change in the other, e.g. as age increases so might stress, but ageing doesn't necessarily **cause** stress.

Advantages
Causal relationships — these can be ruled out if no correlation exists.
Ethics — can study variables that would be unethical to manipulate, e.g. is there a relationship between the number of cigarettes smoked and incidences of ill health?

Disadvantages
Causal relationships — these cannot be assumed from a correlation, which may be caused by a third, unknown variable. Sometimes the media (and researchers) infer causality from a correlation.

Designing Psychological Investigations

Experiments can be done in a laboratory or in the natural environment.

Laboratory Experiments are Controlled and Scientific

1) The aim is to **control** all relevant variables except for **one key variable**, which is altered to see what its effect is. The variable that you alter is called the **independent variable**.
2) Laboratory experiments are conducted in an **artificial setting**.

Advantages

Control — the effects of extraneous variables (those that have an effect in addition to the key variable) are minimised.
Replication — you can run the study again to check the findings.
Causal relationships — it should be possible to establish whether one variable actually causes change in another.

Disadvantages

Ecological validity — experiments are artificial and might not measure real-life behaviour.
Demand characteristics — participants' behaviour changes when they know they're being studied. They may respond according to what they think is being investigated, which can bias the results.
Ethics — deception is often used, making informed consent (see p.116) difficult.

Field Experiments are Conducted Outside the Laboratory

In **field experiments**, behaviour is measured in a **natural environment** — like a school, the street or on a train. A **key variable** is still altered so that its effect can be measured.

Advantages

Causal relationships — you can still establish causal relationships by manipulating the key variable and measuring its effect. However it's very difficult to control all the variables in a field experiment.
Ecological validity — field experiments are less artificial than those done in a laboratory so they reflect real life better.
Demand characteristics — these can be avoided if participants don't know they're in a study. They will behave as they usually do in real life.

Disadvantages

Less control — extraneous variables are often much more likely in a natural environment.
Ethics — often can't give informed consent and can't be debriefed. Observation must respect privacy.

Natural Experiments Measure but Don't Control Variables

A **natural experiment** is a study where the independent variables **aren't** directly manipulated by the experimenter. In other words, things are left as they naturally would be.

Advantages

Ethics — it's possible to study variables that it would be unethical to manipulate, e.g. you can compare a community that has TV with a community that doesn't to see which is more aggressive

Disadvantages

Participant allocation — you can't randomly allocate participants to each condition, and so extraneous variables (e.g. what area the participants live in) may affect results. Let's face it — you've got no control over the variables so it's ridiculously hard to say what's caused by what.
Rare events — some groups of interest are hard to find, e.g. a community that doesn't have TV.
Ethics — deception is often used, making informed consent difficult. Also, confidentiality may be compromised if the community is identifiable.

Practice Questions

Q1 Why might you get an unrepresentative sample when carrying out questionnaire-based research?

Q2 Describe a disadvantage of correlational research.

Q3 What are the main advantages of laboratory experiments?

Exam Questions

Q1 Outline three methods that could be used to selected a sample. [6 marks]

Q2 Outline the advantages that field experiments have over laboratory experiments. [4 marks]

Designing Psychological Investigations

All research studies involve testing or measuring participants. If you want the results to be meaningful, the tests need to be reliable and valid. And if you want to pass your exam you need to know what reliability and validity mean.

Reliable Tests Give Consistent Results

Reliability refers to how **consistent** or **dependable** a test is. A reliable test carried out in the **same circumstances**, on the **same participants** should always give the **same results**. There are different types of reliability:

 Internal reliability — **different parts** of the test should give **consistent results**. For example, if an IQ test contains sections of supposedly equal difficulty, participants should achieve similar scores on all sections.

> The internal reliability of a test can be assessed using the **split-half method**. This splits the test into two halves, e.g. odd and even numbered questions, and the results from each half should produce a **high positive correlation**.

 External reliability — the test should produce **consistent results** regardless of **when** it's used. For example, if you took the same IQ test on two different days you should achieve the same score.

> The external reliability of a test can be assessed using the **test-retest method**. This involves **repeating** the test using the **same participants**. A reliable test should produce a **high positive correlation** between the two scores. A problem with this is that the participants may have changed in some way since the first test, e.g. they may have learnt more. To avoid this, external reliability can be checked using the **equivalent forms test**. This compares participants' scores on two different, but equivalent (equally hard), versions of the test.

 Inter-rater reliability — the test should give **consistent results** regardless of **who** administers it. For example, if two researchers give the same person the same IQ test they should both record the same score.

> This can be assessed by **correlating** the scores that **each researcher** produces for **each participant**. A **high positive correlation** should be found.

Valid Tests Give Accurate Results

Validity refers to how well a test measures what it **claims to**. For example, an IQ test with only **maths questions** would not be a valid measure of **general intelligence**. There are different types of validity:

1) **Internal validity** — the extent to which the results of the test are caused by the variable being measured, rather than extraneous variables.

2) **External validity** — the extent to which the results of the test can be generalised, e.g. to a larger population.

3) **Ecological validity** — the extent to which the results of the test reflect real-life.

Validity can be **assessed** in different ways:

- A quick (but not very thorough) way of assessing validity is to simply **look** at the test and make a judgement on whether it **appears** to measure what it claims to. For example, an IQ test that just consisted of maths questions could be identified as having low validity by this method.

- **Comparing** the results of the test with the results of an **existing measure** (that's already accepted as valid) can help to determine the validity of the test.

- The results of the test can be used to **predict** results of **future tests**. If the **initial** results **correlate** with the **later** results it suggests that the test has some validity and can continue to be used.

Designing Psychological Investigations

Reliability and Validity Can Both be Improved

There are several ways that the **reliability** and **validity** of tests can be **improved**:

Standardising research

Standardising research involves creating **specific procedures** which are followed every time the test is carried out. This ensures that all the researchers will test all the participants in **exactly the same way**, e.g. in the same sequence, at the same time of day, in the same environment, with all participants receiving exactly the same instructions. This reduces the possibility of extraneous variables affecting the research. Therefore it will help to improve **internal validity**, **external reliability** and **inter-rater reliability**.

Mark had spent all morning standardising the procedure and was feeling pretty smug about the end result.

Operationalising variables

1) **Operationalising variables** involves **clearly defining** all of the research **variables**.

2) For example, in a study of whether watching aggressive TV influences aggressive behaviour, the terms **'aggressive TV'** and **'aggressive behaviour'** need to be defined.

3) 'Aggressive TV' could include cartoons or human actors. One of these might influence human behaviour and the other might not — this needs to be taken into account when planning, carrying out and drawing conclusions from the investigation.

4) Similarly, 'aggressive behaviour' could refer to physical and verbal aggression, or just physical aggression.

5) Clarifying this from the start improves the **reliability** and **internal validity** of the test.

Pilot studies

Pilot studies are small scale **trial runs** of the test. They're used to check for any problems before the test is carried out for real. They also give researchers practice at following the procedures. Pilot studies allow the **validity** and **reliability** of the test to be **assessed in advance**, which then gives the opportunity for **improvements** to be made.

Practice Questions

Q1 Explain the difference between internal reliability and external reliability.

Q2 How does the split-half method test for internal reliability?

Q3 Why does standardisation help to improve the reliability and validity of research?

Q4 What is a pilot study?

Exam Questions

Q1 Describe how validity could be assessed in any two pieces of psychological research that you've studied. [6 marks]

Q2 Describe how reliability could be improved in any two pieces of psychological research that you've studied. [6 marks]

Reliable tests? Who cares. Reliable results are what you need right now.

So, it turns out that 'reliable' and 'valid' are more than just terms to bandy around and throw into answers with some sort of vague idea that they're good things for studies to be. They've got specific meanings and you need to know them. These examiner types are so demanding — it's like they've got nothing better to do than sit around thinking up stuff for you to learn.

Ethics

Remember Milgram's obedience research from AS? The one that made participants think they were giving lethal electric shocks to others. It was a bit... "unethical", some might say. If you're not sure what that means, worry not, just read on...

Ethics *are an* Important Issue *in Psychology*

1) Psychological research and practice should aim to improve our **self-understanding**, be **beneficial** to people and try to **improve the quality of life** for individuals.
2) As professionals, psychologists are expected to do their work in an **ethical manner**.
3) **Ethical guidelines** are **formal principles** for what is considered to be acceptable or unacceptable.
4) In the UK these are produced by the **British Psychological Society (BPS)**.
   However, questions are raised about whether the guidelines are **adequate** and **appropriately applied**.

Ethical Guidelines *Must Be Followed During Research*

1 Informed Consent
- BPS guidelines state that participants should always give **informed consent**.
- They should be told the aims and nature of the study before agreeing to it.
- They should also know that they have the **right to withdraw** at any time.

1) **BUT** if the participant is under 16 years of age they **can't give consent** (although a parent can).
2) In **naturalistic observation** studies, consent is not obtained. In this case the research is acceptable provided that it is done in a **public location** where people would expect to be observed by others.
3) Even when informed consent is supposedly obtained, issues may be raised. **Menges (1973)** reviewed about 1000 American studies and found that **97%** had not given people all the information about the research.

2 Deception
- If participants have been deceived then they cannot have given **informed consent**.
- However, sometimes researchers must **withhold information** about the study because the participants wouldn't behave **naturally** if they knew what the aim was.

1) The BPS guidelines state that deception is only acceptable if there is strong **scientific justification** for the research and there's **no alternative procedure** available to obtain the data.
2) Researchers can also ask **independent people** if they would object to the study. If they wouldn't, then the study may be done with naïve participants (although the naïve participants **may not agree** with others' opinions).
3) Participants could just be given **general** details — although if too little is said they may feel **deceived**, but if participants know too much then they may not behave naturally.
4) The **severity** of deception differs, e.g. research on memory may involve **unexpected** memory tests (that participants weren't informed about). This is **less objectionable** than the deception involved in Milgram's study.

3 Protection from harm
- The BPS guidelines say that the risk of harm to participants should be **no greater** than they would face in their normal lives. It's hard to **accurately assess** this.

1) Research procedures can involve physical and psychological discomfort, e.g. **Glass and Singer (1972)** exposed participants to noise to make them stressed, and participants in **Milgram's** research suffered extreme distress.
2) Some people face **risks** in their work (e.g. soldiers) but that doesn't mean they can be exposed to risks in research.
3) Researchers don't always **know in advance** what might be distressing for participants.

4 Debriefing
- Debriefing is supposed to return participants to the state they were in **before the research**.
- It's especially important if **deception** has been used.

1) Researchers must fully explain what the research involved and what the results might show.
2) Participants are given the **right to withdraw their data**.

Ethics

5 **Confidentiality**
- None of the participants in a psychological study should be **identifiable** from any reports that are produced.

1) Data collected during research must be **confidential** — researchers can't use people's **names** in reports.

2) Participants must be **warned** if their data is not going to be completely anonymous.

3) However, some groups or people might be **easily identifiable** from their **characteristics** — more so if the report says where and when the study was carried out, etc.

Some Research Raises *Sensitive Social Issues*

1) Findings from psychological research may highlight **social issues** and create negative effects or reactions in society.

2) Socially sensitive research can be defined as research that may have implications for the individuals in the research, or for groups in society — e.g. the participants' families, or particular cultural groups.

e.g. Research into **genetics** raises many issues:

1) Research into whether there are genetic influences on **criminal behaviour** raises important questions, e.g. whether genetics could be used as a **defence** against being convicted for a crime.

2) Also, there's the possibility of **compulsory genetic testing** to identify people with a particular gene.

3) Such **screening** could also identify genes linked to psychological disorders such as **schizophrenia**.

4) Although this may potentially help people it could also lead to **anxiety** and **social stigma**, especially as people may have a **genetic vulnerability** for a disorder but not actually **develop it**.

e.g. Using a factor like **race** as an **independent variable** is a very sensitive issue:

1) Some studies using **IQ tests** have shown possible **racial differences** in **intelligence**.

2) The issue is whether this is an **appropriate topic** for research because of **social tensions** that the results and conclusions may produce.

3) Such research is often **discredited** because of **methodological problems** with the IQ tests that were used. For example, they may have been **biased** towards some social-cultural groups — this shows that we need to be careful about the **conclusions** that we draw from research methods.

Practice Questions

Q1 What are 'ethical guidelines' and why are they needed in psychology?
Q2 Why is it sometimes impossible to obtain informed consent from participants?
Q3 When is it permissible to deceive participants?
Q4 What is the purpose of debriefing?

Exam Question

Q1 a) Outline three BPS guidelines for psychological research with human participants. [8 marks]

b) Discuss why ethical guidelines are important in psychological research with humans. [16 marks]

It's the debriefing part that bothers me — I'd rather stay clothed, thanks...

There's absolutely no getting around it — ethics and psychological research are inextricably linked. So you really can't blame those pesky examiners for making you learn about it. Well, you probably could, but it would be a bit harsh. Anyway — learn it, then if anyone tries any nasty research on you at least you know your rights. Knowledge is power, my friend.

Probability and Significance

Inferential statistics let you make an 'inference' (or educated guess) about whether your results show something significant, or if they're due to chance. "Marvellous", I hear you cry. "Just what I've always wanted to learn about..."

Inferential Statistics are about Ruling Out Chance

1) You can never be 100% certain that results aren't all down to chance. So instead of 'proving' a hypothesis, you have to be content with finding out whether it's **likely** to be true. This is called **statistical significance**.

2) If your results are statistically significant, it means that you can **read something into them** — they're unlikely to be just down to chance.

3) If your results are **not statistically significant**, it means they could have happened by chance rather than being the effect of changes in your independent variable, so you can't really read anything into them.

Use Statistical Tests to Find Out if Your Results Mean Anything

OK, it's not easy, this bit — so stop texting people and concentrate...

1
- The first thing you do is write out your **null hypothesis** — this is the theory you want to **test**.
- In a statistical test, you assume your null hypothesis is **true** (for the time being, at least).
- (So a null hypothesis might be *"rats that eat poison and rats that eat sugar pellets are equally likely to be ill"*.)

2
- Next you choose a **significance level** — this is a **'level of proof'** that you're looking for before you read anything into your results.
- The smaller the significance level, the stronger the evidence you're looking for that your results aren't just down to chance.
- A significance level is a **probability**, and so is a number between 0 and 1.
- (Probabilities near 1 mean things are very **likely**, and probabilities near 0 mean things are very **unlikely**.)
- Significance levels are always **very small** — usually 0.05 (5%) or less. (Because a significance level is very **small**, events with probabilities smaller than the significance level are very **unlikely** to happen.)

I didn't inhale, honest.

3
- You then turn all your experimental results into a single **test statistic** (p.120-123).
- Then you can find out how likely this test statistic is (and so how likely your results are), **assuming the null hypothesis is true**.

4
- If the probability of getting your results (assuming the null hypothesis is true) is **less than the significance level**, then they must be **really unlikely** — and so it's pretty safe to say that your null hypothesis **wasn't true** after all.
- This is what stats-folk mean when they talk about 'rejecting the null hypothesis'. (If you reject your null hypothesis, you assume your **alternative hypothesis** is true instead.)

5
- If you reject your null hypothesis, you can proudly shout out that your results are **statistically significant**.
- (So rejecting the null hypothesis above would mean that *"rats that eat poison and rats that eat sugar pellets are not equally likely to be ill"*.)

6
- If you **don't reject** the null hypothesis, it means that your results could have occurred **by chance**, rather than because your null hypothesis was wrong.
- If this happens, you've proved **nothing** — not rejecting the null hypothesis doesn't mean it **must be true**.

7
- Using a significance level of **0.05** (5%) is okay for most tests.
- If the probability of your results is **less** than this ($p \leq 0.05$), then it's **pretty good evidence** that the null hypothesis **wasn't true** after all.
- If you use a significance level of **0.01** (1%), then you're looking for **really strong evidence** that the null hypothesis is untrue before you're going to reject it.

Probability and Significance

There are Two Types of Potential Error

It's possible to make errors when you're deciding whether or not to reject the null hypothesis.

A **Type 1 error** is when you **reject** the null hypothesis when it was **actually true**.
The significance level gives you the **probability** of this happening.
This is why significance levels are **small**.

A **Type 2 error** is when you **don't reject** the null hypothesis when it was **actually false**.
This can happen if your significance level is **too small** (e.g. if you want very strong
evidence of the need to reject a null hypothesis and so use a 0.01 significance level).

Choosing significance levels is a **compromise** — if the level you choose is **too big** you risk making a Type 1 error.
If the significance level you choose is **too small**, you could make a Type 2 error.

There are Various Ways to Test Significance

1) Remember that you can never be 100% sure that a hypothesis is correct — it's always possible that results are just due to **chance**.
2) Significance levels are assigned to establish the **probability** of the result being due to chance, and if this is acceptably low (e.g. 5%), then you can reject the **null hypothesis**.
3) **Inferential statistical tests** help to decide whether to accept or reject the null hypothesis. However, there are many **different tests** and it is crucial that you use the **correct one** for your data. We'll get to the specific tests over the next few pages.
4) You use inferential tests to calculate what's called an **observed value** (the value you get when you carry out the test on your results). The observed value is then **compared** against a **critical value**, which is provided for each test in a **critical value table**. This indicates whether or not the results are significant.
5) In some tests, if the observed value is **more than** the critical value, the results are considered to **be significant**. In others, the observed value must be **equal to or less than** the critical value to **show significance**.

Her date's significant lack of arms, legs and head was no matter to Julie, who just needed someone to lean on.

Practice Questions

Q1 What does it mean if the results of an experiment or study are not statistically significant?
Q2 What two significance levels are commonly used in statistical tests?
Q3 Name the two types of error that can be made.

Exam Questions

Q1 Outline what is meant by $p \leq 0.05$. [2 marks]

Q2 Outline the two types of errors that can be made when deciding whether to reject the null hypothesis. [4 marks]

Q3 Describe the role of a critical value table in interpreting the results of an investigation. [2 marks]

There's a high probability that you'll be able to infer this stuff is important...

So, got all that? If not, have a read back over the pages again until it sinks in. In a very small nutshell, you can't ever rule out the fact that your results are down to chance, but you can ensure that the likelihood of that is as small as possible. And, joy of joys, there are some lovely statistical tests over the page to show you how it's done. I know, I know, I'm spoiling you.

Inferential Statistics

If the thought of maths in general, and statistics in particular, makes you want to run for the hills, then take a ticket and get in line. Unfortunately the hills aren't an option, but really, the stats bit isn't so bad if you stick with it. Honest.

Several Things Determine Which Inferential Test Should be Used

Inferential statistics allow you to make an educated guess about whether or not a hypothesis is correct. Deciding which inferential test you use for your data is determined by the following factors:

Research Design

Research may have either **related measures** (if a repeated measures or matched participants design was used), or **unrelated measures** (if an independent measures design was used).

Research Aims

Some inferential statistics test whether there is a **significant difference** between two (or more) groups of scores:
- For example, 'did the participants in group A have significantly higher average scores than those in group B?'.
- This is what happens in an **experiment**. The IV is manipulated to see if it produces **changes** in the DV that are significantly different from the **control condition** (or other experimental conditions).
- Some inferential statistics test to see if there is a **significant association** between two (or more) variables:
- For example, whether they occur together more than would be expected by chance.
- This is what we look for in **correlation studies** — to see if two variables are positively or negatively associated, more than would be expected by chance factors alone. If they are, a **significant** correlation has been shown.

Level of measurement / type of data

The results of a study can be collected in different ways, which affect how they can be analysed.
- **Nominal data** — This is the most basic level of measurement — a **frequency count** for completely **distinct categories**. For example, in a study where a confederate pretends to need help, you could assign each passer-by to either an 'altruistic' category (if they helped) or a 'non-altruistic' category (if they did nothing).
- **Ordinal data** — All of the measurements relate to the **same variable**, and measurements can be placed in ascending or descending **rank order**, e.g. on a **rating scale** for aggression where 1 = 'not aggressive' and 10 = 'extremely aggressive'. But you can't say a person with a score of 10 is twice as aggressive as a person with a score of 5, just which one was **more** or **less** aggressive.
- **Interval data** — Measurements are taken on a scale where **each unit is the same size**, e.g. length in centimetres. Interval data places participants in rank order **according to the differences** between them, e.g. in a race, participant 'F' was quickest, in 15.8 seconds and participant 'B' was second, in 16.5 seconds. Technically, an **absolute zero point** is needed to make judgements about whether one score is twice that of another. When we have this (e.g. 0 seconds, 0 centimetres, etc.) then we call it a **ratio scale**.

Spearman's Rho is a Correlation Coefficient

To work out (and then test the significance of) **Spearman's rho** correlation coefficient, you need values for two different variables (e.g. hours of revision and average test scores for 10 students).

a) The values for each variable are placed into **rank order** (each variable is ranked separately). The lowest value for each variable gets rank 1 (and in the above example, the biggest value will get rank 10).

b) The **difference** (d) in ranks for each student's variables is calculated. (So a particular student may have done the most revision, but got the 3rd best results, in which case the difference in ranks will be d = 3 − 1 = 2.)

c) The value of d for each student is **squared**, then the results are added together (to get $\sum d^2$).

d) Then the special **Spearman's correlation coefficient** calculation is done, which is $r_s = 1 - \dfrac{6 \times \sum d^2}{N \times (N^2 - 1)}$

            (where N is the number of students, or whatever).

e) To find out whether the result is **significant** (and so whether the variables are linked), you compare the outcome of that nightmarish calculation with a **critical value** that you look up in a **statistics table**.

Inferential Statistics

The *Wilcoxon Signed Ranks* Test — *A Test of Difference for* **Related** *Data*

The Wilcoxon Signed Ranks test is used when a hypothesis states that there'll be a difference between two sets of data, when the data is ordinal, and when the experiment is a repeated measures or matched pairs design.

> **Example:** A group does a memory test with two methods of memorising, in a **repeated measures** design:

Participant no.	1	2	3	4	5	6	7	8
No. words recalled — Method 1	6	5	10	6	8	5	9	8
No. words recalled — Method 2	7	7	8	8	7	6	9	9

1) The **difference** between each participant's two scores is calculated:

Participant no.	1	2	3	4	5	6	7	8
Difference	1	2	2	2	1	1	0	1
Sign (+/-)	-	-	+	-	+	-		-

> Always subtract in the same direction, noting if the result is a positive or negative value. Any differences of zero are removed from the results.

2) The differences are given a **rank** to show their **order** — the lowest gets rank one. Ignore +/- signs.

Difference	1	2	2	2	1	1	0	1
Rank	2.5	6	6	6	2.5	2.5		2.5
Sign (+/-)	-	-	+	-	+	-		-

> When there are a few of the same number, calculate their mean rank. e.g. Here, there are four 1s, which should be rank 1, 2, 3 and 4, so they all get the mean rank 2.5.

3) **Total** the ranks for the positive differences and for the negative differences. The smallest is the **observed value of 'T'**.

> Total negative differences = 2.5 + 6 + 6 + 2.5 + 2.5 = **19.5**
> Total positive differences = 6 + 2.5 = **8.5**
>
> So, the **observed value of T = 8.5**.

4) The observed value must be **less than or equal to** the **critical value** to be significant.

> • Critical values for each number of participants can be found in **a special table** that you'll be given.
> • The number of participants is the actual number of people **taking part** in the trial, so 8 in this case.

Sarah wanted to work out the observed value but had totally forgotten which bottle was which.

Practice Questions

Q1 Why do differences in research aims determine which inferential test to use?
Q2 Name the three different types of data.
Q3 What do you need to be able to work out Spearman's Rho?

Exam Questions

Q1 Discuss the factors that need to be considered when deciding which statistical test should be used.	[12 marks]
Q2 Outline when the Wilcoxon Signed Ranks test would be appropriate.	[2 marks]

I guess stats why they call it the blues...

Actually, that's a bit unfair. I'm sorry. All this stats stuff is dead useful — a good understanding of research methods and how they can affect your results is really important for this course as a whole. And even better than that, there's only a few more pages to go to the end of the section, after which point you can have a lie down until you recover. See, it's not so bad.

Inferential Statistics

Just two more inferential tests to learn on these pages and then you can move on, I promise. To make it a bit easier, there's a worked example for each. Breathe in, breathe out, breathe in, breathe out, rank, significance, data, easy.

The **Mann-Whitney U Test** is Used with **Ordinal Data**

The **Mann-Whitney U Test** is a test of difference (or of similarity) for **unrelated data**.
It focuses on **ranks** and is used when you have **ordinal** data.

Take a look at the following example:

> Two groups took part in a study investigating whether drinking a **vitamin drink** once a day for 4 weeks improved performance on a **verbal memory** test compared to a group who had not had any vitamin drinks.

Number of words recalled	Vitamin group	19	13	9	12	21	15	14
	No vitamin group	7	5	10	8	6	11	18

Firstly, the Data Needs to be **Ranked**

The data is ranked regardless of the group each score is in. Start with the **lowest score** (in the example it's 5) and give it a rank of '**1**'. Then the next lowest score gets a rank of '2' and so on.

Number of words recalled	Vitamin group (A) (rank)	19 (13)	13 (9)	9 (5)	12 (8)	21 (14)	15 (11)	14 (10)
	No vitamin group (B) (rank)	7 (3)	5 (1)	10 (6)	8 (4)	6 (2)	11 (7)	18 (12)

If some of the data values are the **same** then you have to use an **average** rank. E.g. if the 3rd and 4th values are the same then you'll use 3.5.

The **Ranks** for **Each Group** are then **Added Up**

Look at the **ranks** associated with the vitamin group's scores and **add** them up.
Then do exactly the same for the no vitamin group.

- Sum of ranks in **vitamin group** (R_A) = 13 + 9 + 5 + 8 + 14 + 11 + 10 = 70
- Sum of ranks in **no vitamin group** (R_B) = 3 + 1 + 6 + 4 + 2 + 7 + 12 = 35

When you think about it, if the vitamin group really did show **better** verbal recall then their scores will be **higher** than the no vitamin group. This means that the **ranks** of the scores in the vitamin group will also be **higher**.

The Mann-Whitney U test then uses the following scary-looking formulas:

$$U_A = N_A N_B + \frac{N_A(N_A + 1)}{2} - R_A$$

$$U_B = N_A N_B + \frac{N_B(N_B + 1)}{2} - R_B$$

N_A is the number of people in group A
N_B is the number of people in group B
R_A is the sum of the ranks for scores in group A
R_B is the sum of the ranks for scores in group B

$$U_A = (7 \times 7) + \frac{7(7 + 1)}{2} - 70$$

$$U_A = 7$$

$$U_B = (7 \times 7) + \frac{7(7 + 1)}{2} - 35$$

$$U_B = 42$$

You need to select the **smaller** of these, 7, and call it '**U**'.

The observed U must be **less than or equal to** the **critical value** to be **significant**.
Critical values can be found in a table that you'll be given in the exam. In this case, the critical value is **6**, so there's **no significant difference** between the two groups.

Inferential Statistics

The **Chi-square Test** is Used with **Nominal Data** and **Independent Samples**

There's no better way of explaining this than showing you an example. So, hey presto...

> A student is interested in seeing whether finding reality TV programmes **entertaining** is related to being either **male** or **female**. His results are shown in the table below.

The **chi-square test** tests the **null hypothesis**. In this example, the null hypothesis would be that there's **no association** between finding reality TV entertaining and being male or female — this is shown by the **expected frequencies**. Under the null hypothesis, the expected frequencies show that **equal amounts** of men and women find reality TV entertaining, and equal amounts do not.

	Men	Women	Totals
Finds reality TV entertaining	19	35	54
(expected frequency)	(27)	(27)	
Does not find reality TV entertaining	41	25	66
(expected frequency)	(33)	(33)	
Totals	60	60	120

The expected frequencies are worked out using the following formula:

$$E = \frac{\text{row total} \times \text{column total}}{\text{overall total}}$$

You Then Just Have to Put the Numbers into a **Formula**

John was stunned that the "chai test" involved more than just "add boiling water and brew for 4 minutes".

The chi-square (χ^2) is calculated using yet another scary-looking equation:

$$\chi^2 = \Sigma \; \frac{(O - E)^2}{E}$$

O is the observed frequency
E is the expected frequency

So, for each pair of observed and expected frequencies, take the expected score away from the observed score, square this and then divide by the expected score. Do this for all the observed and expected pairs — then add up all your answers (that's what the Σ means).

If you work through this example, χ^2 turns out to be **8.62**. You can then use a critical value table to see if this is significant (it is, so the null hypothesis is **false**).

For a reminder on critical value tables, take a look at p.119.

Practice Questions

Q1 What type of data is a Mann-Whitney U test used on?
Q2 When would a researcher use a chi-square test?
Q3 How do you calculate an expected frequency?

Exam Question

Q1 Ian is interested in whether there is an association between being an only child and having a pet. Suggest a null hypothesis and a suitable inferential test for this study. [4 marks]

Just to throw another spanner in the works, you say "kai", not "chi"...

...but this isn't an inferential statistical test speaking exam (and thank goodness for that, by the way), so that's useless info. What will help, though, is knowing what each statistical test is used for. So, the Mann-Whitney U test is for ordinal data and the chi-square test is for nominal data. Mann-Whitney, ordinal, chi-square, nominal. Breathe in, breathe out, easy.

Analysis of Qualitative Data

Qualitative data is data that involves anything other than numbers. It could be words, sounds or pictures, for example.

Observational Methods *Can Provide Qualitative Data*

1. **NATURALISTIC OBSERVATION** Participants are observed in their **natural environment**, normally without their knowledge.

   Several design issues are involved:

   1) **Sampling of Behaviour**. Researchers may use **event sampling**, where they only observe and record the particular events of interest. **Time-interval** sampling is used if the observation is over a long period of time.

   2) **Recording Behaviour**. Researchers may make notes, or complete pre-made forms to record how often something happens. A problem with this method is that researchers may **miss** some behaviours or **disagree** over behaviours, so video or audio recordings may be made.

   3) **Rating Behaviour**. Behaviours need to be described and placed into **categories**, e.g. solitary play, cooperative play, etc. Researchers can do a **frequency count** of how many times each behaviour is observed.

   ADVANTAGES / DISADVANTAGES

   a) The observation is in the participants' natural environment so there is **ecological validity**.

   b) Participants don't know they're being observed so should behave naturally and not show **demand characteristics**.

   c) There is **no control** over any of the variables so **cause and effect relationships** cannot be established.

   d) Observers may be biased in how they interpret behaviours. So, it's important to establish **inter-observer reliability** by comparing two or more observers' recordings to ensure that they're similar.

   e) For **ethical reasons** naturalistic observations can only be done where people would **expect to be observed**.

2. **PARTICIPANT OBSERVATION** An observer **joins the group** they are studying. They may be known to the group or hidden.

   ADVANTAGES/DISADVANTAGES

   a) Insights about groups may be found that other methods couldn't show, but it can be more difficult to record data.

   b) However, 'hidden' observation raises **ethical issues**.

   c) If the researcher is known to the group then they won't **behave naturally**.

   d) Equally the researcher may get emotionally **attached** to the group, and become **biased**.

3. **INTERVIEWS** The structure of an interview can vary.

   1) **Fully structured** — a set sequence of questions with **closed answers**, i.e. multiple-choice (this is quantitative).

   2) **Informal/Unstructured** interviews — the interviewer asks questions with no set structure and answers are **open**, i.e. the person being interviewed can respond in any way.

   ADVANTAGES/DISADVANTAGES

   a) Fully structured interviews are **quick** and **easily analysed**, but the structure **limits** how the interviewee responds.

   b) Unstructured interviews can provide lots of **detailed**, **insightful** qualitative data, but this is **hard to analyse**.

   c) To **compromise**, both open and closed questions can be used.

   d) Researchers must make sure that questions are not **ambiguous**, **double-barrelled** (combining more than one issue in a single question) or **leading**.

4. **CASE STUDIES** These involve the **detailed study** of an individual, or small group using many different methods*.

   ADVANTAGES/DISADVANTAGES

   a) Lots of **data** may be obtained, providing detail that other methods can't give.

   b) This may give insight into unique cases and **unusual situations** which may help to develop theories, e.g. case studies on children who were **socially privated** have shown its **effects on their development**.

   c) Researchers have very **little control** over variables in the study and can mistakenly identify **causal relationships**.

   d) Results can't be **generalised** to the rest of the population.

*E.g. interviews (structured and/or unstructured), observations, psychometric tests (e.g. intelligence tests), experiments, etc.

Analysis of Qualitative Data

*It's Difficult to **Objectively Analyse** Qualitative Data*

1) Once **quantitative data** is collected it can be **easily** and **objectively** analysed.

2) However, **qualitative data** (such as an interview transcript) is much more difficult to analyse **objectively**.

Qualitative Analysis Involves Subjective Decisions

Qualitative analysis can involve making **summaries** and identifying key **themes** and **categories**. For example:

1) Analysis of a transcript or video involves identifying statements — e.g. feelings, jokes, criticisms, etc. Different researchers may read different things into the statements.

2) Such analysis may give the basis for **hypotheses**, e.g. about what may be found in other sources / other things the participant may say — the hypothesis formation is therefore **grounded in the data** (but could still be subjective).

Criticisms

1) How do you decide **which categories to use** and whether a statement fits a particular category?

2) How do you decide what to **leave out** of the summary, or which quotations to use?

These are **subjective** decisions and researchers may be **biased**, possibly showing statements or events **out of context**.

Strengths

1) Qualitative analysis preserves the **detail** in the data.

2) Creating hypotheses during the analysis allows for new **insights** to be developed.

3) Some **objectivity** can be established by using **triangulation** — other sources of data are used to check conclusions (e.g. previous interviews). With more sources researchers can cross-check their interpretations.

*Content Analysis is a Way to **Quantify Qualitative Data***

1) When analysing a transcript, **coding units** can be established, e.g. 'references to cultural stereotypes'. These phrases are given **operationalised definitions**, e.g. 'defining a cultural stereotype'.

2) A **frequency count** of how many times each coding unit occurs in the transcript can be done, producing **quantitative data**, which can then be **statistically analysed** — this is known as **content analysis**.

Strengths — A **clear summary** of the patterns in the data may be established. Statistics provide a more **objective basis** for comparisons and statistical tests may show, for example, that a coding unit is **significantly** more frequent in one source of data than in another.

Criticisms — Subjective judgements are still made to define coding units. Also, reducing the data to particular coding units removes detail, and the true meaning of things may be lost when taken **out of context**.

Practice Questions

Q1 What is naturalistic observation?

Q2 Explain the difference between structured and informal/unstructured interviews.

Q3 What are the advantages and disadvantages of case studies?

Q4 What is content analysis?

Exam Questions

Q1 Explain why the analysis of qualitative data can be subjective. [2 marks]

Q2 Give one advantage and one disadvantage of content analysis. [4 marks]

Case study — leather, brown, handle, wheels... but thinks it's still a cow...

Phew, that's a whole lot of stuff on analysis of qualitative data. Which makes me think it must be important. It shouldn't be too bad to learn — four observational methods, a little bit on objectively analysing the results and an even littler bit on quantifying them. Learn that and it's job done. For now that is — there are still a few pages left before you can totally relax.

Presenting Data

It's all very well investigating the effects of the 'sarcastic clap' on a live interpretive dance show, but you also need to be able to present the results clearly. Results can be presented in different ways and you need to know what they are...

Data Can Be Presented in Various Ways

1) **Qualitative** data from observations, interviews, surveys, etc. (see pages 124-125) can be presented in a **report** as a 'verbal summary'.

2) The report will contain **summaries** of what was seen or said, possibly using **categories** to group data together. Also **quotations** from participants can be used, and any **research hypotheses** that developed during the study or data analysis may be discussed.

3) When **quantitative** data is **collected** (or **produced** from qualitative data, e.g. by a **content analysis** — see p.125), it can be **summarised** and presented in various ways. Read on...

Tables are a Good Way to Summarise Quantitative Data

Tables can be used to clearly present the data and show any **patterns** in the scores.

Tables of '**raw data**' show the scores **before** any **analysis** has been done on them.

Other tables may show **descriptive statistics** such as the mean, range and standard deviation.

Table To Show the Qualities of Different Types of Ice Cream

Type of ice cream	Quality (score out of 10)		
	Tastiness	Thickness	Throwability
Chocolate	9	7	6
Toffee	8	6	7
Strawberry	8	5	4
Earwax	2	9	8

Bar Charts Can be Used for Non-continuous Data

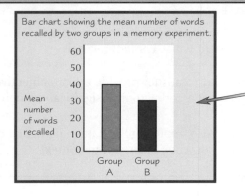

Bar chart showing the mean number of words recalled by two groups in a memory experiment.

Bar charts (bar graphs) are usually used to present '**non-continuous data**' — when a variable falls into **categories** rather than being measured on a numbered scale.

This bar chart shows the number of words recalled by two different groups in a memory experiment.

Note that the columns in bar charts **don't touch** each other. Also, it's preferable to always show the **full vertical scale**, or **clearly indicate** when it isn't all shown (otherwise it can be **misleading**).

Histograms are for When You Have Continuous Data

Histograms show data measured on a '**continuous**' scale of measurement.

This histogram shows the time different participants took to complete a task.

Each column shows a **class interval** (here, each class interval is 10 seconds), and the columns **touch** each other.

All intervals are shown, even if there are **no scores** within them.

It's the **height** of the column that shows the number of values in that interval.

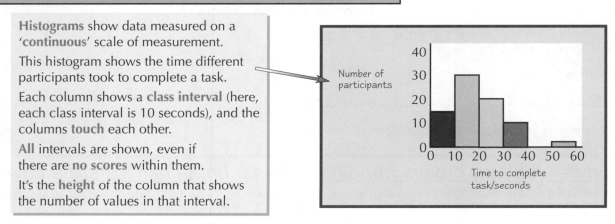

Presenting Data

Frequency Polygons are Good for Showing More Than One Set of Data

Frequency polygons are similar to histograms, but use **lines** to show where the top of each column would reach.

It can be useful to combine **two or more** frequency polygons on the same set of axes — then it's easy to **make comparisons** between groups.

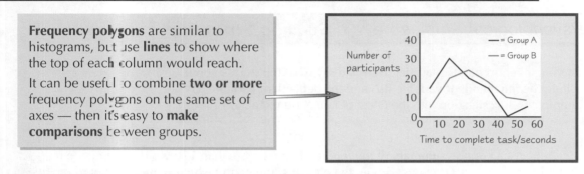

Scattergraphs Show Relationships Between Co-variables

Correlation is a measure of the relationship between **two variables**, e.g. how closely **exam grades** are related to **amount of revision**. A correlational coefficient is produced — these range from **–1** (a perfect linear **negative** relationship) to **+1** (the same, but **positive**). In a **correlational study** data can be displayed in scattergraphs.

1) **Positive correlation** — this means that as one variable rises, so does the other (and likewise, if one falls, so does the other).
Example: hours of study and average test score.
The correlation coefficient is roughly **0.75** (close to +1).

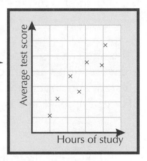

2) **Negative correlation** — this means that as one variable rises, the other one falls (and vice versa).
Example: hours of TV watched each week and average test score.
The correlation coefficient is roughly **–0.75** (close to -1).

3) **No correlation** — if the correlation coefficient is 0 (or close to 0), then the two variables aren't linked.
Example: a student's height and their average test score.
The correlation coefficient is roughly **0.01** (close to 0).

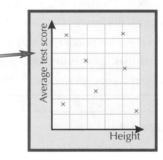

Practice Questions

Q1 What kind of data is shown on bar charts?
Q2 What type of data do histograms represent?
Q3 What is the difference between a negative correlation and no correlation?

Exam Question

Q1 Describe three ways of summarising quantitative data. [6 marks]

What? They want numbers and charts as well? Are you having a graph?

Producing a graphical representation of results means that you can identify trends and correlations without having to trawl through endless reams of numbers. There's nothing worse than trying to work out 'what it all means' when all you really want to do is go downstairs and have a bowl of soup. But if you pop it on a graph, you can be at your saucepan in seconds.

Reporting on Psychological Investigations

Once the research study has been done you'd think that'd be the end of it and the poor overworked psychologist could have a break. But no — the study has to be written up and it has to be done in a certain way. Some people are so picky.

Reports on Psychological Studies Have a Specific Structure

Title   The first thing a report needs is a **title**. It should say what the study's **about** and include the **independent variable** (**IV**) and the **dependent variable** (**DV**). For example, 'An Investigation into the Effect of Hunger on Reaction Times'.

Abstract   The abstract's a **concise summary** of the report (often no more than 120 words), telling the reader about the research and findings without them having to read the **whole report**. It should include brief descriptions of the **aims** and **hypotheses** of the study, the **method**, and a summary of the **results**. The abstract should also contain interpretations of the findings and any significant **flaws** in the study. A lot to fit into a small space...

Introduction   The introduction is a general **overview** of the **area** being studied, including **existing theories**. It should also discuss a few **studies closely related** to the current study.

Aim and Hypotheses   The aim is a sentence stating the **purpose** of the study. For example, 'To investigate whether reaction times are affected by hunger levels'. The hypothesis is what's actually going to be **tested**, and should include the **independent variable** and the **dependent variable**. For example, 'There is no relationship between hunger levels and reaction time'.

Method   The method describes **how** the research was **carried out**. Someone should be able to **replicate** the study by following the method, so it needs to be **detailed**. The method should include information on:

The **design of the investigation**, for example:
- The **research method** used, e.g. field experiment, interview.
- The **research design**, e.g. repeated measures, and any potential problems with the design.
- How **variables** and **order effects** were **controlled**, e.g. counterbalancing, randomisation.
- How **word-lists**, **questions**, etc. were chosen.
- How **ethical issues** were dealt with.

The **procedure used**:
- This should be a blow-by-blow account of **what happened** each time a participant took part.
- It should start with **how** the researcher and the investigation were **introduced** to the participant and how **informed consent** was obtained.
- It needs to include what was **said** to the participants (the standardised instructions), how the study was **carried out** and how the participants were **debriefed**.
- The method should also contain details of how the **data** was **recorded**.

The **use of participants**, for example:
The **number** of participants used.
The **demographics** of the participants, e.g. age, employment, gender, etc.
The **sampling method** used (see p.112).
How participants were **allocated** to **conditions**.

The **resources used**, for example:
The **materials** used, e.g. questionnaires, pictures, word lists, etc.
Any **apparatus** used — it's often useful to include diagrams or photographs of these.

Reporting on Psychological Investigations

Results The results of the study can be reported as **descriptive** or **inferential** statistics. Descriptive statistics include **tables**, **graphs** and **charts** (see p.126-127). Inferential statistics (see pages 120-123) involve doing **statistical tests** on the data. The results section needs to include explanations of **why** certain tests were chosen, e.g. because the study was looking for a correlation. The **results** of the test — including the observed value, the critical value and level of significance should also be included.

Discussion The discussion covers a range of things including:

- **An explanation of the findings** — **summarising** the results and **relating** them to the **aim** and **hypothesis**. The null hypothesis should be accepted or rejected in the discussion. Any **unexpected** findings should also be addressed and explained here.
- **The implications of the study** — for example, whether the study relates to **real-life situations**, e.g. interviews, exams, etc.
- **The limitations and modifications of the study** — any **problems** or **limitations** need to be explained, along with modifications that could **improve** the study.
- **The relationship to background research** — the results need to be related to the **background research** covered in the introduction. The data should be compared to other data and comments made on whether or not the findings of the study support the findings of other studies.
- **Suggestions for further research** — at least two ideas for further research should be included.

References The references section contains a list of all the books, articles and websites that have been used for **information** during the study. It allows the reader to see where the information on the **research** and **theories** mentioned in the report (e.g. in the introduction) came from. References should be presented in **alphabetical order** of first author's surname.

Appendices Any **materials** used, e.g. questionnaires or diagrams, can be put in the appendix. **Raw data** and **statistical test calculations** also go here.

When Ellie said she needed help with her appendix, a hospital trip wasn't what she had in mind.

General Tips The report should be written in the **third person**, e.g. 'the participants were asked to recall numbers' rather than 'I asked the participants to recall numbers'. The language used should be **formal**, e.g. 'the participants in the study were an opportunity sample', rather than 'the participants were basically anyone we could get hold of.'

Practice Questions

Q1 What should be included in an abstract?

Q2 In which section of a report would you find an overview of the research area?

Q3 List six things that should be included in a method.

Q4 Name two types of statistics that could be included in the results section of a report.

Q5 In which section should materials such as questionnaires be included?

You've achieved your aim and reached the end of the section — result...

If you're the kind of person that has their own special celebratory dance for moments of crowning glory or achievement, I suggest you perform it now — because this is the end of the book. If you've made it this far and learned everything in between then you are now (unofficially) an unstoppable psychological research machine. And very smart, too.

Do Well in Your AQA Exam

These pages are about how to ace the exam. Which is, after all, the name of the game. And what a fun game it's been.

There are **Two Units** in AQA A2 Psychology

The Unit 3 (Topics in Psychology) exam has eight questions

1) There'll be **one question** on each of the following topics — Biological Rhythms and Sleep, Perception, Gender, Relationships, Aggression, Eating Behaviour, Intelligence and Learning, and Cognition and Development.

2) Don't worry though — you just need to choose **three** of these questions to answer. Each one is worth **24 marks** and could be either a **single question** or a **two-part question**.

3) The exam lasts for an **hour and a half**.

You'll be marked on the quality of your written communication in all three answers.

The Unit 4 (Psychopathology, Psychology in Action and Research Methods) exam is split into three sections

1) **Section A** is on **Psychopathology** and you'll have to answer **one 24 mark question** out of a choice of **three**.

2) **Section B** is on **Psychology in Action** — again, you need to answer **one 24 mark question** out of **three**.

3) **Section C** has one **compulsory** question on **Research Methods**. It's worth **35 marks** and is split into **several parts**.

4) The exam lasts for **two hours**.

You'll only be marked on the quality of your written communication in section A.

The **Number of Marks** Tells You **How Much to Write**

1) The number of marks that a question is worth gives you a pretty good clue of **how much to write**.

2) You get **one mark per correct point** made, so if a question's worth four marks, you need to write four decent points.

3) In the Research Methods Section (Unit 4) there's no point writing a huge answer for a question that's only worth a few marks — it's just a **waste of your time**.

4) For the longer essay-style questions, make sure that you've written **enough** to get good marks, but don't waffle.

You Need to Meet Certain **Assessment Objectives**

Just as in AS, there are three assessment objectives covered by the two units — **AO1**, **AO2** and **AO3**. The way that a question is **worded** can give away which assessment objective is being tested.

AO1 is about the facts and theories

These questions test your **knowledge and understanding of science**. You get marks by **recalling** and **describing** psychological knowledge, such as theories, studies and methods. For example, you might get asked to **describe a theory** of depression. To get the marks, you'd simply need to describe what the theory proposed and describe its key features. What you don't need to do is evaluate the theory — that'd just be a waste of time that you could use elsewhere, and you wouldn't get any extra marks.

AO2 gets you to apply your knowledge

AO2 questions are slightly different in that they get you to **apply your knowledge and understanding** of science. It's likely that these questions will begin with '**discuss**' or '**evaluate**'. Rather than just recalling stuff, e.g. listing relevant experiments, you've got to **apply your knowledge** to the situation in these questions. So, you'd need to use the experiments you've come up with to **support your argument**. You also might have to apply your knowledge to situations you've not come across before. For example, you could be asked to assess the **validity**, **reliability** or **credibility** of a study that's new to you.

AO3 is about 'How Science Works'

'**How Science Works**' focuses on how scientific experiments are carried out. You need to be able to suggest appropriate **methodology** and know how to make sure measurements and observations are **valid** and **reliable**. You could also be asked to **analyse** and **evaluate** the **methodology** and **results** of a study described in the exam. When you're doing this, don't forget about things like **ethics** and **safety**.

Do Well in Your AQA Exam

An *Example Answer* to Show You What to Aim for...

See pages 14-15 "Development of Perception" for more about this answer.

1 (a) Outline one cross-cultural study into the development
        of perceptual abilities.   *(8 marks)*

   (b) Outline the nature-nurture debate in relation to explanations
        of perceptual development.   *(16 marks)*

(a) Segall et al (1966) investigated whether the Müller-Lyer illusion has a cross-cultural effect. They showed the Müller-Lyer illusion to a group of South Africans and a group of rural Zulus, and asked them which line was the longest. Most of the urban South Africans identified the line with the inwardly pointing arrows as being longer than the line with the outwardly pointing arrows, even though the lines were actually the same length. Segall et al believed this was because they were used to an environment dominated by straight lines (e.g. in their buildings) and interpreted the diagram in 3D. In other words, they saw one line as a corner receding away from them, and the other as a corner projecting towards them. The brain interprets the line receding away as being further away, so interprets it as being larger than the image it forms on the retina.

The Zulus were less susceptible to the Müller-Lyer illusion than the urban South Africans — a large proportion of them identified the lines as being the same length. Segall et al believed this was because they were less familiar with an environment made heavily from straight lines (e.g. their huts were circular) so didn't apply size constancy in the same way as the urban South Africans. This meant that they didn't perceive any difference in the length of the lines. Segall et al saw this cross-cultural difference in perception as evidence that perceptual abilities are developed in response to the environment. In other words, perception is the result of nurture.

(b) Some psychologists believe that the development of perceptual abilities such as depth perception and visual constancies are the result of nature — they're innate abilities. Others believe that they are the result of nurture — we learn them through interaction with our environment. There are studies to support both sides of this debate.

For example, Gibson and Walk (1960) investigated the development of depth perception in babies. They created a 'visual cliff' and investigated whether six-month old babies would crawl over the 'deep' side. They found that babies were reluctant to crawl over the deep side, and concluded that babies could perceive this as a drop. From this, they concluded that depth perception is the result of nature. However, the babies that Gibson and Walk tested were 6 months old so could have learnt depth perception by this age.

Campos (1970) addressed this problem by using a different measure of depth perception. He measured the heart rate of babies who could and couldn't crawl on both sides of the cliff. He found that the heart rate of babies who couldn't crawl didn't change on either side of the cliff, suggesting that they are not aware of the depth. However, the heart rate of babies who could crawl dropped on the deep side, suggesting that older babies are aware of the change in depth. Campos concluded that as only the older babies appeared to be aware of depth this shows that depth perception is learned and therefore down to nurture.

The conflicting findings of these studies and many more (e.g. Segall et al (1966) suggests perceptual development is the result of nurture, Bower (1985) suggests it's the result of nature) mean that no conclusion can yet be drawn on whether perceptual development is the result of nature or nurture. In fact, many psychologists now believe that perceptual abilities could come about by a combination of the two.

Get straight into gaining marks by introducing the study you're going to outline.

This question is worth 8 marks so make sure you write enough — a couple of sentences won't do.

*The question's about the nature-nurture debate so include evidence for nature **and** for nurture.*

Sum up your answer with a brief conclusion — but don't just repeat everything you've said.

... And Some Pointers About What to *Avoid*...

1) It's important to remember that it's not just a case of blindly scribbling down **everything** you can think of that's related to the subject. Doing this just **wastes time**, and it doesn't exactly impress the examiner.

2) You only get marks for stuff that's **relevant** and **answers the question**.

3) So, read the question a couple of times before you start writing so that you really understand what it's asking.

4) Try to **structure** your answer in an **organised** way. If there's one thing that examiners find worse than a load of pointless information, it's being unable to make head or tail of an answer. So, before you start, jot down a **plan** of what you want to write so you don't end up with a really jumbled answer.

Index

Index

Index